The Best Pitcher in Baseball

THE
BEST PITCHER
IN
BASEBALL

THE LIFE OF
RUBE FOSTER, NEGRO LEAGUE GIANT

Robert Charles Cottrell

New York University Press

New York and London

To Jordan, a Rube Foster fan

NEW YORK UNIVERSITY PRESS
New York and London

Copyright © 2001 by New York University
All rights reserved

Library of Congress Cataloging-in-Publication Data
Cottrell, Robert C., 1950–
The best pitcher in baseball : the life of Rube Foster, Negro League giant /
Robert Charles Cottrell.
p.   cm.
Includes bibliographical references (p.   ) and index.
ISBN 0-8147-1614-8 (cloth : alk. paper)
1. Foster, Rube, 1879–1930. 2. Baseball players—United States—
Biography. 3. African American baseball players—United States—
Biography. 4. Baseball team owners—United States—Biography.
5. Negro leagues—History. I. Title.
GV865.F63 C68 2001
796.357'092—dc21   2001003175

New York University Press books are printed on acid-free paper,
and their binding materials are chosen for strength and durability.

Manufactured in the United States of America

10 9 8 7 6 5 4 3 2 1

CONTENTS

Contents

All illustrations appear as a group following page 136.

ACKNOWLEDGMENTS

In the midst of another writing project, I became increasingly enamored of Andrew "Rube" Foster, who has been termed both the father and the godfather of black baseball. To my amazement and somewhat perverse author's delight, I discovered that only one biography of Foster had been produced; moreover, as matters turned out, the scope of that lone book was quite limited. By contrast, any number of essays, articles, and book chapters on Foster were in print, including those by Robert Peterson and John Holway, who during the 1970s helped to rekindle interest in the blackened version of the national pastime.

In my journey to make sense of Foster's life and times, I devoured scores of books on baseball, the Negro Leagues, African Americans, and general United States history. I also delved into archives at the National Baseball Hall of Fame Library in Cooperstown, the Sporting News Archives in St. Louis, and the Chicago Historical Society. I am particularly appreciative of the many kindnesses and the professionalism displayed by Tim Wiles and his staff in Cooperstown, who enabled me to explore numerous Players, Officials, and Ashland Collection Files. I am similarly thankful for the assistance afforded by James R. Meier and Steven Gietschier at the Sporting News Archives. Once again, I am enormously grateful to George Thompson and Jo Ann Bradley of the Interlibrary Loan Department at California State University, Chico. The folk at CSUC handled my countless requests for copies of various articles, books, and, above all else, microfilm rolls from a succession of black newspapers. Larry Lester of NoirTech Sports provided the photographic images contained in this book.

As I was completing the manuscript, my literary agent, Robbie Anna Hare of Goldfarb & Associates in Washington, D.C., began shopping it around. She and I had the good fortune to land a contract with New York University Press, where I have received enthusiastic support from Eric Zinner, Emily Park, and Niko Pfund.

One of the greatest pleasures in undertaking this project involved the fascination displayed by my now-eight-year-old daughter, Jordan, who herself was enthralled by the tale of Rube Foster. She was taken less by his baseball genius than by the travails he had to endure. Jordan never quite understood why Rube, notwithstanding extraordinary skills recognized by the likes of John McGraw and other baseball aficionados of the era, had to compete in a segregated game. Yes, she was well aware of the Jim Crow edifice that hemmed in black Americans; still, she didn't "get it." Nor does her father, even though he has been teaching American history for more than two decades now.

Yet again, I have to convey my grateful thanks to Jordan and my wife, Sue, who endured my extensive research ventures and the long hours at the computer and on the couch, where I typically read, edit, and rewrite.

INTRODUCTION

Rube Foster, it can readily be argued, was black baseball's greatest figure, although many claim that distinction for Jackie Robinson, who played but one season with the Kansas City Monarchs. Robinson's place in the annals of baseball and American history is, of course, secure. The minor league contract he signed with Branch Rickey in 1945 shattered the segregation barrier that had long soiled the national pastime. Then, as the first African American to perform in organized baseball in the twentieth century, Robinson starred as a member of the famed "Boys of Summer"; he helped to lead the Brooklyn Dodgers to six National League pennants, and, in 1955, to their first and only World Series championship. But as baseball historians have come to acknowledge, the story of Jackie Robinson and a procession of splendid African American major leaguers was possible only because of the earlier struggles and enduring accomplishments of Rube Foster and his black compatriots.

Foster was a true triple threat: he was black baseball's top pitcher during the first decade of the twentieth century, its finest manager, and its most creative administrator. But the 6'1" tall, 200-plus-pound Foster was still more: he was the man, more than any other individual, who all but single-handedly ensured black baseball's continuance in a period when it demanded all his legendary skill, acumen, and energy to remain in existence.

Striding out of Texas, where he was born in 1879, three years after the National League was established, Foster passed through Arkansas and the Upper Midwest before temporarily settling along the East Coast. Boasting a blazing fastball, an exceptional curve, a deadly screwball-like pitch, and impeccable control, Foster established a reputation as the finest ebony-skinned hurler in the land. He pitched for the game's top black teams, the Cuban X-Giants and the Philadelphia Giants, steering them to consecutive "colored" championships from 1902 to 1906. His superb performances in the 1903 and 1904 series, along with a triumph over the Philadelphia Athletics' Rube Waddell, led to the acquiring of a nickname and a nearly larger-than-life reputation.

The barrel-chested Foster, with an ever-expanding waistline, then headed for Chicago to serve as player-manager for the Leland Giants, considered to be the finest black baseball club in the Midwest. After vying with his former boss Frank C. Leland for the right to retain that name for his own ball club, Foster headed a squad that went 123-6 in 1910 before compiling a winning record in a series of exhibition contests in Cuba. Foster, with his strong Texas accent and calm, deep voice that invariably could be heard referring to someone as "Darling," controlled virtually all his team's operations before he acquired a white partner, John C. Schorling, the son-in-law of Chicago White Sox owner Charles A. Comiskey. Their newly renamed ball club, the Chicago American Giants, attracted substantial crowds, occasionally outdrawing the city's major league squads.

For the next dozen years, the American Giants, featuring a thinking man's, race horse brand of play, dominated black baseball. Foster adapted readily to the kinds of players his teams boasted, ranging from high-average power-hitters like Oscar Charleston, Cristobal Torriente, and Pete Hill, to weak batsmen who relied on speed to support the stellar moundsmen the Giants invariably featured. Among the other stars who performed on Foster's units were shortstop John Henry Lloyd, second baseman Bingo DeMoss, and pitchers Smokey Joe Williams, Frank Wickware, Big Richard Whitworth, and Dave Brown. Not surprisingly then, the American Giants competed successfully against major and minor league players in barnstorming tours that took them across the land and, on occasion, to the Caribbean. His team traveled first class, riding Pullman cars, whose porters hawked the *Chicago Defender,* a paper that spread the gospel of the American Giants. Foster's squad played winter ball in Florida, residing in swanky hotels, while performing before the idle rich and readying for another season of black baseball.

All the while, Foster awaited the day when racially restrictive edicts would dissolve, thereby opening the door, in a manner he had once envisioned for himself, to the stellar ballplayers found on his American Giants. Unfortunately, ragtime America proved afflicted with the triple blight of racism, segregation, and class chasms, as was starkly apparent in Chicago. Parts of Chicago were blackening as African Americans, stung by the worsening of Jim Crow practices, attracted by supposedly greater economic opportunities, and drawn by wartime exigencies, migrated out of the Deep South. Tensions between whites and blacks heightened, resulting in a horrific race riot in 1919, the very year Foster again plotted, as he had earlier, to create a league of his own.

The following February, Foster, meeting with other black baseball moguls at the YMCA in Kansas City, established the Negro National League. Appropriately enough, Foster's American Giants, with their manager characteristically ordering his players about as smoke wafted from an ever-present pipe, early dominated the league, winning the first three championships. The teams in the Negro National League were among the most important institutions in black communities across the Midwest, as were other squads situated back east that made up the Eastern Colored League; that circuit, patterned after the Negro National League, had been founded in 1923. For a brief spell, the pennant winners of the two leagues met in the Colored World's Championship, thereby fulfilling another enduring dream of Foster's.

Increasingly, however, Foster's autocratic ways resulted in sharper and more sustained criticisms. Some black baseball leaders resented the 5 percent fee he obtained for booking league games and the additional 5 percent from gate receipts that was to be mailed to the organization's Chicago headquarters. Others were distressed by the league president's attempts to direct their every move, including decisions to hold back star pitchers for Sunday contests when crowds were invariably larger. His colleagues must have been troubled too by the mental problems that began to afflict Foster, which eventually led him to deliver signals openly.

Those difficulties were undoubtedly intensified by the tragic death of his young daughter and by the continued disappointment engendered by organized baseball's refusal to discard its rigid color barrier. A meeting with two friends, New York Giants manager John McGraw and American League president Ban Johnson, raised Foster's hopes that racial strictures might at last be overcome on the playing field. Foster suggested that his American Giants be allowed to compete against major league ball clubs, in Chicago to play the White Sox or Cubs, when open dates could be found on their schedules. Soon, however, an edict from Commissioner Kenesaw Mountain Landis ensured that Foster's lads would not have such an opportunity. The blow, another in a series regarding

Foster's long-standing attempts to challenge baseball's segregation practices, proved all but fatal. As his mind began to lose its hold on reality, Foster was confined to a state institution in Kankakee, Illinois. There he remained until his death in late 1930 at the too-early age of fifty-one. An outpouring of grief and recognition followed, with thousands lining up in the Chicago winter to pay their respects.

The affection accorded the father of organized black baseball demonstrated the importance that the sport and the Negro National League held for the African American community. Numerous references at the peak of his career were made to Foster as the best-known black man in America. Contending that such a characterization was exaggerated, some would have reserved that distinction for Booker T. Washington, the president of Tuskeegee Institute; W. E. B. Du Bois, editor of *Crisis,* the magazine of the National Association for the Advancement of Colored People; or boxer Jack Johnson, the world heavyweight champion from 1908 to 1915. No matter, the celebrity Foster achieved during his lifetime and the response to his death proved heartfelt and demonstrated the pride that African Americans possessed in the creation of a baseball league of their own.

Foster's importance ultimately reached well beyond his own lifetime, as his league, other than a yearlong hiatus at the height of the Great Depression, remained in existence until the color barrier was broken in organized baseball. From the time of its founding, the Negro National League served as a vehicle through which many of the finest black baseball players could showcase their considerable talents. Black baseball, which owed so much to Foster, did survive, along with tales of John Henry Lloyd, Oscar Charleston, Smokey Joe Williams, and Rube's own Chicago American Giants. Other stories of seemingly epochal feats were about to be woven by a new crop of black ballplayers, led by Satchel Paige and Josh Gibson, and such teams as the Pittsburgh Crawfords and Homestead Grays. Down the road, another generation arrived, including the likes of Roy Campanella, Monte Irvin, and a twenty-six-year-old shortstop on the Kansas City Monarchs named Jackie Robinson; later, they would be joined in the major leagues by onetime Negro League performers Willie Mays, Hank Aaron, and Ernie Banks. More than any other individual, Rube Foster provided the bridge between the largely unorganized brand of baseball played by dark-skinned players around the turn of the century and the game performed in hallowed venues like the Polo Grounds, Fenway Park, Wrigley Field, and Yankee Stadium.

By contrast, Rube Foster, tragically, had proven unable to compete on those ballfields. That inability, notwithstanding his enormous talents as player, manager, and administrator, eventually proved too taxing for such a driven individual. Segregative practices thus cost him mightily, but the American public paid an enormous price as well. On the most elementary level, some of black baseball's finest performers were not permitted to face their white counterparts on an even playing field. Thus, the national pastime, as baseball was viewed, lacked a certain integrity that it purportedly exemplified. Its moguls refused to allow all to participate, a failure too seldom denounced as a violation of the seemingly inherent American right to compete, to demonstrate one's individual worth. That failure, unfortunately, was all too characteristic of the race-, class-, and gender-based nature of American society. People of color, among them folk of African ancestry; those who were less-well-heeled financially; and women had to wrestle with all sorts of restrictions concerning opportunities and, at times, even physical movement.

Throughout his lifetime, Rube Foster experienced the racial restraints that so typified turn-of-the century America. He suffered that treatment unhappily and worked mightily, in his own fashion, to contest it. To compound that indignity, Foster's efforts on the baseball diamond repeatedly escaped the notice of supposed experts of the sport, but those feats eventually proved too consequential to be ignored any longer. On March 12, 1981, Foster was selected for induction into the National Baseball Hall of Fame; still, even that historic moment was marred, to a certain extent, by the fact that seven ballplayers who had been excluded altogether from organized baseball, and two whose finest performances had occurred in the Negro leagues, had been so honored before Foster.

It was, of course, Jackie Robinson who became the pathfinder that Foster had long aspired to be, and the first African American baseball player to be inducted into the Hall of Fame; Satchel Paige was the initial admittee whose most storied days took place in the Negro leagues. But without Foster's vision and organizational acumen, Paige, Gibson, Buck Leonard, and even Robinson would likely have remained mere footnotes in American sports history. The country and its often tortured race relations would, as a consequence, have been more troubled still. For sports—and particularly major league baseball, ironically enough, given its own tainted history—proved instrumental in challenging long-held racial stereotypes.

Foster's own challenge to discrimination and racial stereotypes was his most significant accomplishment, setting the stage for future efforts to contest Jim Crow where it unfortunately stood: throughout large pockets of the United States. As an athlete, manager, sports organizer, administrator, and businessman, Foster deliberately and consciously battled against the mind-set sustaining the "Whites Only" signs that disgraced the American landscape. Taking those matters into consideration, his efforts to create viable black teams and a black baseball league become more noteworthy still. In the very era when baseball was lauded as the national game, Rube Foster helped to provide a forum where African American players, field bosses, and executives could demonstrate athletic brilliance that eventually could no longer be ignored. Black baseball's most prominent individual, like that version of the sport, thus added a great deal to the American experience.

The story of Andrew "Rube" Foster embodies a still-too-little-acknowledged chapter, and a telling one it is, of this nation's lore. His life and times provide a lens to examine how determined African Americans, battling against demeaning racial restrictions, demonstrated grace under the most telling of circumstances. Operating inside a darkened version of America's game, Foster helped to lead the fight against the kind of segregation that blacks, over the span of several generations, were compelled to contend with. Driven by an oversized ego, unbounded pride, and a prophetic, although not unblemished sense of his own destiny, black baseball's dominant personality sought to eradicate the Jim Crow barriers that long afflicted some of the greatest American athletes.

ONE

The Best Pitcher in
the Country

In the final stages of the nineteenth century, Calvert, Texas, experienced tremendous growth, thanks to railroads and to cotton planters who established large plantations in the Brazos River bottoms that exuded prosperity and southern warmth. With the passage of time, many of those planters headed into town, where they constructed stately Victorian mansions, some of which are still standing today. Situated in Robertson County, Calvert became a trading center in eastern Texas, trafficking in "King Cotton," alfalfa, vegetables, and livestock. By 1871, Calvert possessed the world's largest operating gin. As the town, one hundred miles northeast of the state capital, Austin, grew, it briefly became Texas's fourth largest, boasting a population of more than ten thousand. Along with fine Victorian homes, Calvert featured hotels, theaters, opera houses, and many other businesses. Virtually daily, upwards of one hundred mule-driven freight wagons, packed with goods to be sent to the Texas coastal region, stood ready at the train depot. Eventually, some thirty thousand immigrants passed through Calvert on their way out west.

The Reverend Andrew Foster, presiding elder of the American Methodist Episcopal Church in the region, also served as minister of its local congregation. A devoutly religious man, the good reverend favored temperance and abhorred smoking. On September 17, 1879, two years after Reconstruction ended, resulting in the steady decline of the condition of African Americans in the South, the Reverend and Mrs. Foster welcomed their fifth child into the world. Named after his father, young Andrew, by all accounts, readily adopted the moral precepts of his family's faith and regularly attended Sunday services at the Methodist Episcopal Church. By the time Andrew was ready to attend school, Calvert had some three thousand residents, five churches, gins, mills, a foundry, machine shops, an opera house, a pair of banks, two free schools, several private ones, and a weekly newspaper, the *Courier*.

At the time of Andrew's birth, expectations still existed in the black community that the promises of Reconstruction could be sustained. Those hopes had been piqued earlier by Abraham Lincoln's emancipation proclamations and the ratification of the Thirteenth, Fourteenth, and Fifteenth Amendments to the United States Constitution. The Thirteenth Amendment terminated slavery on land possessed by the United States; the Fourteenth established that citizens are entitled to privileges and immunities that are shielded from state abridgement, and that both due process and equal protection of the law are to be provided to all on American soil; and the Fifteenth afforded suffrage to eligible black citizens. Reconstruction governments throughout the South, including in Texas, had striven to improve conditions for blacks and poor whites alike. Education was viewed as a means to uplift the downtrodden and dispossessed. The Republican Party in Texas helped blacks to acquire citizenship, the suffrage, and, on several occasions, elective office.

In 1878, Harriel G. Geiger and R. J. Evans, both African Americans from Robertson County, captured seats in the state legislature, with the backing of the Republican Party. Two years later, another black man, Freeman Moore, served as a county commissioner, but Geiger lost his bid for re-election. After winning a special election in 1881, Geiger was shot and killed by an irate judge, O. D. Cannon, who was offended by remarks that the black legislator had made in his courtroom. Evans, in 1884, was the Republican candidate for commissioner of the General Land Office. In 1889, Alexander Asberry, a foe of segregation, was chosen to represent Robertson County in the state capital. Following a closely contested election in 1896, Asberry was wounded by the same judge who had murdered Representative Geiger.

Such elected officials, along with their black colleagues in the state legislature, failed to prevent disenfranchisement's taking hold. Increasingly, African Americans were restricted from participating in the affairs of various political organizations and denied the right to vote. Intimidation and violence were called on to curb the political activities of blacks in Texas. More and more, segregation was also resorted to, as evidenced by discrimination in railroad passenger cars, marriage, and jury duty, among other matters.[1]

Consequently, Andrew's formative years, both inside and beyond the classroom, occurred in the very period when Jim Crow practices were lengthening. Schools became a particular battleground where segregationists demanded that white and black children not be allowed to "mix." Calvert's schools, by the time little Andrew Foster came of age, were already segregated; Andrew attended the only local school that welcomed African American children.

One story had Andrew "operating a baseball team in Calvert while he was still in grade school." The Reverend Foster discouraged his son from playing ball but to no avail; indeed, following morning church sessions, on Sunday afternoons, Andrew could be found on the playing field. Barely a teenager, he refused to go back to school after the eighth grade, opting to play baseball instead; his mother had died and his father, now remarried, headed to southwest Texas. By 1897, the now strapping, 6'1" tall (various reports have Foster listed at anywhere from 5'10" to 6'4"), 210-pound Andrew, who packed an ivory-handled gun under his belt, was pitching for the Waco Yellow Jackets, an itinerant squad that traveled throughout Texas and nearby states. Class and racial prejudices were sometimes encountered, with the players occasionally "barred away from homes . . . as baseball was considered by Colored as low and ungentlemanly." By contrast, that year's highlight saw the right-handed Foster go up against white major leaguers in Fort Worth during spring training.[2]

As the Yellow Jackets performed throughout the region, Foster's reputation grew. Having watched him on the mound, a white sportswriter in Austin condemned the racial stereotypes that prevailed in the South, which he found unfathomable because "Foster had him intoxicated with his playing." A tale was spun that in an eleven-day stretch, Foster pitched daily, allowing his foes only fifty hits while holding them scoreless. Regarding that story, one journalist declared, "It sounds like a myth but if it is, the Southern white press wove the myth."[3]

Word of Foster's pitching prowess continued to spread. In 1902, following an appearance in Hot Springs, Arkansas, he received an invitation from W. S. Peters, who headed the Chicago Unions, to join his ball club. When Peters failed to deliver traveling money, Foster, who possessed a terrific fastball, a sharp curve, a vicious screwball-styled pitch, and impeccable control of his tosses, opted to remain home. Soon, however, Frank C. Leland asked Foster to play for his newly formed Chicago Union Giants, who planned to compete against top-notch white teams. Cockily responding, Foster wrote, "If you play the best clubs in the land, white clubs, as you say, it will be a case of Greek meeting Greek. I fear nobody." He received forty dollars a month and a fifteen-cents-a-meal stipend.[4]

After hurling a shutout his first time on the mound for the Union Giants, Foster floundered and, along with teammate David Wyatt, left the squad at midseason; such player movement was all too characteristic of black baseball during the early twentieth century. Teams possessed little recourse as players freely joined or departed from their ranks. Foster and Wyatt headed for Otsego, Michigan, where they joined a white semipro nine; there, Foster's luck proved little better as he dropped five consecutive games. Wyatt informed the Otsego management "that Foster was just a wild young fellow right out of Texas, and if they would give me a chance to smooth the rough spots down he would yet surprise them." Thanks to Wyatt's backing and coaching, Foster soon starred in the white Michigan State League. However, he was unable to beat a black squad, the Page Fence Giants from Big Rapids, Michigan, whose members goaded him unmercifully. Wyatt remembered, "Foster would engage in personalities while pitching, and they always took him for a ride. Foster had a reputation as a gunman and was never seen without his Texas pistol. All the colored players formed a decided dislike for Foster and declared he couldn't pitch."[5]

With Otsego's season concluded, Foster, obviously displaying considerable potential, linked up with the Cuban X-Giants, who were playing in Zanesville, Ohio. The Cuban X-Giants had been the most potent squad in black baseball for the past five years or so. Never lacking for confidence, Foster soon referred to himself as "the best pitcher in the country." The match thus appeared to be an ideal fit. As X-Giants' manager E. B. Lamar Jr. later recalled, Foster "had as much speed as Amos Rusie and a very good curve ball." Still, "he depended on his windup and speed to win games. Foster thought he knew more than anyone else and would take that giant windup with men on bases." In his first outing, he suffered a 13-0 shellacking at the hands of a team from Hoboken, New

Jersey, which ran wild on the base paths. Lamar declared, "That taught Rube a lesson. From then on he made a study of the game, and every chance he got he would go out to the big-league parks and watch the big clubs in action."[6]

Lamar's patience paid off and Foster soon became one of the finest black pitchers in the land. Records for black baseball are notoriously incomplete, but the Cuban X-Giants competed with the Philadelphia Giants for the title of the premier African American team along the East Coast. Top players on the Cuban X-Giants included catcher-outfielder William Jackson, first baseman Ray Wilson, and first baseman-outfielder Ed Wilson. The monthly payroll was a then-princely $700.[7]

Black baseball was becoming a bit more organized, as evidenced by a brief note in the April 23, 1902, edition of the *Philadelphia Item,* a white-run newspaper. The city now boasted, the *Item* reported, a "star team of colored ball players": the Philadelphia Giants. The squad was reportedly made up of some of the country's top players, who, "were it not for the fact that their skin is black . . . would to-day be drawing fancy salaries in one or the other of the big leagues." Veteran ballplayer Sol White and white sportswriter H. Walter "Slick" Schlicter of the *Philadelphia Item* had put together the Giants, who opened the 1902 season that day at Columbia Park, the Athletics' ballpark, where they triumphed over Camden City 12-4. Philadelphia went on to compile an 81-43-2 mark that first year.[8]

By the following campaign, Foster was an established star on the powerful Cuban X-Giants; the team was paid $850 monthly. One of the few box scores surviving from the season had Foster throw a 3-0, five-hit shutout against Penn Park in York, Pennsylvania, on July 16, 1903. The report of the game indicated that his opponents were "at the mercy of Foster." The next day, teammate Charles "Kid" Carter hurled a perfect game against Penn Park, winning 5-0. Starters for the X-Giants included second baseman Charlie Grant, shortstop Grant "Home Run" Johnson, and catcher George "Chappie" Johnson, along with pitcher Danny McClellan. Just two years earlier, John McGraw, then managing the Baltimore Orioles of the newly formed American League, had sought to sign Grant by presenting him as an Indian called "Chief Tokahoma." Chicago White Sox owner Charles Comiskey exposed the subterfuge, thereby maintaining baseball's color barrier.[9]

In September, following "two years of squabbling, challenges and counter challenges," the Cuban X-Giants battled against the Philadelphia Giants to decide the "colored championship of the world." Philadelphia, led by manager-shortstop Sol White, second baseman Bill Monroe, outfielder Pete Hill, and pitchers Carter, William Bell, and Harry Buckner, put together an 89-37-4 mark in 1903. Nevertheless, the Cuban X-Giants prevailed in five of seven games; Foster won four contests, consequently establishing a reputation as black baseball's best pitcher. The Cuban X-Giants took the opener 4-2 on September 12 at Columbia Park in Philadelphia, before nearly four thousand spectators as Foster scattered six hits, while walking three and striking out five. Foster was reported to have "pitched magnificent ball for the 'Cubes,'" holding the Philadelphia Giants to only two hits through the first seven innings. He gave up a pair of runs—only one earned—in the eighth but held on for the complete game victory. Foster also contributed two hits, including a double, and drove in a run.[10]

Some three thousand fans showed up in Ridgewood, New Jersey, the next day to watch the two teams split a doubleheader: the Cuban X-Giants won the opener; the Philadelphia Giants prevailed in the second contest, 5-2. Foster led the X-Giants to another victory in game four, but Philadelphia, with Kid Carter on the mound, blanked its opponents 3-0 in the next affair. On September 18, the Cuban X-Giants triumphed 12-3, as Foster allowed seven hits, walked only one, and struck out a handful. Foster belted the lone extra-base hit, a triple, along with a pair of singles, and scored three runs in the romp at the Island Park grounds in Harrisburg, Pennsylvania. The final game was played a week later in Camden, New Jersey, with Foster besting Carter and Philadelphia 2-0, while relinquishing but three hits; Foster banged out one of the five hits the X-Giants got off Carter.[11]

The series concluded with the Cuban X-Giants proclaimed black baseball's finest team and Foster's reputation soaring, thanks to his four complete game victories. Referring to the contests, Sol White declared, "These games were of the utmost importance and were fought with the bitterest feeling at every stage of the series."[12]

During the off-season, Foster and a number of his teammates, including batterymate Chappie Johnson and Charlie Grant, moved to the Philadelphia Giants; Foster, who was hardly averse to jumping from one ball club to another, would now be paid a purported $90 a month. As the 1904 season opened, the *Philadelphia Item* indicated that the hometown Giants "will be faster and stronger than ever." After all, "the acquisition of Pitcher Foster will give them the strongest staff of pitchers of any team in the Independent Association."[13]

In the first decade of the twentieth century, black baseball thrived in Philadelphia, thanks to its surging African American population. Census reports indicate that in 1890, forty thousand resided in the city of approximately one million residents; by the time Foster moved to Philadelphia, the number of black residents in the metropolitan area had nearly doubled. Only Washington, D.C., New York City, New Orleans, and Baltimore, had greater numbers. Many of the new Philadelphians, like Foster himself, had migrated from former Confederate states; there, Jim Crow practices remained in place, while increasingly the right to vote was restricted and lynching had become an all-too-common occurrence. Most of the new arrivals in Philadelphia settled in the southern sector of the city, particularly in the Seventh Ward. There, middle-class enclaves could be found, but also a large number of homeless blacks. The sharing of outdoor toilets was common, sanitation problems worsened, and the incidences of tuberculosis, pneumonia, and venereal diseases mounted. Pay for black workers generally was considerably less than that for white counterparts, and employment opportunities remained limited; playing blackball for pay, although hardly as lucrative as the major league variety, must have seemed like a godsend for black baseball players. Many families supplemented their incomes by accepting boarders, including some of those same black ballplayers.[14]

The leading African American newspaper in the city was the *Philadelphia Tribune,* which was linked up with black political figures who tended to belong to the Citizens Republican Club; another newspaper, the white-run *Philadelphia Item,* actually proved far more attentive to the sporting world, including black baseball. Nevertheless, both newspapers provided a forum in which African American editors and writers could discuss contemporary events and challenge discriminatory practices. On the surface at least, another matter of great importance was taking place in the City of Brotherly Love. By the middle of the new century's first decade, the great black intellectual W. E. B. Du Bois estimated, some twenty-five thousand black Philadelphians were registered to vote. As Du Bois saw matters, even those voters were basically disenfranchised, for they were beholden to a political machine that proved little concerned for their interests. Churches, on the other hand, along with the Home Missionary Society, provided the kinds of social welfare functions that even progressive governments of the area appeared little inclined to.[15]

Still, the general tenor of the times, in the North as well as the South, was exemplified by President Theodore Roosevelt, a progressive Republican, who considered blacks "a backward race" generally afflicted with "laziness and shiftlessness." Not surprisingly then, Roosevelt contended that "race purity must be maintained."[16]

It's unknown how fully Foster was affected by the social, economic, and political currents that were swirling throughout Philadelphia and the United States, yet, as indicated by later autobiographical sketches, he must have been scarred by the same kinds of discriminatory treatment endured by so many African Americans of this era. Obviously, the bulk of his time and energy was expended in the segregated brand of the national pastime in which he was allowed to participate. There, he encountered the "whites only" signs that restaurants, hotels, and other places of public accommodation in the North resorted to as their proprietors sought to maintain a color barrier.

In an ironic turn of events, John McGraw, manager of the New York Giants and a friend of Foster's, contested organized baseball's Jim Crow edifice in his own fashion. McGraw's Giants had finished the 1903 National League season six and a half games behind the pennant-winning Pittsburgh Pirates. Believing that his immensely talented but still raw right-hander, Christy Mathewson, required tutoring, McGraw supposedly hired black baseball's best pitcher to do the job. Foster is credited by some baseball historians with helping Mathewson to perfect the famed fadeaway—later known as the screwball—that enabled him to become the top major league hurler. Going from a 14-17 mark, Mathewson, beginning in 1904, reeled off three consecutive seasons in which he won thirty or more games.[17]

In the opening game for black baseball in Philadephia in 1904, Kid Carter on April 5 tossed a one-hitter at Murray Hill (N.J.), winning a seven-inning contest 5-0. Left-fielder Foster rapped out one of the six

Philadelphia hits, a double, the game's only extra bagger. Throughout the season, when not on the mound, Foster played in the field, working all the outfield positions, first base, second base, and even behind the plate. On April 10, Foster won his first game for the Philadelphia Giants, defeating Ridgewood 6-3 on a six-hitter, as he struck out eleven; Foster also contributed three hits to his own cause.[18]

Suffering his first loss of the season, Foster dropped a 6-5 affair on April 25 to Camden, which scored two in the opening frame and added three in the fifth. Camden garnered nine hits and one walk off Foster, who struck out four batters. Four days later, the Giants and Foster nipped Pottstown (Pa.) 11-10, with the pitcher scoring twice and belting both a double and a triple; he gave up eleven hits, struck out seven, and walked three. Foster fired a five-hit, seven-strikeout, three-walk shutout at Wilmington A.A. on May 9, as Philadelphia won 7-0, with the Giants' new star pitcher scoring one run and producing three hits, one a triple.[19]

The *Philadelphia Item* applauded the Giants' early season performance, declaring that they had "been universally successful in defeating the semi-professionals of the metropolitan area." The winning skein ended ingloriously on May 30, when Camden swept a doubleheader, with Foster dropping the second contest 4-3 in eleven innings, despite scattering only six hits and giving up only two earned runs. He struck out six, walked only one, and produced two hits himself. Foster threw nine scoreless innings before giving up a pair of runs in each of the next two frames. He bounced back against Hoboken on June 4, throwing a six-hitter, in which he struck out eight, walked five, and relinquished one earned run; the Giants won 9-2, with Foster scoring twice and stealing a base. Foster went to 5-2, besting Johnstown 4-1 on June 10, in giving up only five hits, while producing one of his own. On June 14, the Giants avenged themselves by defeating Harrisburg 10-2 behind Foster's five-hitter, with the pitcher contributing a run and two hits. Tossing his second shutout of the season on June 19, Foster allowed Hoboken only seven hits, while striking out five and walking only two in a 7-0 contest; he also scored once and smacked a single. Foster's own winning streak ended on June 26, as Murray Hill beat him 5-3.[20]

Back on the mound on June 30, Foster beat Edgewood Park 7-2 on a five-hitter, while scoring once and belting four hits. Four days later, he pitched again as Philadelphia and Williamsport (Pa.) dueled to a 2-2 tie in ten innings. Foster gave up eight hits, while producing two himself and scoring one run. Pitching on only three days' rest the next time out, Foster no-hit Mt. Carmel A.A. in a 4-0 game called after seven innings because of rain; Foster managed two hits and scored once. On July 9, Philadelphia prevailed again, as Carter no-hit Atlantic City 3-0, with right fielder Foster going hitless. In the second half of a doubleheader on July 11, after Philadelphia dropped the opener, Foster held Pottstown to four hits, struck out eight, walked only one, and smashed a home run, to record a 5-1 victory. The next day, Will Horn struck out twelve and fired the Giants' third no-hitter of the season, beating Oxford 2-0, as second baseman Foster stole one base and scored one of the Philadelphia runs.[21]

Foster's record improved to 11-3-1 on July 15 as he held Atlantic City to eight hits and two earned runs, while striking out six, with the Giants prevailing 6-3. He scored one run and got three of Philadelphia's seven hits. With only two days' rest before his next outing, Foster was beaten by Hoboken 5-2, although his opponents managed but six hits along with three earned runs, while striking out six times; Foster went hitless at the plate. On July 21, Foster again failed to win, as the Giants and Mt. Carmel battled to a 4-4 tie in a seven-inning contest. Foster, who got a pair of hits, held his foes to seven, but Philadelphia had to produce single runs in the last two innings just to knot the score.[22]

In a masterly display of pitching on July 25, Foster produced his second no-hitter of the season, as he struck out seventeen and walked four in beating Trenton YMCA 1-0. Foster, who managed three hits, scored the game's only run as Trenton's pitcher threw errantly to second base. The next day, the Giants beat the Mohicans 4-1, although Foster went hitless. Four days later, Foster relinquished only four hits in defeating Atlantic City 4-1, allowing only one unearned run in the top of the seventh, while striking out five and walking four; Foster managed two hits himself. On August 1, Foster struck out eleven and walked two, while scattering nine hits and one earned run, in a 3-2 contest. Contributing two hits, including his second homer of the season, Foster helped Philadelphia to defeat Clayton, a topflight team from South Jersey, 6-1, on August 2.[23]

Foster smashed his third homer of the 1904 season, added a single, and saved a 6-5 win against Atlantic City for the Giants on August 5. He dropped to 15-5-2 in losing to Pottstown the next day, relinquishing the game's lone run in the top of the first. He gave up eight hits, struck out six, walked three, and was hitless at the plate. On August 10, Foster managed a triple as he held Haddington to six hits and triumphed 5-2, striking out three and issuing four walks. In his next start, on August 14, Foster threw his fifth shutout of the year, beating Hoboken in "a brilliant pitchers' duel." Foster allowed only seven hits, struck out seven, and walked but one batter. He notched a hit, and the Giants scored the game's only run in the top of the ninth. Despite issuing only six hits on August 23, Foster failed to help out his own cause, going hitless as Atlantic City beat the Giants 1-0, scoring the lone run in the top of the ninth. Philadelphia lost again the next day, dropping a 6-4 contest to Pottstown, although Foster batted cleanup and got a pair of hits, including his fourth home run of the season.[24]

At this point in the season, Foster stood at 16-6-2, with five shutouts and a pair of no-hitters. But greater acclaim still was about to come his way. Once again, he starred in "the colored championship of the world," this time doing battle against the team he had guided to the title in 1903 and had helped to claim the crown for the previous year, the Cuban X-Giants. That squad, moreover, had just won eighteen straight contests, equaling the record set by the National League's New York Giants. The three-game set, manager Sol White related, was greatly anticipated. "Both players and spectators were worked to the highest pitch of excitement. Never in the annals of colored baseball did two nines fight for supremacy as these teams fought."[25]

If anything, Foster shone even brighter this time in leading Philadelphia to the title. Four thousand spectators gathered at Inlet Park in Atlantic City on September 1 to watch him throw, as the *Philadelphia Item* reported, "a sensational ball game. . . . Foster's work was, of course, the great feature of the game. He was in wonderful form and the Cuban X-Giants could do nothing with him." This was somewhat unexpected because an ailing Foster had been ordered by a physician to remain confined to bed; his manager Sol White supposedly begged him to accompany the team to Atlantic City. Gloating, the Cuban X-Giants promised to knock Foster out of the box if he pitched; indeed, they indicated that he wouldn't dare to show up. In the 8-4 affair, the error-riddled X-Giants managed seven hits, including a pair of doubles and homers, and received five free passes. But Foster was backed by ten hits off the X-Giants' Danny McClellan and Walter Ball, led by a triple of his own and a homer by left fielder Payne; Foster managed three hits in all, scored one run, and stole a base. But most noteworthy, he fanned eighteen batters, establishing a black baseball record and surpassing the major league mark by three. Foster's performance, the *Item* noted, "excelled any . . . of the big League twirlers." The Philadelphia Giants' star pitcher thus received plaudits from the white press, which would help to craft the Foster legend.[26]

Surprisingly, Will Horn, not Kid Carter, was selected to pitch the next day's game. Horn pitched well before giving way to Foster but was outdueled by the X-Giants' Harry Buckner, who gave up no extra-base hits among only six safeties produced by Philadelphia. In the pivotal game played the following day, Foster returned to the mound, where he quickly fell behind 2-0, allowing a single and a two-run homer in the bottom of the third. The Giants chipped away at the lead, scoring single runs in both the fourth and the fifth before notching a pair in the seventh. In the meantime, Foster shut down the X-Giants on three hits; he walked only one and struck out six over the full nine innings. That performance earned the title for the Philadelphia Giants and their superlative right-hander, who led his team with a .400 series batting average.[27]

The Giants' success, the *Philadelphia Item* reported, was somewhat surprising to even their biggest supporters. Those backers, the paper declared, "felt that the team was made of the right sort of timber" but "did not for a moment even dare to think that the team was really as fast an aggregation as they proved to be." The *Item* particularly singled out Foster for praise.[28]

On September 21, the *Item* reported that the Philadelphia Giants were slated to battle the All-Cubans, reputedly the top team on the Caribbean island, in the fifth and deciding game to determine "the colored world's Championship." Before the game began, each member of the Philadelphia Giants was presented with a gold medal stamped "Champions of 1905" [*sic*]. Playing at Columbia Park, the Giants, behind Foster's five-hit, fourteen-strikeout performance, crushed the All-Cubans 13-3; Foster's pitching, the *Item* suggested, "was entirely too much for the Cubans." Among the crowd of 1,200, the newspaper noted, was "all the colored aristocracy." In his next outing, Foster defeated the Kingston Colonials, champions of the Hudson River League, 3-2.[29]

By the end of the month, reports were bandied about that the Giants sought to play the New York Highlanders, then vying for the American League title. Those efforts proved unsuccessful, to the Giants' chagrin. The best that black baseball had to offer, the Philadelphia Giants, thus completed a 95-41-6 season. Foster, in games that could be tracked, went 20-6-2, including his championship outings. Now standing as the finest pitcher in black baseball, Foster had won seven such games in a row, and had established a new single-game strikeout mark. Not surprisingly then, he eagerly awaited the next baseball season. One postseason contest against the Athletics saw Foster go head-to-head against Connie Mack's star southpaw, Rube Waddell. Foster won 5-2, and as a consequence, he later recalled, "they gave me the name of the colored Rube Waddell." News accounts, starting in 1905, first began referring to the Philadelphia Giants' ace as Rube Foster.[30]

At the Top of His Game

Prior to the start of the 1905 season, Foster and several other Philadelphia Giants spent part of the winter in Palm Beach, competing for the Royal Poincians, which went up against top players in both black baseball and the organized professional game. In a stellar matchup at the Palm Beach diamond in early March, Foster threw a terrific shutout, defeating Ormond 1-0. Many of the Ormond players, who worked for the hotel of the same name, were pro ballplayers from the New York State League. In past seasons, Ormond had dominated the Palm Beach winter league and was expected to do so once again. With two outs in the seventh, Danny McClellan's sharply hit grounder drove in the game's lone run.[1]

The *Philadelphia Item,* where sportswriter–Giants' owner Slick Schlicter helped to craft editorials, discussed Foster's outing.

> Foster, the Great, was in prime form. A girl in the grandstand proclaimed him "Procrastination" Foster. He had such an aggravating way of taking his time. He is a man of huge frame. His arms are like those of a windmill. He would swing them like the pendulum of a clock, looking the while, about the diamond. Suddenly he would twist up like a Missouri grasshopper about to make a spring and the ball would shoot from the pitcher's box. Time and again he struck out his men and not a single Ormondite got his base on balls.[2]

The regular season again proved enormously successful for both Foster and the Philadelphia Giants. The team went 134-21-3, amassing an .865 winning percentage. The Giants featured a potent lineup that included first baseman Sol White, Charlie Grant at second, Bill Monroe at the hot corner, shortstop Home Run Johnson, left fielder Pete Hill, center fielder Mike Moore, right fielder Danny McClellan, catcher Chappie "Rat" Johnson, and pitchers Scotty Bowman, McClellan, and Foster.

On April 2, Foster bested Murray Hills 5-1, giving up only five hits; he defeated the same team 6-1 six days later, allowing only five hits yet again, while striking out nine; he also scored once and got two hits himself. After playing right field in the first two rounds of a three-game series against Newark of the Eastern League, Foster won an 8-4 contest on April 8, scattering nine hits in an affair where he "did not extend himself"; he again scored one run and managed a pair of hits. On April 22, Foster, in a "brilliant" performance, shut down Ingersol-Sergeant 3-1, giving up but three hits, striking out nine, and issuing only two walks; Ingersol's lone tally in the bottom of the sixth inning was unearned.[3]

As April neared a close, the *Philadelphia Item* asserted that the Giants' record was "a most remarkable one." Having won the "undisputed" title of "colored world's champion" in 1904, the Philadelphia Giants, the *Item* reported, "stand in their class without a peer to-day." The paper particularly singled out for praise infielders White, Grant, Home Run Johnson, and Monroe, along with catcher Chappie Johnson. Grant was termed "one of the most dependable second basemen in the game to-day" and "one of the heaviest stick artists in the bunch of hard hitters." White was proclaimed "one of the ablest of baseball tacticians on the diamond," and Home Run Johnson was applauded for making a run at his own longball mark. Monroe was said to be both "playing the best ball of his career" and a terrific drawing card. Chappie Johnson, known as the "Beau Brummel" of backstoppers, was deemed "without a peer as a one-handed catcher."[4]

April concluded with the Giants having won eighteen of twenty games during the month, in competition against "some of the strongest teams outside of the major leagues." Philadelphia's batting stars included Bill Monroe, who hit .440 while stealing ten bases, and Home Run Johnson, who produced a .405 mark. Pete Hill, Chappie Johnson, and Danny McClellan also batted better than .300, and Johnson scored thirty times during the Giants' run. Among those playing regularly, Foster was proving to be something of a weak link, hitting only .252, with fifteen runs scored and five stolen bases. The *Philadelphia Item* referred to the team as "the most remarkable batting aggregation of colored ball players ever gathered together."[5]

The great black heavyweight boxer Jack Johnson was the subject of considerable attention on May 11 when his Pets battled the Philadelphia Giants at Haddington Ball Park. The Giants easily bested Johnson's Pets 13-4, with both first basemen, Johnson and Foster, who was starting to heat up at the plate, contributing a pair of hits. Two days later, Foster went eleven innings to defeat Haddington 4-3, having allowed only four hits while striking out eight. The Haddington runs were all unearned as the Giants committed four errors. Foster won again on May 17, beating Wilmington 5-2, while relinquishing the first earned run he had given up in three games. Foster, who struck out five and walked a like number, again held his opponents to four hits. Three days later, Foster dropped a 4-2 contest to Plainfield (N.J.), despite allowing only one earned run and holding his foes to five hits, as he struck out a pair, walked three, and plunked one batter with a pitch. Back on the mound on May 22, he shut out Manhattan 7-0, giving up only five hits in the process.[6]

Through forty-nine games, the Giants had won forty-three, for a superb .837 winning percentage. Chester was the latest victim, on June 6, falling before Foster 11-3, while collecting only seven hits and one earned run. He struck out three and issued two walks. On June 18, during the fourth game of a series against the Manhattans played at Olympic Field, the Giants, behind Foster, who smacked two hits, including a home run, waltzed to a 13-0 triumph. Foster allowed only four harmless singles, while striking out seven and walking three, as Philadelphia won for the thirteenth straight time. Four days later, Foster took a six-inning, rain-shortened contest, 3-1, against Lynn, in that Massachusetts community. Pitching with only three days' rest, Foster just managed to last through a 14-13 slugfest that ended with the Giants scoring ten in the top of the ninth to beat Murray Hills. In an atypical performance, he gave up seventeen hits and eleven earned runs, while striking out four and walking three. Again pitching on short rest, Foster defeated Chester 8-3 on June 28, by scattering nine hits.[7]

Playing at the 16th and Vine Street grounds on July 1, Philadelphia, behind Foster's five-hitter, stopped Haddington's winning streak, 6-1. Giving up only an unearned run in the top of the ninth, Foster struck out eight as he "performed in brilliant style." Again allowing no earned runs, he bested the Trenton YMCA, which managed eight hits, 9-2, on the Fourth of July. Wilder than usual as he went to the mound three days after his last outing, Foster issued six free passes, while striking out four and leaving eleven Trenton runners stranded. Back on the pitcher's mound on July 7, Foster held Glassboro (N.J.) to six hits and one earned run in winning 11-2. Playing right field, Foster pounded four hits, including a triple, as the Giants swatted the P.R.R. YMCA 19-4 on July 15; Foster's extra-base smash was called "the longest hit of the season, on which, however, he made but three bases, owing to his shoes being filled with feet." The next day, Foster pitched well, giving up only four hits, walking one and striking out four, but the Giants were beaten by Hoboken 2-1. On July 20, Foster again failed to win, despite giving up only three hits and striking out eight in a thirteen-inning contest against the Royal Giants that was called because of darkness; the Royal Giants didn't score after tallying twice in the top of the fifth. Foster, Moore, and White all homered as Philadelphia ripped Quakertown 9-1 in that Pennsylvania town on July 22. After losing to Lynn 8-7 on July 25, the Giants' record for the season stood at 73-14. On July 28, the Giants defeated the Walkovers from Brocton, Massachusetts, 4-1, behind Danny McClellan's eleven-strikeout performance and Foster's home run.[8]

Despite allowing ten hits, Foster defeated Medford F.C. on August 2, as he struck out two and walked a pair of batters. A twenty-hit attack triggered Philadelphia's 17-4 romp, with Foster getting six himself, including a double, and scoring four runs. On August 11, he gave up thirteen hits and three earned runs, while recording five strikeouts and three walks, but defeated Pottstown 11-4. On August 14, Foster went eleven innings before Home Run Johnson's "screaming" double drove in Pete Booker with the winning run to nip Atlantic City 4-3. Foster "pitched a strong game," chalking up ten strikeouts and three walks; he also rapped a pair of hits, including a double.[9]

Matched up against Camden on August 22, Foster was sharper still, tossing yet another no-hitter and striking out five as Philadelphia, relying on only four hits of its own, prevailed 3-0. Foster, the *Item* noted, "had the Jerseymen at his mercy throughout," facing a mere thirty batters and allowing only three base runners because of walks, with but one reaching second base. A record 7,500 fans gathered at Olympic Field to watch the Giants defeat the hometown Manhattans 7-5, with right-fielder Foster scoring one run and getting a hit. Playing at Inlet Park, Foster again pitched extra frames, as a fourteen-inning contest with

Atlantic City was stalemated at four runs apiece. Atlantic City managed all its runs, two earned, in the top of the second and then proved "powerless" against Foster, who allowed only seven hits, struck out ten, and gave up four bases on balls. On September 7, Philadelphia bested the Royal Giants 6-1, behind Foster's six-hitter. He struck out only one, walked two, threw a pair of wild pitches, but held his foes to a solitary unearned run that was tallied in the bottom of the sixth. Five days later, he was even sharper, shutting out Allentown on three hits.[10]

The 1905 version of the battle to determine blackball's best team was kicked off on September 14, when Philadelphia, behind Scotty Bowman's eight-hitter, shut out the Royal Giants 2-0 in Atlantic City. Betting was plentiful the next day, as Foster went against the Royal Giants' slow-ball ace, Pop Andrews. Both hurlers "were hit hard," with the Royal Giants taking a 3-0 lead into the top of the fifth. A porous defense, coupled with four hits, enabled Philadelphia to put five runs on the scoreboard. The Royal Giants came back with one in the bottom of the sixth and two more in the seventh, on a homer over the center-field wall, to go ahead 6-5. Philadelphia knotted the contest in the top of the eighth and neither team could break the deadlock in the ninth. But in their half of the next inning, the Philadelphia Giants scored, thanks to a single by Grant, a sacrifice, and two errors, which produced the game-winning run. Foster held off the Royal Giants in the last of the tenth to win his eighth straight game in a "colored world's championship" series. The third and final bout was also captured by Philadelphia, 7-2, on September 16, as Danny McClellan again spaced eight hits while his teammates mounted a fourteen-hit attack, led by Pete Hill with four, including a homer.[11]

A superb performance was in store for Foster during his next outing on September 18, when he held Harrisburg to a single hit, delivered by the leadoff man in the bottom of the first. That runner eventually scored, but the Giants bounced back for lone runs in the fourth and sixth to win 2-1, as Foster struck out eleven and walked only two. On September 24, he replaced McClellan on the mound, struck out six, and produced a pair of hits, as Philadelphia defeated Manhattan 5-1. On October 1, Foster dropped a 3-1 contest to a championship Holyoke team, despite giving up only three hits. He struck out two and walked three, while pounding out two of the Giants' four safeties, including a double, the game's only extra-base hit. Three Philadelphia errors hurt Foster's cause.[12]

On October 25, the *Philadelphia Item* charted the Giants' 1905 record. Their performance, the *Item* declared, was "remarkable," with a still-incomplete mark of 132-21-3. Moreover, nine of the defeats had been by a single run, while one required eleven innings for Atlantic City to inflict. Only one shutout had been suffered by the Giants all season long, that at the hands of a team from Hudson, New York. By contrast, the Giants had recorded twenty-six shutouts of their own. In the 153 games that ended conclusively, Philadelphia had amassed 1,145 runs, while relinquishing but 467. The performance of the Giants pitchers, the *Item* noted, had been "truly remarkable." Only three men—Danny McClellan, Scotty Bowman, and Rube Foster—had handled Philadelphia's pitching assignments. In spite of that fact, only once during the season had a Giants pitcher failed to go the distance.[13]

That fall, Foster, along with teammates McClellan, Pete Hill, and Mike Moore, traveled to Havana to play for the Cuban X-Giants. On the roster were former Philadelphia Giants outfielder Bobby Winston, third baseman Danger Talbert, first baseman Ray Wilson, and shortstop John Hill. Matched against the All-Cubans in late October, Foster, despite three errors by the Cuban X-Giants, "pitched a good game," allowing only one earned run. Foster scored once and banged out two hits, while managing to withstand a three-run assault in the bottom of the ninth. The crowd of 4,500 watched as the Cuban X-Giants came out on top, 8-6. Sloppy fielding cost Foster another bout against the All-Cubans, when they beat him 4-1.[14]

Near the close of the year, the *Philadelphia Telegraph* applauded the Giants' top hurler:

> If Andrew Foster had not been born with a dark skin, the great pitcher would wear an American or National League uniform. Rube Waddell, Cy Young, Mathewson, McGinnity and others are great twirlers in the big leagues and their praises have been sung from Maine to Texas. Foster has never been equalled in a pitcher's box. Out of forty-nine games pitched this season he has won forty-five. Aside from his twirling ability, he is a heavy hitter and a fine fielder and ranks among the foremost of the country.

The *Indianapolis Freeman* agreed, adding, "Andrew Foster deserves every word of praise ever said of him. He is undoubtedly among the very best pitchers that America affords."[15]

Box scores available for the 1905 campaign indicated that Foster, in other than the Cuban exhibition games, compiled a 25-3-2 mark. His earned run average for those thirty contests was a sparkling 1.66. Later, Foster related that he lost only four of fifty-five games that year, competing against top semipro teams and squads from organized baseball as well. "We . . . cleaned 'em all up," as Foster put it.[16]

By now, Foster had acquired a reputation as a crafty ballplayer who relied as much on his brains as on his gifted right arm. One contest in Phila-delphia, where the Giants were a solitary run ahead of the Athletics, vividly demonstrated as much. The bases were loaded, with the potential tying run stationed on third base and the winning one on second. An exhausted Foster desperately needed a third out. At the plate was a dangerous hitter, left fielder Topsy Hartsel. The fans were in an uproar, hollering all sorts of epithets at Foster, including "scared," "yellow," and undoubtedly more charged ones. Foster motioned to Pete Booker, who was behind the plate, to come out to the mound. "Now you get out of the box," Foster declared, "like I'm going to walk him, like I'm afraid of Harry, and I'm going to walk him. And then I'm going to throw the fast one right through the middle. So you be ready." Returning to his backstop position, Booker hollered out to Foster, "Take your time, big boy, and walk him because he'll break up the game."[17]

The first pitch was fired down the center of the plate and the umpire called, "Strike one." Stirring, the fans in the grandstand asked, "What's going on?" After throwing over to first base several times, Foster tossed the ball to the second baseman and then began walking around. The grandstand erupted: "Make the big smoke pitch. Make him pitch!" Instead, Foster called out to Booker once again, before the catcher took his position and bellowed out, "Rube, be sure this time!" Foster hurled another fast ball in the same location and "Strike two" rang out. Booker leapt up and headed back toward the pitcher's box, shouting at the pitcher, "What'd I tell you to do? I signalled for a ball and you chucked over a strike. Do you want him to break up the game?" Reasoning that he couldn't fool Harstel yet again, Foster started stalling some more. As David Malarcher, later one of Foster's favorite players, put it, "He was quite a showman, you know."[18]

The fans were in an uproar, pounding the stands with their feet while applauding furiously. Turning to the umpire, Hartsel asked him to order the battery mates to stop delaying the game. The Athletics' first-base coach cried, "Make him pitch ball." From the other side of the diamond, the coach declared, "Don't let him stall, he's scared." Following their lead, the umpire, who had gone out to where Foster and Booker were standing, exclaimed, "All right, big fellar. Quit your stalling and play ball or I'll call the game." Foster calmly asked the umpire, "How much nerve have you got?" The reply was "I've got plenty." Foster then informed the man with the mask, "Well, if you have, I'll see because I'm going to put the next one right through the heart of the plate."[19]

As he readied to pitch, Foster questioned the ump, "Why don't you make him stand back off that plate? He'll get hit. MAKE him stand back." Hartsel looked down at his feet and pivoted to inform the umpire that he was properly stationed. As he did so, Foster, relying only on wrist action, flung the ball toward the middle of the plate and the call was "Yer out!" Hartsel went over to Foster, where he admitted, "I might have known you were up to something. You slipped one over on me that time." Grinning all the while, Foster headed for the dressing room.[20]

On April 1, the Philadelphia Giants opened their 1906 season by swamping the Brightons 10-4, with Bill Monroe pounding a homer and Scotty Bowman holding the opposition to seven hits. Despite rumors "that nearly all the last year's cracks were to join a new team," the *Philadelphia Item* noted, "they were all found in their places with the champions." In fact, one key member was missing: Rube Foster, who had been playing with the Philadelphia Quaker Giants, based in New York. Nevertheless, as the Philadelphia Giants readied for a contest at Marquette Oval in south Brooklyn, the *Item* declared that "the visitors are composed of nothing but stars." In mid-April, the paper, which was covering the Giants much less regularly than in previous years, reported that Foster, "last year's phenomenal pitcher," was rejoining his old squad in Altoona.[21]

Foster's first outing of the year, on April 19, hardly proved auspicious, however: Altoona pounded him for seventeen hits and won the contest 5-4, with a run in the top of the eleventh. The umpire was said to have "materially helped the home team in the last two innings." Foster tossed a two-hitter on May 20 against the mighty Leland Giants from Chicago; Philadelphia triumphed 9-1, thanks to a thirteen-hit attack. On May 31, Foster and Pop Andrews of the Royal Giants pitched scoreless ball for ten innings until the game was halted because of rain. Foster struck out five, walked one, and scattered eight hits in the brilliantly pitched ballgame. He again pitched against the Royal Giants on June 4, giving up ten hits and two walks, while striking out only one, but proved victorious 7-4 when Philadelphia plated three runs in the top of the ninth. On June 13, the *Item* termed Foster "as good as ever." Certainly, that appeared to be the case when Foster tossed a four-hit shutout against Hazleton on June 22. In the opening game of a doubleheader against Roebling on June 30, Foster gave up only three hits but walked five, while striking out two, as he managed to overcome five Philadelphia errors to win 6-5. Through July 9, Philadelphia had amassed a 66-12-3 record. On July 18, Foster, after giving up two runs in the bottom of the first, held Rockville scoreless. The Giants finally tied the game with a pair in the top of the ninth, and then scored the winning run in the tenth.[22]

In midsummer, the International League of Independent Professional Ball Players was formed, and eventually included the Philadelphia Giants, the Cuban X-Giants, the Wilmington Giants, the Philadelphia Professionals, and Riverton-Palmyra; the Philadelphia Quaker Giants and the Cuban Stars dropped out because of scheduling difficulties. Both the Philadelphia Professionals and the Riverton-Palmyra were white ball clubs. The Philadelphia Giants and the Cuban X-Giants jumped off to an early lead in the fight for the Frelhofer Cup, with each team compiling a 6-1 mark. Continuing to play outside their "league" as well, the Philadelphia Giants, behind Foster's six-hitter, defeated Millville (N.J.) 5-3 on August 23; he silenced his opponents until the final frame, when three runs crossed the plate to spoil his shutout bid. Philadelphia won the Frelhofer Cup and was again proclaimed "the Champion colored team of the world." In mid-September, the Giants prepared to play the All-Philadelphia Police squad, with Foster slated to pitch; he was said to possess "his usual speed and good curves." On September 18, the Giants defeated York, pennant winner of the Tri-State League, 6-0, as Danny McClellan scattered seven hits. On October 1, Philadelphia won three games, beating Brooklyn's Royal Giants 6-1, the Cuban X-Giants 8-2, and Brighton 5-2. Eleven days later, the Philadelphia Giants rallied for three runs in the top of the ninth to tie the score, before giving up one in the bottom of that frame to fall to the Philadelphia Athletics 5-4. Scotty Bowman gave the A's only three hits, while striking out six. Four errors proved costly for the Giants, who managed five hits, including two by Pete Hill and a homer by Harry Buckner, off Eddie Plank. Umpiring was the A's ace left-hander, Rube Waddell, whose calls were supposedly "off in several instances."[23]

In winning a third straight championship in 1906, the Philadelphia Giants compiled a 108-31-6 record. Giants owner H. Walter Schlichter issued a challenge to the major league teams, calling for a three- or five-game series to determine "who can play base ball the best—the white or the black American." On October 22, Schlichter was elected president of the National Association of Colored Baseball Clubs of the United States and Cuba; the Royal Giants' J. W. Connors was picked as vice-president, the Cuban Giants' J. M. Bright as treasurer, Nat C. Strong as secretary, and the Cuban Stars' Manuel Camps and the Cuban X-Giants' E. B. Lamar Jr. were placed on the Board of Trustees, along with Schlichter. The organization included four of the top teams in black baseball: the Philadelphia Giants, the Cuban X-Giants, the Royal Giants, the Cuban Giants, and the Cuban Stars. Patterned after the major leagues, the National Association was intended to ensure "the perpetuation of colored base ball" by fostering "absolute public confidence in its integrity and methods and maintaining a high standard of skill and sportsmanship in its players." Its founders sought to safeguard "the property rights of those engaged in colored base ball as a business, without sacrificing the spirit of competition in the conduct of the game." The National Association, it was reported, also desired to promote "the welfare of colored ball players as a class by perfecting them in their profession and enabling them to secure adequate compensation for expertness."[24]

The moguls of the leading clubs in black baseball considered the organization essential because reportedly all had lost money during the 1906 season. They pinpointed the "exorbitant salaries" received by the players and the spirited competition that existed among the teams. Consequently, they hoped, the *Philadelphia Item* reported, to put black baseball on a firm financial footing. To that end, it was essential to prevent the kind of player jumping that had characterized the previous season. Ultimately, "unscrupulous" teams, the *Item* declared, should be "cut out" from competition altogether.[25]

The determination of Schlichter and other leaders of black baseball to keep salaries in check, however, soon cost them dearly. An exodus of ball-players was about to occur, with the midwestern metropolis of Chicago, another baseball center, the beneficiary. Heading that migration was the greatest star in black baseball, Rube Foster.

That winter, Foster again performed in Cuba, leading the Fe ball club with nine victories. Cuban baseball was often first-rate, with major league squads, even pennant winners, frequently bested during visits to the is-land. E. B. Lamar Jr.'s Cuban X-Giants had gone to Cuba in 1900 and 1903, but another couple of years passed before another major influx of talent from the mainland traveled to Cuba to play winter ball. Fe featured some of the top players in black baseball, including Pete Hill, Charlie Grant, Home Run Johnson, Bill Monroe, and Foster. Cuban newspapers castigated the Fe players as "the interventionists," with the Almendares team, featuring almost all Cuban athletes, defeating Foster in the season finale.[26]

In early 1907, Sol White's *Official Guide: History of Colored Base Ball* was published. An invaluable source of information about black baseball, White's compendium contained several references to Rube Foster, as well as an essay written by him. White's *Official Guide* spoke of Foster's performances in the 1903 and 1904 championship series and contained box scores of some of his finest outings. Foster's team-mate and manager referred to him as "one of the best colored pitchers the game has produced." White also indicated that Foster had hurled "several no hit games" and had twice struck out as many as eighteen in a single contest: once against the Trenton YMCA (that total was ac-tually seventeen) and again against the Cuban X-Giants in the 1904 "colored world's championship."[27]

At the conclusion of his later-to-become-classic work, White con-tended that earlier black ballplayers had clearly "possessed major league qualifications." He singled out catcher Fleet Walker, who had played briefly in the old American Association, along with pitcher George Stovey, second baseman Frank Grant, and second baseman Bud Fowler, who all had starred in the International League. He also pointed to in-fielder George Williams, who had captained the original Cuban Giants, pitcher Billy Whyte, catcher Arthur Thomas, catcher Clarence Williams, center fielder–infielder Ben Boyd, third baseman Ben Holmes, and pitcher William Selden.[28]

Given the same opportunities as their white counterparts, White argued, "there would be a score or more colored ball players cavorting around the National League or American League diamonds at the present time." With his boundaries far more limited, however, the black ballplayer, White contended, "loses interest. He knows that, so far shall I go, and no farther, and, as it is with the profession so it is with his ability." Furthermore, the dearth of black teams also served as a deterrent. This was unfortunate, White suggested, because there were "many colored pitchers who would no doubt land in the big league." Among the pitchers he named were those often considered the era's finest: Danny McClellan, George Walter Ball, Harry Buckner, and Foster. The top position players included Foster's teammates Charlie Grant, Billy Francis, Nate Harris, Pete Hill, Grant "Home Run" Johnson, Bill Monroe, and Mike Moore, along with "many others."[29]

White's *Official Guide* also contained Johnson's study "Art and Science of Hitting" and Foster's essay "How to Pitch." Quality pitching, Foster suggested, was a baseball team's greatest need. To become a professional pitcher, he argued, "the essentials" had to be learned. Pinpoint control should be aspired to, although wildness afflicted every pitcher. Yet in contrast to others, when a full count was reached, Foster himself often resorted to the curve ball. "In the first place, the batter is not looking for it, and secondly they will hit at a curve quicker as it may come over the plate, and if not, they are liable to be fooled."[30]

To Foster, the greatest test for a pitcher occurred when men were on base. The pitcher, he offered, should strive "to appear jolly and unconcerned," as he himself frequently did with the bases loaded and a three-ball, two-strike count in place; that unnerved batters. Also, delaying the game often succeeded against those who waited anxiously at the plate.[31]

Foster concluded: "The three great principles of pitching are good control, when to pitch certain balls, and where to pitch them. The longer you are in the game, the more you should gain by experience. Where inexperience will lose many games, nerve and experience will bring you out victor." And "if at first you don't succeed, try again."[32]

THREE

A Return to the Midwest

Once back in the States, it was clear that Slick Schlichter's championship nine was about to be transformed. Team magnates Schlichter and Sol White were encountering considerable resentment from ballplayers like Foster and Pete Hill, who considered themselves woefully underpaid. The Giants were a powerful unit, featuring second baseman Charlie Grant, shortstop Grant "Home Run" Johnson—drawn from the Cuban X-Giants—outfielder Hill, and pitchers Danny McClellan and Foster. However, Foster, along with many of his compatriots, was increasingly disgruntled. As he saw matters, "The whole team was making only $100 out of Sunday games and a proportionate amount for other games. In spite of the fact that we were the best colored team in baseball, that was all Walter Schlichter, the owner, could or would do for us." Even worse, in the fall of 1906, Schlichter, like other white operators of black baseball on the East Coast, determined to cut costs. Henceforth, only fifteen cents a day would be provided for two meals, players were required to furnish their own uniforms, and no salaries would be issued before a full month in which games were regularly played had passed.[1]

Foster soon called together several of his teammates and informed them that in contrast to their situation, his contract had not been altered, nor his salary reduced. Nevertheless, he considered what Schlichter and other white moguls were doing to be unfair and urged that the ballplayers unite and, if necessary, "starve together." He promised to match their current salaries, along with the opportunity to do better, if they headed with him to join the Leland Giants in Chicago. Consequently, Foster, along with several other star players, departed from the Philadelphia Giants, the team they had led to three straight black baseball championships.[2]

Once again then, sensing that greater opportunities lay ahead, Foster opted to depart from a title-winning ball club. Like others players, both great and mediocre, Foster demonstrated only limited loyalty to the black baseball teams where he had first attracted notice as a topflight hurler. This is noteworthy, particularly given Foster's own professed aversion to player jumping, once he became involved in management. In reality, Foster's record remained decidedly mixed in that area, as first evidenced by his enticement of other leading Philadelphia Giants to head out west.

Spurred by the hardening of Jim Crow practices in the South and industrial growth up north, African Americans, in greater numbers, moved during the early part of the twentieth century to cities like Philadelphia, New York, and Chicago. The number of blacks residing in Chicago neared forty thousand by the time Foster returned there in 1907; at the same time, African Americans still constituted only about 2 percent of the city population. Most blacks settled in Chicago's South Side, which, as it became densely crowded, experienced soaring rents. Lacking choices, blacks had to make do with increasingly dilapidated housing. They also witnessed new gambling joints and prostitution dens spring up; a red-light district, to which W. T. Stead's 1893 expose, *If Christ Came to Chicago,* had called attention, continued to flourish on the South Side. Reputable economic opportunities remained limited. More than two-thirds of the businesses in the area were owned by whites. Compounding problems, many employers refused to hire black workers, who also were little welcomed by most labor unions. This proved to be the case although many of the black migrants were educated or semieducated; indeed they made up a cohort of what W. E. B. Du Bois referred to as "the talented tenth," who eventually helped to lead an assault against segregation.[3]

Protest against such conditions as prevailed on the South Side and still more blatant racism was not altogether absent in Chicago. The year before Foster moved back to Chicago, the local chapter of the Niagara Movement, an all-black civil rights organization founded by Du Bois, had denounced a theatrical presentation that involved an adaptation of Thomas Dixon's novel, *The Clansman.* In highlighting the Civil War and the period of Reconstruction, Dixon's work painted African Americans as sex-crazed imbeciles determined to have their way with southern white womanhood; by contrast, the author cast the Ku Klux Klan in a heroic light.[4]

Back in seemingly ever-changing Chicago in 1907, Foster carried with him a reputation as black baseball's finest pitcher. For five consecutive years, he had guided his teams—first, the Cuban X-Giants, and then the Philadelphia Giants—to "the colored world's Championship." In the process, he had compiled a noteworthy record, albeit one that can only partially be documented because of the irregular reporting of black baseball contests. Nevertheless, it is clear that his mound work was superlative, often featuring high-strikeout, low-walk performances, and included any number of low-hit games, topped off by at least three no-hitters. Most important, Foster's celebrity was ensured by exceptional performances in championship bouts, especially the 1903 and 1904 black baseball world series; indeed, he won all eight title games that he pitched.

At the same time, Foster had become increasingly discontented with his lot, particularly the relatively low salary he continued to draw, notwithstanding his brilliant play. It was hardly surprising, then, that the ever-ambitious Foster eagerly agreed to join the Leland Giants as player-manager; his stature and persuasiveness enabled him to bring along some of the finest performers in black baseball. Making the move with Foster were catcher Pete Booker, second baseman Nate Harris, outfielders Pete Hill and Mike Moore, plus pitchers Bill Gatewood and Bill Bowman.

Before the season began, the *Indianapolis Freeman* columnist John L. Footslug suggested that African Americans were becoming more enamored of "America's great game." He then posed the question "So far as his ability at playing the game, where do you find any better players among the big white leagues of this country than are found in such far-famed clubs as the Philadelphia Giants, Cuban Giants, Chicago Giants, Leland (Pa.) Giants, Cleveland (O.) Blues, Indianapolis (Ind.) ABCs, and several other clubs?" Soon, Footslug and others placed Chicago's Leland Giants in that elite circle.[5]

As the 1907 season unfolded, Footslug examined the color barrier that kept some of the finest ballplayers out of organized baseball. "The African brother," he declared, "has found the color line in the big leagues a barrier that is insurmountable." Yet many black ballplayers were performing as capably as top minor leaguers and, if given the chance, might have done well in the majors. Footslug concluded, "Today we have Foster, Williams and a number of others who would be major-league stars if their color was not against them."[6]

Skippered by Foster, the 1907 Leland Giants produced a 110-10 record, purportedly including forty-eight straight wins at one point, while capturing the Chicago city league title. Operating at 79th and Wentworth Avenue, the Giants played in the Chicago municipal semipro circuit but also battled top black baseball teams from throughout the region. In the opening contest of a three-game series against the Indianapolis ABCs, Foster, on August 22, triumphed 7-4, despite giving up ten hits. The *Freeman*'s account of the battle indicated that Foster, "one of the greatest pitchers in history, sent them over in such style that the boys could not tap him for some while." In the next day's affair, Foster's readiness to resort to trickery was again evidenced. The ABCs held a 7-4 lead heading into the bottom of the eighth inning, but the Giants scored once and loaded the bases. At that point, Foster, who was coaching alongside third base, asked the pitcher to toss him the ball. As the pitcher did so, Foster simply stepped aside, the ball bounded away, and all three Leland runners scored. Three more runs came across that inning and Chicago ultimately prevailed 14-8.[7]

After the Giants took the last game, the *Freeman* again discussed Foster's baseball acumen and that of his team. The ABCs were a good ball club, the newspaper noted, but had competed against a vastly more experienced squad. Furthermore, the Leland Giants were led by a man who for ten years had battled against the nation's top teams. "This man has taken time to teach the arts of the game, and why should they not play good ball. Mr. Foster is one of the best pitchers in this country, so say the big critics, 'and if he were white would belong to the biggest league in America.'"[8]

In the early September issues of the *Freeman,* Frederick North Shorey spun the almost apocryphal tale of Andrew "Rube" Foster in reporting the results of a series between the Leland Giants and Mike Donlin's All-Stars. The six-game set, in Shorey's estimation, engendered greater excitement than the previous year's World Series that had featured Chicago's two major league teams. Shorey began by declaring, "If you have never seen 'Rube' Foster, captain and manager of the Leland Giants, the aggregation of colored ball players that is the pride of the entire population of Dearborn street, in action, you are not qualified to discuss baseball, first degree fan though you may be." Or at least that was how African American baseball fans in Chicago saw matters, as the Leland Giants battled perhaps the finest semipro team in the land, which included the likes of Jake Stahl, Jimmy Callahan, Jimmy Ryan, and Mike Donlin. A favorite of John McGraw's, Donlin nevertheless had left the New York Giants in 1906, a year removed from a season in which he had batted .356 and led the National League with 124 runs scored. Among the All-Stars were Stahl, whose nine-year major league career was temporarily halted in 1907; and Ryan, a lifetime .306 hitter whose eighteen year stint in the big leagues had ended in 1903.[9]

A spirited crowd of four thousand gathered for the opening contest on August 27, with money being waged freely. For weeks, Shorey reported, anticipation had mounted about the impending series between the Leland Giants and the All-Stars. In the black community, the general impression was "that it all depended upon Rube Foster." The All-Stars, who knew of Foster's legendary pitching performances back east, hoped "that the colored team might do something to undo the efforts of the twirler." "The entire colored population of the city," Shorey wrote, "who were interested in baseball were there, occupying grandstand and box seats." African Americans turned out in large numbers, ready to bet on the Giants as Foster took the mound for the first game; "they did not see how it could be lost." The All-Stars also had considerable backing, with one "well-known ball player," who was standing amid a large group of blacks, chortling, "I've got $20 that says the chocolates won't win." The response was immediate: "I'll take $5 of that money, white man." "Heah, gimme $2." "An' I'll take another $5."[10]

As the Leland Giants took the field, Shorey reported, a riot nearly broke out in the grandstand. The Giants confidently went to their positions, with Foster waiting until his teammates were all in place. When Foster was spotted, a roar coursed through the crowd. "Rube Foster was the whole thing," Shorey noted, "and, what is more, he knows it." The journalist continued:

It is well worth a trip to the North, South or West Side to see Foster in action. In appearance he is almost the typical stage darke—husky, black as coal, with a halting stride, a head sunk between his shoulders, and without any ostensible neck. When he enters the box he takes a calm survey of the field to see that his men are in place, sizes up the batter, and suddenly, before the batter realizes what has happened, the ball is over the plate for one strike. This is the most frequent of "Rube's" tricks, and he has plenty of them. He has the faculty of whipping the ball across the plate with or without the preliminary winding up, which is the most painful performance of so many pitchers, and he can do it underhand, with a side-wheel motion, overhand, or apparently snap it with his wrist. And when he is in a tight place he seemingly can pitch so that the ball will be batted to a certain place.[11]

Foster took the opening game—played on August 27, 1907—holding the All-Stars to three hits and a lone run in winning 3-1. He struck out five, walked only one, scored a run, and contributed a single to his own cause. He appeared to grow stronger as the game progressed and, along with his first baseman, resorted to trickery yet again to catch a runner off base; the fans happily demonstrated their appreciation of the feat. Foster's celebrity was so great, Shorey declared, that "if it were in the power of the colored people to honor him politically or to raise him to the station to which they believe he is entitled, Booker T. Washington would have to be content with second place."[12]

After the contest, Shorey waxed eloquent about black baseball's most renowned player.

> Rube Foster is the pitcher of the Leland Giants, and he has all the speed of a Rusie, the tricks of a Radbourne, and the heady coolness and deliberation of a Cy Young. What does that make of him? Why, the greatest baseball pitcher in the country; that is what the best ball players of white persuasion that have gone up against him say. But his color has kept him out of the big leagues, and that is why the Leland Giants, the Philadelphia Giants, and other colored teams for the last ten years have had the advantage of a pitcher who otherwise would be a priceless boon to the struggling White Sox or the ambitious Highlanders just now.[13]

The All Stars rebounded to take the second game by the same 3-1 score, with Foster, who was playing right field, managing one of only two hits by the Leland Giants. The third game of the series engendered the greatest enthusiasm yet, especially after it became evident that Foster was going to pitch once again. Some six thousand exuberant spectators showed up at South Side Park, exceeding the attendance figures for Cubs' games that had been recently played on Chicago's West Side. The fans came with noise-making devices in hand, and bets were, once more, freely delivered. In a crowd of black patrons gathered under the stands, one dark-skinned gentleman stated, "If Rube don't win today Ah suah will walk home. Ah've put up mah last dollah on mah preference." A backer of the All-Stars retorted, "You fellows back there ought to give odds." The black better responded, "Where's youah spo'tin' blood, man? Are you afraid to bet on youah All-Star team?"[14]

In the meantime, Foster was warming up, resulting in an observation by a fan: "That boy suah can shoot them over." The game began with a pitcher's duel, although the Giants managed a first-inning run. Attempting to upset Foster, a spectator shouted as Donlin came to bat, "At 5 o'clock Mr. Foster will eat a dog½." Another cried out, "Here's where the chocolate loses his horseshoe." When a fan sought to bolster the All-Stars by attempting to affect a supposed black dialect, an African American spectator admonished him, "Befo' you try to imitate someone else you ought to learn the English language." Through it all, Foster continued his masterly pitching. A fine hitter, Donlin liked to stride up to the plate and quickly swing at pitches offered his way. Consequently, Foster delayed his tosses, causing Donlin to complain, "Here, you pitch that ball and pitch it quick." Foster retorted, "You'll get dat ball all right, don't you worry." The impatient Donlin flied out.[15]

In the ninth inning, an All-Star reached base with one out and took third after stealing second and advancing thanks to a poor throw from the Giants catcher. The always-dangerous Jake Stahl came to bat. Foster, clinging to a one-run lead, pitched deliberately. Stahl flied to right, and the runner on third tagged up and headed for home plate. The ball arrived, along with the runner, and umpire "Pipes" Conly exclaimed, "Out!" Giants fans poured onto the field, while Foster was hoisted onto the shoulders of a pair of strong black men. That Friday night, a celebration ensued along Dearborn Street.[16]

After the game, Frederick North Shorey conducted an interview with the winning pitcher. Foster was asked how long he had been playing ball. "Well, about ten years, I should say. You know, I play most of the time, in the winter going to Cuba or down to Palm Beach or somewhere. It seems like it's the only thing I can do." Foster discussed both his pitching techniques and his overall career.

I don't rely on any kind of ball, and I don't use any kind of system. I just kind of size up the batter and give him what I think he can't hit, sometimes it's a curve, sometimes it's a straight ball, but I can most always tell, sort of by instinct, what's coming off behind me. Five or six years ago, I think, I'd have been a first-class pitcher, but I found then I'd got as far as I could go and that there was no hope of getting into the big league, so I kind of let myself go. I was playing with the Philadelphia Giants then, and I played with them for five years.

In 1905 I won fifty-one out of the fifty-five games I pitched for that season, and that was doing pretty well. We played the New York Giants, the Philadelphia Athletics, the Nationals, the Brooklyns, the teams of the New England and Tri-State leagues, and cleaned 'em all up. It was when we beat the Athletics, with Rube Waddell pitching, that they gave me the name of the colored Rube Waddell. This is my first season in Chicago, and if I'm here another year I'll have even a stronger team than the one I've got now, and you'll allow that those boys can play pretty good ball. If we only had the chance that the white teams do, the opportunity to train and to go up against good teams all the time, I wouldn't be afraid to play against any teams in the country.

Generally exceptionally adept at cultivating interest in blackball, Foster was equally proficient in staking a claim for his own team's preeminence outside the realm of organized baseball.[17]

Then, Foster related a kind of general philosophy of life, with baseball always at the forefront of his explorations.

The only trouble with baseball is that it makes a man kind o' triflin'. He don't feel like going out and working all day for what he used to get for three or four hours' work. I get kind of that way myself after playing ball all the year round. But if it hadn't been for playing ball and living outdoors I don't suppose I'd been here today. All the rest of my family died of consumption, and I suppose I'd gone the same way if it hadn't been for baseball. I'm going to keep at it until I get too old, and then I guess I'll retire.[18]

The same issue of the *Freeman* featuring both the Giants' latest game with the All-Stars and the Foster interview contained an intriguing article indicating that organized baseball's color barrier might be ebbing. The Boston Braves were reported to have signed "a colored pitcher," Bill Joy, a very dark-skinned Malay, for the 1908 season. The announcement, the *Freeman* noted, had initiated "a little zephyr along the baseball circuit which is liable to develop into a hurricane" before the quandary of hotel and travel accommodations was resolved. The newspaper editorialized, "The fact that baseball is strictly an American game has caused a general resentment against foreigners, except the Irish and Germans, by players as well as the public." Although skillful managers had helped to smooth things over for certain ballplayers, the hiring "of this Negro from Honolulu," the *Freeman* insisted, "is like a match in a powder magazine."[19]

Sportswriter David Wyatt, formerly a teammate of Foster's on the Chicago Union Giants, discussed baseball's segregated nature in the *Freeman*'s next edition. The series between the Leland Giants and Mike Donlin's All-Stars had ended with the black players prevailing, thanks largely to the four games Foster had won. Some "20,000 lovers of baseball" had attended the games, Wyatt declared, with "no color line drawn anywhere." Whites and blacks, men and women, had congregated in the box seats and bleachers, readily discussing the relative merits of the two teams and the key performers and how the series might impact "the future of the Negro in baseball." Only praise for the Giants was heard, with Foster, hardly surprisingly, "coming in for the lion's share."[20]

The results of the series had not been fully anticipated because several baseball critics had considered the Leland Giants "overrated." After witnessing the first game, White Sox owner Charles Comiskey was no longer so skeptical. "Commy" declared, in fact, that "if it were possible he would have annexed the signature of at least three of the boys to contracts." Furthermore, he was so impressed by "the fast, snappy work of the Lelands" that he sent his world championship unit over to watch them perform.[21]

The Giants, Wyatt suggested, had surprised many.

The colored boys demonstrated clearly that they were not a bunch of overgrown corn-fed athletes, despite appearances, and many who thought they would see a gang of "piano movers" instead of ball players were greatly surprised, because the colored boys played so fast, pulled off so many tricks and outwitted the All-Stars to such an extent that their friends were compelled to express their sympathy in an open manner.

In the series against the All-Stars, the Giants had played before the largest crowds yet to witness semipro ball.[22]

Baseball afforded black folk all sorts of opportunities, Wyatt insisted. "That there is a great open field in baseball for the colored man there is [no] disputing, and the sooner we get the facts into the print so that they may reach the eyes of the people, the more credit we will receive and we will have less of the old 'bogy' that we haven't got a chance." The Leland ball club reputedly had no chance to succeed financially, but despite two months of poor weather, had done well. "All we need," Wyatt wrote, "is the courage; we have the talent and the ability is well known."[23]

All those attributes were obviously possessed by black baseball's leading performer. Foster and George Wilson—known as the "Black Rusie," a reference to major league star Amos Rusie—were considered by astute baseball observers, Wyatt noted, "to be the equal to any white pitchers." Living up to that reputation, Foster hurled another no-hitter—at least his fourth—the following week against the South Chicago Rooters' Association, striking out seven and walking three, to win a 1-0 contest that determined the South Side championship. The Giants managed only three hits but punched across a run in the top of the sixth. Forty-five hundred fans witnessed Foster's feat against the club operated and managed by Jake Stahl; the *Freeman* likened Foster's latest accomplishment to another masterpiece he had tossed against Newark's Eastern League squad. He was said to have hurled "the pigskin across the plate with such terrific speed, that the southsiders showed actual terror." The atmosphere for the game appeared electric because Foster was on the mound. "'Rube' Foster is now to baseball," the *Freeman* asserted, "what [Joe] Gans is to prizefighting," referring to the black world lightweight champion.[24]

The 1907 season was viewed as a tremendous boon for black teams from Chicago to St. Louis. The Leland Giants, in particular, had drawn large crowds composed of both whites and blacks. "They wanted to see

Rube Foster pitch," the *Freeman* declared, "as much so as they would care to see Waddell do the stunt, the result being heavy receipts."[25]

That was important to Foster, who, on moving over from the Philadelphia Giants, had been appalled to discover that his new team was paid only $150 for a holiday doubleheader. Foster persuaded Frank C. Leland to allow him to take over the squad's booking arrangements; he proceeded to demand a 40 percent cut for the ballplayers. "After some argument," Foster later remembered, "we got it and made over $500 that day instead of the piffling $150." He then began to insist that the gate be evenly divided between host teams and the Leland Giants. From this stage onward, he was involved in booking arrangements. A shrewd business operative, Foster typically was determined to cut a better deal for both his players and himself.[26]

Foster, for his part, purportedly was approached by white semipro teams, who, seeking to boost their attendance figures and impressed by his pitching skill, sent "attractive contracts" his way. Believing that black baseball would suffer from such a defection, however, he refused those offers. Rather, he desired to help blackball thrive until organized baseball was compelled to discard its racial barriers.[27]

Following the 1907 season, discussion occurred regarding possible formation of a National Colored Baseball League. In mid-November, the *Freeman* indicated that interest in such an organization was mounting. The league, one correspondent argued, would allow all to witness "the National Game played in its best form. We will have the pleasure of enjoying good ball playing with the air of freedom that the white man does in his park." Most important, it would spur professionalism among black teams and players. Among the black baseball figures who favored establishment of such a league were Frank C. Leland, Ran Butler, Elwood C. Knox, J. D. Howard, and Rube Foster; from this point forth, Foster became involved in a series of endeavors to organize blackball. Also supportive were top African American actors, such as Bert Williams, George Walker, Bob Cole, J. Rosamond Johnson, Ernest Hogan, and S. H. Dudley.[28]

On December 18, representatives from premier black teams gathered in Indianapolis to discuss the proposed formation of the new league, with Frank C. Leland selected as president. The impressive turnout, Cary B. Lewis suggested, demonstrated the likelihood that "a national colored baseball league" could be constructed. Plans were afoot to begin the league in 1908. However, the high hopes quickly petered out and this latest attempt, like earlier ones, to birth a black baseball league, withered away.[29]

As the 1908 season unfolded, Foster remained a topflight pitcher. On July 20, he left his right field post to replace a struggling Walter Ball on the mound during the seventh inning of a tight contest with the Normals. Foster, who smacked four hits, went nine innings, relinquishing only two hits, while striking out eight and walking but one. The bottom of the ninth was tension laden as the Normals loaded the bases with no outs, but Foster wriggled free. Finally scoring in the top of the fifteenth, the Giants escaped with a 6-5 triumph.[30]

The July 25 edition of the *Indianapolis Freeman* referred to the Leland Giants as "the best organized semi-pro team in the world today." As a consequence, it would be unfair to single out any one player "as a star," for all who made up the team, from the owner to the batboy, were tops in their fields. Moreover, all operated like parts of a well-oiled machine. Finally, "These gentlemen's male forte is 'gentlemen on and off the ball field,'" and thus the Leland Giants were said to garner universal respect wherever they appeared.[31]

Equally important to the *Freeman,* the Leland ballplayers were "of high moral character and not the ball players of years ago." The operators of the Leland franchise, the paper contended, were "some of the best colored people in the State of Illinois commercially, politically and professionally." The team was backed by at least $100,000 in financial capital, its own ball park, a roller-skating rink, and the Air Dome of Amusement capable of seating two thousand. The team's management reportedly was constructing an amusement park that would dwarf Chicago's Luna Park. "A club with such foundation," the *Freeman* noted, "is enough to make any one 'sit up and take notice.'"[32]

Foster won his next outing, striking out ten, walking only one, and scattering nine hits, while getting one of his own, to defeat the Spaldings 4-3. Nearly 7,500 spectators attended the contest, which was decided only when the Giants scored in the top of the ninth and Foster shut down the opposition in the bottom of the frame.[33]

The August 1 edition of the *Indianapolis Freeman* contained a letter from Frank C. Leland, in which he extolled the virtues of "the world's colored champions, the Leland Giants." As of late July, the 1908 version of the Giants had taken fifty-three of fifty-seven contests, winning all their games in the recently disbanded Chicago City League, defeating the New York Cuban Giants five straight, Cuba's All Havanas in eleven of thirteen matches, and Jimmy Callahan's Logan Squares in eight of nine encounters. The ballpark at Auburn Park, built to hold seven thousand spectators, was, in Leland's words, "not large enough to accommodate our following." Virtually every home game resulted in a sign out front indicating "Standing room in the field only." Leland singled out for particular praise "the world's greatest, Rube Foster, who has lost only one game out of twenty pitched thus far."[34]

At the start of an eagerly anticipated six-game set against the renowned Philadelphia Giants, the Leland Giants, with first baseman Foster contributing a single, defeated his former team 6-4. With four hits, including a home run, Foster powered Leland to a 10-7 win over West Innis on August 2. In the next day's contest against the Philadelphia Giants, Leland won easily, 11-1, as Foster tossed a five-hitter, struck out five, and issued only one walk. Foster, who shut out Philadelphia until the ninth, was said to have been "wonderfully effective" against a lineup that featured shortstop John Henry Lloyd and catcher Bruce Petway. Six days later, Foster lost for only the second time all season, despite giving up only two hits to the Logan Squares. Foster, who again garnered five strikeouts, also doled out seven free passes in the 4-3 loss; he shut out Logan after the first two innings, but a ninth inning rally left Leland just short. The series ended in a tie: Leland had won three of the first four contests, but Philadelphia bounced back to take the last two games when Leland shortstop George Wright and second baseman Nate Harris were lost to injuries.[35]

After Foster and his Leland Giants made their first trip together to Detroit, the *Detroit Free Press* sports editor declared,

> Several of them would be in the big league, were it not for their color, notably among these is "Rube" Foster, who is considered among the best pitchers in the world, barring nobody. He has worked against the leading batters of both leagues and they have found his offerings as vivid a propo-

sition as anything in the hurling line ever cut loose. He played all over the United States; also invaded the Island of Cuba. He managed a Cuban Club [in] the Cuban National League. He is the best known Colored man in the world today.[36]

In February, Leland Giants president Beauregard Mosely and Foster determined to take the team south for spring training, reportedly the first time a semiprofessional squad, black or white, was to take such a venture upon itself. This followed an announcement that minor league units in Chicago, Milwaukee, and Joliet were going to establish "a league of star clubs" headed by a commissioner associated with organized baseball. As the *Indianapolis Freeman* saw matters, "[T]his bit of news startled the baseball world." Depending on the results of the impending season, the Leland Giants, the "biggest drawing card" in the Midwest, could well "break that strong barrier of race prejudice." Predicting that many smaller leagues might soon add black teams, the *Freeman* declared, "It looks like the colored baseball players will get just a peep into that long looked for promised land." However, "a lot depends not only on the Leland Giants, but all colored clubs, for their knockers will be busy. The smallest detail will be laid before the commissioners." In the meantime, the Leland Giants readied to travel southward, with Texans said to be eagerly awaiting the appearance of "their native son"; Foster, the paper contended, "would be a drawing card for any club, let alone the Leland Giants." Cities along the eastern seaboard were also preparing for the Giants, who were shaping up to be a twenty-one-man contingent, "the largest aggregation of colored baseball players in the world."[37]

The tour, spanning almost 4,500 miles, proved to be markedly successful. Reportedly, the Leland Giants won every game, despite playing top teams across the South and in Texas, appearing in Memphis, Birmingham, Fort Worth, San Antonio, Prairie View, and Houston. Among their opponents was a young pitcher with the San Antonio Black Bronchos named Joseph "Smokey Joe" Williams, also known as "Big Cyclone Joe," who sported a blazing fastball. A warm greeting awaited the Giants, with the outpouring of affection particularly striking in east Texas, where Foster had last played in the Lone Star State. As the Giants arrived at the train depot in Fort Worth just after noon on April 18, a station filled with both black and white supporters awaited them. Moreover, when Foster was spotted, "he was given a welcome that would have done honor to the President of the United States. The people had carriages, automobiles and an opera coach for the club, and long before time to play the grounds could not accommodate all the people." Similar scenes unfolded in Austin, San Antonio, and Houston. In Houston, a large contingent from Foster's hometown of Calvert was present.[38]

"The ovation from men of every walk of life given Foster," declared the *Freeman*, "gives prominence to the high esteem of the people all over the country." Foster "is without a doubt the most popular ball player in the country." He had also proven to be an astute administrator, thereby ensuring the success of the tour, despite repeated warnings that it could never succeed.[39]

The 1909 season was another fruitful one for the Leland Giants, although it was marred by a broken leg Foster suffered that summer, a setback induced by another top black baseball squad, and defeat at the hands of the Chicago Cubs, who finally agreed to meet his team in a postseason series. The physical ailment placed Foster on the sideline, an unfortunate occurrence for both him and the Leland Giants because he had opened the campaign with eleven straight wins, including four shutouts. In an extended series that year, Leland easily bested the Cuban Stars, taking eleven of sixteen games, the only American team able to do so. In the process, the Giants snapped the winning streak of the Stars' ace pitcher José Méndez; Leland was the lone ball club on the mainland to beat him. All that occurred despite the loss of both Foster and outfielder Bobby Winston with crippled legs. With Foster on the sideline, his Giants battled doggedly in late July against the St. Paul Gophers. The Gophers took the opener 10-9, scoring twice in the top of the eleventh and holding the Giants to one run in the bottom of the frame. In reporting the first game results, the *St. Paul Pioneer-Press* termed the Giants "far-famed as the best in the land," and the Gophers "the record-breakers of the Northwest." After Leland won the next two, the Gophers bounced back to win the last couple of games and the series. Characteristically, Foster refused to acknowledge that his injury-depleted Giants had been bested by a superior team.[40]

In mid-October, Leland faced off against the Chicago Cubs, then a perennial National League power. In 1906, Frank Chance's team had won a record 116 games, then was stunned by the cross-town White Sox in the World Series. The next two seasons resulted in the Cubs' being crowned world champions. During the past season, Chicago had won 104 games but finished six games back of the Pittsburgh Pirates. The Cubs featured the famed double-play combination of shortstop Joe Tinkers and second baseman Johnny Evers, along with their superb first baseman–manager Chance. Heading a deep pitching staff were the great Moredecai "Three Finger" Brown, Orvie Overall, Ed Reulbach, and Jack Pfiester, all at least seventeen-game winners.

On October 18, the Cubs, without Evers and Chance—who supposedly refused to play—in the lineup, prevailed 4-1, scoring once in the second and three times in the third to defeat Walter Ball, who allowed only seven hits. The Leland Giants, who had won the City League championship, managed but three singles off twenty-seven-game winner Brown, who gave up a lone run in the bottom of the sixth. The second game, played on October 21, pitted Foster, who hadn't pitched since July 12, against Reublach, who won nineteen games during the regular season. Chance would refer to Foster as "the most finished product I've ever seen in the pitcher's box," but the Giants' star, due to the extended layoff, was clearly not in the best condition. The Giants dominated the contest until the very end, scoring five times in the last of the third. The Cubs got one back in the top of the fourth but failed to tally again until the eighth, when they managed another run. Still, going into the ninth, they trailed 5-2 and appeared, in the words of the *Chicago Daily Tribune,* "hopelessly beaten." After getting Tinker out, an obviously fatigued Foster, who had struck out only three batters, an uncharacteristically low number for him, gave up consecutive hits to Pat Moran, Overall, and Heine Zimmerman. Jimmy Sheckard walked, the only free pass Foster issued all afternoon, forcing in a run. Frank Schulte grounded sharply to third baseman Dick Wallace, who threw out Overall at home plate. Needing only one more out to close out the game, Foster allowed Del Howard to smack a single, the Cubs' thirteenth hit, against the right-field fence, scoring Zimmerman and Sheckard and enabling Schulte to reach third.[41]

Foster began delaying, the *Tribune* reported, operating "about as fast as a hippopotamus would run on skis." After throwing a pair of tosses over to third, Foster headed for the Giants' bench to confer with pitcher

Pat Dougherty regarding whether he should remain on the mound. Foster then asked the umpire for the score of the game, now tied at five runs apiece. The Cubs objected to the delay, as did the umpire, and Dougherty was ordered back to the sideline. As a band of Giants, including Foster, and a number of Cubs gathered around the umpire, Schulte raced for home and was declared safe. An irate Foster asked how Schulte could be allowed to score while a group of Cubs was conversing on the playing field. A debate raged well into the night about the game's concluding moments. During the first two contests, even many white fans in attendance had questioned a series of calls by the umpire, bellowing out, "Beat them squarely, or quit playing."[42]

The next day's contest was also hard fought and proved to be the best-pitched match of the series. Three Finger Brown shut out the Giants 1-0 on four hits, topping Dougherty, who gave up only three hits. A lone run by the Cubs in the top of the third won the game, which was called after seven innings because of darkness.[43]

The closeness of these games, along with disappointing attendance figures, undoubtedly persuaded the Cubs' management not to play Foster's ball club again. That was, of course, terribly unfortunate in so many ways. His team was unable to compete against the very best organized baseball had to offer. Fans missed the opportunity, consequently, to witness how good the finest practitioners of black baseball could be. And Foster was left with bittersweet memories of these lone encounters, which saw him go head-to-head against some of major league ball's finest, despite lacking his usual polish and stamina because of his midsummer injury and ensuing layoff.

FOUR

The Leland Giants

By the advent of the Cubs' series, Frank C. Leland, due to a power struggle with Rube Foster, had departed from the team he had founded four years earlier. Foster was initially backed by two former Leland associates, Major R. R. Jackson and Beauregard Mosely. Leland went to court, seeking to prevent Foster from using the team name, and Foster countersued. The court ruling was curious, to say the least. Foster was allowed to retain the name Leland Giants, although the team's namesake maintained the existing lease at Auburn Park. Foster, moreover, was enjoined from raiding the Leland roster; Leland had formed a new club of his own, terming it the Chicago Giants. Initially, Leland also kept Foster's team from participating in the Chicago City League. Foster, relying on attorney Mosely, obtained a lease at Normal Park, situated at 69th and Halstead, only a half mile from where the Leland Giants had been playing. Foster also raided his old team, the Philadelphia Giants, hiring some of the greatest stars in black baseball, including shortstop John Henry Lloyd, third baseman Home Run Johnson, catcher Bruce Petway, and pitcher Frank Wickware.[1]

The breakup with Leland was a contentious affair, with Foster later asserting that his former boss sought to drive him from the game. In the process, Foster demonstrated one of his less noble traits: a propensity to lash out at those who vied with him for control of a baseball organization. At such a point, he frequently hurled embittered invective even at onetime compatriots and colleagues. Now, Foster charged that Leland insisted on being credited with his team's remarkable success on the playing diamond and the general ascendancy of black baseball. His former boss, Foster insisted, demanded to control "the destiny of the game" and to become, in effect, "Czar of the baseball universe." Leland sought to take over the managerial reins from Foster, a move opposed by the team's investors. They, however, determined to retain Foster, who claimed to have "accomplished in one year what [Leland] failed to do in a lifetime." All the while, the man who had brought him back to the Midwest, Foster bristled, engaged in "low, dirty, undermining tactics against me."[2]

In typical fashion, Foster, looking ahead to the 1910 season, laid claim for his team to be considered the finest in black baseball; it was characteristically also the best paid, pulling down weekly salaries of $250 for the full squad. Amazingly enough, he now asserted that the Cuban X-Giants had long boasted of that status, despite their having lost two of three games to his Philadelphia Giants in 1904. The Philadelphia management, Foster declared, had refused to play any more games against the X-Giants. The New York team had disbanded, never having dropped a best-of-seven series, so no team, in his estimation, currently deserved the title of "colored world's champion." The St. Paul Gophers, having defeated Leland in a best-of-five set, proclaimed their right to be so crowned, but Foster contested that notion, declaring that those games were "only exhibition contests." Furthermore, he continued uncharitably, "no man who ever saw the Gophers play would think of classing them as world's colored champions."[3]

Hardly surprisingly, Foster stood ready to field the question "Who and where is the best colored team in the world?" He declared, "I could answer you with a smile, and as a fact: the Leland Giants are head and shoulders above all the teams in all departments of the game. For three years, when the team was intact, no team ever won a series of games from them." Having been a part of all the top black ball clubs, Foster confidently proclaimed that the Leland Giants were the finest. Moreover, his ballplayers, he wrote, "are known far and wide. They have received more recognition from the press, have raised the standard higher than all the other colored teams together."[4]

Announcing that the game had never been as popular as it was at present, Foster warned that black baseball moguls better "get together and quit trying to put each other out of business." Otherwise, "the ball player can no longer speak of his profession with pride, for it won't take it long to get back where it was before the Leland Giants came to

Chicago in 1907." Foster then pointed to the success of the Leland Giants, who, though a crippled squad, had won the Chicago City League championship and battled the Cubs "to a standstill." In competing against the National League team, Foster remarked, "the Lelands accomplished what no other colored club ever accomplished. Their gentlemanly way and good ball playing gained so much prestige that public sentiment forced the Cubs to meet the Lelands."[5]

Now, the Leland Giants would no longer participate in the City League, where they were being replaced by Frank C. Leland's Chicago Giants. Proudly, Foster insisted that he was departing of his own accord. He refused to condemn the very team that he had sacrificed so mightily to build up. He sought only to maintain the high standards that the Leland Giants had established, as represented by the pennant flag that would fly on Chicago's South Side in 1910. Leland sought a court order denying Foster the right to hang that pennant, but the banner soon went up.[6]

Sportswriter David Wyatt worried about a possible baseball war that might be brewing in Chicago's black baseball circles. The Leland Giants, he offered, had placed "Negro baseball . . . upon a higher scale of efficiency"; this was highly appreciated by "all well-meaning patrons of the game." As he had indicated earlier, Wyatt believed that "the Lelands have been piloted by their new manager clear beyond the hopes and expectations of their admirers; never before has a Negro team been able to get on a series with a world's champion big league club, or for that matter with any big league club of championship caliber."[7]

Wyatt had been asked repeatedly why a new ball club was being formed, when the Giants' "efforts as athletes have brought so much praise and honor to bear upon us as a race. Why should the missiles of war be hurled broadcast before our great team has reaped the reward of its earnest efforts?" Wyatt answered bluntly: "Jealousy seems to be at the back of the whole thing." Still, he hoped that internecine battles could be avoided, "if for no other reason, it should be for the good of Negro baseball." Wyatt then pointed out that black ballplayers had hardly advanced until "the brains, money and efforts of a number of well-meaning men produced the now famous Leland Giants, who started Negro baseball on the upward trend." Unfortunately, "some of our most loyal and influential baseball men" were planning to war with that very ball club, which had "just begun to pierce the dense cloud that has hung over our heads for years."[8]

A salary war, Wyatt feared, could well result in "the demise of the game." A similar development earlier in the decade had temporarily wiped out black baseball in Chicago, now the nation's finest. At that time, Foster had departed for the East Coast, where his star rose dramatically. In fact, he "had acquired so much fame," Wyatt noted, "that managers were offering him salaries higher than had ever been heard of in Negro baseball." Subsequently, other players were tendered similar offers. As salaries increased, magnates, striving "to save themselves" by reducing costs, determined to create the National Association of Colored Baseball Clubs. Frank C. Leland refused to go along as the very existence of black baseball in the East was called into question. At that point, Leland, in a move supposedly proven to be "the salvation of the Negro baseball player," consulted with Foster and promised to provide the capital if the pitcher delivered the athletes. Consequently, the East lost a great deal of talent, a fate the Midwest could also suffer, Wyatt warned, if a new salary war were kicked off.[9]

Major R. R. Jackson, who had been named secretary of Frank C. Leland's newly formed Chicago Giants, responded to Wyatt's charges. First, Jackson dismissively referred to Wyatt as "a 'has been,' who has outlived his usefulness as a ball player" and had recently served as the Leland Giants' official scorekeeper. Wyatt, Jackson asserted, knew nothing of the financial dealings of those who had invested thousands "to make the Leland Giants great." Nor was Wyatt familiar with the "inside facts" that had resulted in establishment of the Chicago Giants. Furthermore, Wyatt had it all wrong, Jackson declared, because the majority of baseball supporters "are on Frank Leland's side." After all, "Leland is the 'father' of baseball in Chicago, is honest, eminently fair, and a man who accords everybody a square deal." Pushed out of the National Association of Colored Baseball Clubs, Leland subsequently strove to establish "a first-class ball club and to regain the prestige in the baseball world that he had honestly and conscientiously earned and established during the past fifteen years." It was Leland, not the association, Jackson reminded the *Freeman*'s readers, who had induced "the 'mighty Rube Foster'" to come to Chicago. Moreover, "it was Leland's name that made the team great," along with his deft administration and management of quality ballplayers.[10]

Jackson made light of Wyatt's concerns about an impending salary war. The total amount expended on salaries for the Chicago Giants during the upcoming season, Jackson noted, would remain the same and would not surpass that of the Leland Giants. One major difference, he pointed out, would occur. All the Chicago Giants would be fairly compensated, with no player paid "twice as much as any other man on the team." Obviously referring to Foster, Jackson wrote, "It is easier and much better to pay each man $10 more for his services than to pay $200 per month to one man when other men on the team are playing just as good ball and are just as popular in the public eye."[11]

Responding in his own fashion, Wyatt underscored the importance of demonstrating business and administrative acumen, including the careful tracking of actual performance, in addition to playing prowess. The oldest black teams, like the Cuban Giants, the Page Fence Giants, the Cuban X-Giants, and the Philadelphia Giants, were owned by whites. The Leland Giants and the Chicago Giants, by contrast, were run by blacks. However, for Wyatt, those squads "occupy a position similar to the graphaphone and the singer—the Negro being on the mechanical end of it." Unfortunately, Wyatt declared, much remained "foreign to the average Negro manager, player and promoter. The things in base ball that count for the most are the very things that the average Negro base ball man knows the less of."[12]

The *Freeman* was held up by Wyatt as an example of both a successful enterprise and a great newspaper. This resulted from the fact that the paper "is owned, controlled and operated by Negroes, and its columns are always open to any news or work of merit that a Negro can produce. The news is sought for and written by Negroes. . . ." Unfortunately, however, black baseball clubs had typically been run in a different fashion. "There is no place for you and you can not hope for any consideration if you be other than a player, and woe be unto you, as a player, if you spring an idea that crosses that of the manager. These mistaken ideas must all be removed, and until that time base ball can not be considered in a serious manner." All this had to change, was Wyatt's stance.[13]

Like Foster and several other leaders of black baseball, Wyatt was concerned about the game's general condition. To that end, he returned to a theme that Foster, along with a small band of luminaries, had shortly emphasized and would repeat: the need to organize. In calling once more for the establishment of "a colored league," Wyatt pointed to the success of the Leland Giants in winning the Chicago City League championship and the publicity that team had thereby spawned. Significant too was the difficulty that booking agencies experienced in acquiring favorable terms for independents. Increasingly, leagues were cropping up, which reduced opportunities for traveling squads. Those leagues, in turn, sought to affiliate with organized baseball and quickly drew a color line.[14]

Prior to the start of the 1910 baseball campaign, Foster, who had long determined to retain the kind of administrative control over his team that Wyatt was calling for, planned an extensive barnstorming tour. The 9,072-mile trek carried the Leland Giants from Chicago, where they initially departed in early January for Palm Beach, Florida, before moving on to Georgia, Alabama, Tennessee, Mississippi, Louisiana, Texas, Oklahoma, and Missouri. The last game was played in Kansas City on May 11, at which point the Giants returned home, having been in Chicago for only a brief spell in late March since the trip began. The 1910 Leland Giants included many holdovers from the previous season, although outfielders Bobby Winston and Mike Moore, along with pitcher Walter Ball, had joined the Chicago Giants.[15]

Nevertheless, Foster's squad, which he often termed his finest, was loaded. Foster's pitching staff eventually included Pat Dougherty, Frank "Kansas Cyclone" Wickware, and himself, of course. Behind the plate was Bruce Petway, with Sam Strothers backing him up. The infield featured first baseman Pete Booker, second baseman Home Run Johnson, third sacker Wes "Whip" Pryor, the great shortstop John Henry Lloyd, and utility man Fred Hutchinson. Frank Duncan was placed in left field, Pete Hill in center, and Andrew "Jap" Payne in right.[16]

Stationed in Palm Beach, the Leland Giants battled against one of the top blackball teams: John Connors's Brooklyn Royal Giants, who had claimed the 1909 eastern championship. Leland prevailed 4-1, and a headline in the *Indianapolis Freeman* read, "Rube Foster Back in Form." Foster, described as "the colored champion ball pitcher of the world," was reported to have "added grace and dignity to his title" in hurling a three-hitter while striking out four. Giving up the four Leland runs and eleven hits was Frank Earle, the Royal Giants' top pitcher who had recently defeated the Cuban Stars' José Méndez and Juan Padrone. Foster dropped another contest to the Royal Giants 1-0, despite allowing only two hits.[17]

In the midst of the Leland Giants' extended tour, Foster produced a lengthy essay, "Success of the Negro as a Ball Player," which appeared in the *Indianapolis Freeman* on April 16. Foster was referred to by the paper as "Manager and Captain of the Famous Chicago Leland Giants, World's Colored Champions, Pennant Winners of Chicago Baseball League, Season of 1909." The black ballplayer, Foster declared, had made "great strides . . . in the past few years." With continued backing from "his own kinsmen in a business way," Foster suggested, "the distance between him and the paint designated as wonderful success will be materially lessened." Black baseball's current lack of organization and business know-how greatly disturbed the great pitcher-manager-administrator.[18]

The play of black athletes, Foster remarked, had been notably successful, enabling them to discard comedy routines and witticisms. Consequently, "an exhibition of the national pastime" was expected, "not a farce comedy." Appreciating this fact, black ballplayers had become careful students of the game. Thus, "Now," Foster asserted, "we have players who are classed with the best in the land." This was recognized by leading white baseball men, who were heard to say, "Too bad he is a colored man" or "If so and so was only a white man he would be in the big leagues." Such comments, Foster claimed, demonstrated "that the Negro in a measure has been wholly successful as a player." Indeed, "physically, mechanically or mentally-speaking," the black ballplayer

> has no superior. We have players at this time who can safely be classed with the highest types; and considering our resources for training and traveling in the business, I doubt if any of the big league stars could maintain the high playing standard and preserve their physical make-up in the extent that the colored player has, when you consider that he is compelled to ride in ill-ventilated cars and make long jumps, and is forced to put up with all sorts of inferior hotel accommodations, [and] usually [plays] exhibitions on diamonds that are likened unto the proverbial corn fields.

Despite such impediments, black baseball performers generally appeared ready to contest "the best in the land." With the same financial backing that white players received, many knowledgeable baseball representatives reasoned, black baseball "would far outclass" the paler version.[19]

Foster singled out black pitchers and catchers for particular praise. The moundsmen, he suggested, "are the real students of the game." Ever aggressive, they were striving constantly to devise means "to deceive the other fellow." Foster contended that because "quite a few of our pitchers have shown enough to be classed with the best in the country, it must mean that the player of color is a success." As for the top catchers in black baseball, "were they white, they could name their own salaries." Happily then, Foster concluded, "our best representative players are shining in positions which are considered the head and brains of all clubs." Black baseball also featured great hitters, he noted, but only time would determine how they might fare against top-caliber pitching.[20]

Black baseball would best be served, Foster argued, by establishment of a "colored league." He considered such an organization "absolutely necessary." Despite toiling for some twenty years, black players, managers, and owners were no more closely linked "to our white neighbor than when we first started." Rather, "we are farther apart, as he is going ahead forming leagues in every little hamlet; and the forming of leagues produces a barrier we can not surmount." The participants in black baseball required "proper financial backing and encouragement." At present, however, Foster wrote, "[W]e . . . find ourselves in a dangerous predicament." Good black ballplayers could be uncovered throughout the country, but their opportunities for employment remained terribly limited; moreover, the black teams overall were poorly operated. This was unfortunate, because skilled players, despite enormous obstacles, had "been able to bring our race to the notice of thousands who are interested in the game." Now, Foster asked, "Will our business men and friends of the profession make an effort to help us to reach the coveted goal of complete success, or will they stand by and see us fail? Which shall it be?"[21]

Such an argument, delivered by black baseball's best-known representative, undoubtedly carried considerable weight among his peers. Nor could it be altogether ignored by scribes throughout baseball.

Thus, in the same special supplement where Foster's essay appeared, David Wyatt reported that the merits of black players were being acknowledged "by leading citizens of all races" throughout the country. Wyatt referred to a meeting between Charles Taft, the president's brother, and Foster in which the latter was "congratulated . . . upon his skill as a pitcher." This was hardly surprising to Wyatt, who saw the brand of baseball played by the black athlete as "very good evidence that he is giving his moral and physical welfare the proper amount of attention." Black baseball was now attracting "persons in all walks of life, who appreciate intelligence." Most significant, "these same persons have thrown down the gauntlet to all agitation of the time-worn color line and have openly declared the Negro baseball player the equal of the best and worthy of the same loyal consideration which has been shown the white players."[22]

In his encounters with people from across the country, Wyatt had yet to meet anyone unfamiliar with the Leland Giants. Indeed, reference to the Giants invariably engendered affable talk, demonstrating both baseball's appeal and interest regarding "the progress of the man of color in the game."

The 1910 season, Wyatt predicted, would be a "banner" one. Three or four top black baseball teams, such as the Leland Giants and the Kansas City Royal Giants, would field their strongest units yet. The Philadelphia Giants and Brooklyn Royals, for their part, would, once again, be potent squads. Wyatt was nevertheless concerned about the failure of leading teams, in the midst of barnstormings, to take along baseball correspondents. Such journalists, he suggested, could help to spread the gospel of black baseball. After all, Foster, John Henry Lloyd, and others, he astutely reminded his readers, "would have been lost to the Negro profession" without news accounts.[23]

The *Freeman*'s "Sporting Editor," Thomas I. Florence, predicted that the Leland Giants would win "the world's championship of colored baseball." They were "the greatest organization of Negro ball players that has ever been gathered together in this country." Furthermore, Florence insisted, "[T]hey are the best all-round ball players in the world today, barring none." Rube Foster and John Henry Lloyd, he declared, "are a ball team within themselves." In his estimation, the Chicago Giants' Walter Ball and Jonathan "Steel Arm Johnny" Taylor were "the most sensational pitchers of the race," and Leland's Pat Dougherty and Foster were the other top hurlers in black baseball. The finest catchers were the Chicago Giants' Bill Pettus and Leland's Pete Booker and Bruce Petway.[24]

On May 18, 1910, the Leland Giants officially opened their season in grand style at Normal Park, located at 69th and Halstead Streets in Chicago. A large crowd greeted the Giants, just returned from their extended road trip. With hundreds of friends gathered, Foster appeared elated about the success of that venture. He informed Cary B. Lewis, the *Freeman* correspondent, that he had never been "treated with greater hospitality and courtesy" than during the trek down south. Foster also indicated that he possessed one of America's finest baseball teams and planned to prove it during the upcoming months. The Lelands' secretary Beauregard F. Mosely waxed eloquent about how baseball was such a part of the American pantheon, before praising the Giants and delivering the flag pennant to Foster. Foster "was cheered until the fans were almost hoarse." His Giants got off to a quick start, defeating the Gunthers 5-1, as Frank Wickware hurled a six-hitter.[25]

Five days later, Foster shone on the mound in outpitching José Méndez to defeat the Stars of Cuba 7-1. A still larger crowd had gathered to watch Foster pitch and he hardly disappointed, holding the Stars to five hits, while striking out four and walking only one batter. After giving up a single run in the bottom of the first, Foster shut down the Stars, pitching "with old time vigor and strength." The batting star was Pete Hill, who scored twice and knocked one ball over the fence. On June 3, Foster, despite allowing twelve hits and a pair of walks, struck out two and beat the Gunthers 14-8.[26]

A torrid win streak ended at thirty-five games in mid-June, when Foster lost a 3-1 contest to the Gunthers, who managed nine hits. The Giants headed for Louisville, West Baden, and St. Louis, their first outing away from Chicago since the conclusion of their southern odyssey. Back home, the Giants again battled the Stars of Cuba in late July, as Foster and Méndez locked up in a 4-4 tie that went eleven innings. Both sides managed fourteen hits, with the Stars failing to score after the fourth inning. Foster struck out four and walked two in the then-lengthy two-hour-and-twenty-five-minute contest that was called because of darkness. On August 26, the Giants defeated the Gunthers 9-4 in a benefit game staged for Chicago's Provident Hospital, with Foster striking out four and walking only two batters. One of Foster's best appearances of the year occurred on September 9, when he shut out the Oklahoma Giants 5-0, in a contest featuring a Leland triple play.[27]

The incomplete records for 1910 indicate that Foster ended the season 13-2-1, as his team compiled a staggering 123-6 record. Among its victories were twenty-one straight wins over teams in the tristate area, including the best New York ball clubs. Frank Wickware, who was at the top of his game, contributed an 18-1 mark; Dougherty finished at 13-0. During his one season with the Leland Giants, John Henry Lloyd batted .417, just behind Pete Hill's .428 mark, and barely ahead of Home Run Johnson's .397 and Bruce Petway's .393 averages. John McGraw announced to Foster at one point, "If I had a bucket of whitewash that wouldn't wash off, you wouldn't have five players left tomorrow."[28]

In the aftermath of the 1910 season, Foster's Leland Giants undertook another venture, heading for Cuba where they played ten games against topflight professional teams. Over the span of twenty-five days, the Giants won five times and tied once, as John Henry Lloyd spearheaded the Leland attack with a .400 batting average. Bill Lindsay took two contests, while Wickware, Dougherty, and Foster each split a pair. Following the conclusion of the Giants' games, several Leland players, including Lloyd, Home Run Johnson, Petway, and Hill, remained on the island to participate in a series with the Detroit Tigers. After sweeping three straight American League pennants, the Tigers had come in third, behind the Athletics and Yankees. Hugh Jennings's offense was triggered by Ty Cobb, who had just won his fourth consecutive batting crown with a .385 mark and had stolen 65 bases, along with fellow outfielder Sam Crawford, whose 120 runs batted in had led the league. The top Detroit pitchers included 21-game winner George Mullin; Wild Bill Donovan, who had compiled an 18-7 mark; and Ed Willett, who went 16-11.[29]

After splitting earlier contests, the Tigers won all but one of the five games that Cobb participated in. The great star batted .368 but suffered the indignity of twice being thrown out by Petway while attempting to steal second base. He was equally appalled by the fact that three Leland players, who appeared in six games, outhit him: Lloyd batted .500; Johnson, .412; and Petway, .389. Evidently, Cobb swore that he wouldn't allow himself to be embarrassed in such a manner again, henceforth refusing to join in barnstorming affairs involving black ballplayers.

That winter, black baseball moguls again sought to establish a league of their own; Foster was clearly interested for any number of reasons, including the $2,100 loss the great Leland Giants had chalked up. At the behest of the Leland Giants' Beauregard F. Mosely, they gathered in Chicago at noon on December 28 and selected the attorney as conference chairman. Felix H. Payne of Mobile, Alabama, was chosen as secretary, with Rube Foster seconding the nomination. Mosely proceeded to issue the call for the gathering:

> Whereas, the undersigned, having been and still being interested in the National pastime, baseball, and Whereas, the professional negro ball player is compelled to live and die a semi-pro, there being no other field open to him, thus compelling veteran players to be classed and pitted with amateurs; and, Whereas, the capital invested in the semi-pro parks, and players can be utilized for the active formation and operation of a Negro National Baseball League, therefore . . . the undersigned and such other persons who may be interested in the formation of a league, meet . . . in National conference, for the purpose of organizing, securing park franchises, creating a circuit and appointing a schedule committee, etc.[30]

Signing the call issued by Mosely were S. R. Gibbs of Louisville's Falls City Stars; Frank Walker, representing New Orleans' Frank Polambo; E. H. Cohen of the Cohen Baseball Club, from that same city; and Ralph Clemons of Mobile's Dixie Park Baseball Club. W. T. Johnson of Chicago promised both moral and financial support for such a league, and Kansas City's Tobe Smith expressed his belief that such an organization could succeed. This undertaking, Smith insisted to great applause, "would be regarded as important as anything ever performed by Negroes in this country." Walker underscored the league's importance and promised that the South, guided by "able, clean" leaders," would support the endeavor. Speaking next was Rube Foster, referred to by the reporter covering the event as "the great Negro pitcher of international fame." Discussing "the ups and downs" of blackball, Foster stated that "the time was ripe for organization without which the Negro would soon be regulated out of the game entirely."[31]

A resolution was proposed by Walker urging the formation of "a National League of Ball Players," to be represented in Chicago, Louisville, New Orleans, Mobile, St. Louis, Kansas City, Memphis, and three other spots; each franchise would cost $300. A charter was to be sought from the State of Illinois, with a minimum capital stock outlay of $2,500; the headquarters was to be located in Chicago. Following the meeting, Mosely was chosen president; Payne, secretary; and Mosely, Foster, Smith, Walker, Payne, and Johnson, league commissioners, assigned to request an operating license from the Illinois Secretary of State. Unfortunately, little came of this endeavor; it did, however, sustain Foster's interest in organizing black baseball.[32]

FIVE

The Chicago American Giants and the Making of a Black Baseball Dynasty

The 1910 Leland Giants are one of black baseball's legendary teams. Leland's significance, however, pales in comparison to Foster's next ball club, the Chicago American Giants. For more than a decade following their founding in 1911, the American Giants were unquestionably black baseball's most important squad and, often, its finest. Foster placed his imprint on that team as he had on no other, using a racehorse brand of baseball that the American Giants became noted for. Sportswriters deemed his nine equal to any in the land, including those in organized baseball; its competition against top blackball units, leading minor league teams, and various major leaguers, appeared to merit such an evaluation. At the very least, the American Giants' manager began to acquire still greater stature as both black baseball's leading representative and one of the finest minds to be found on any playing diamond.

After the 1910 season, Foster linked up with a new partner, John C. Schorling, a white saloon keeper and the son-in-law of Chicago White Sox owner Charles A. Comiskey. On July 1, 1910, Comiskey Park, located at West 35th Street and Wentworth Avenue, had been ushered in by the White Sox. Following the move, Schorling—who had been involved with black baseball in Chicago for the past decade—talked to Foster about leasing the old South Side Park, situated at 39th and Wentworth Avenue, as the home field for the Leland Giants; the actual grandstand and bleachers had been removed earlier that summer. Foster indicated, however, that he was under contract to B. F. Mosely, the Leland Giants' majority owner. He spoke with Mosely, who declared that the law was his profession, baseball was Foster's, and he would release him from contractual obligations if the great pitcher-manager believed he could succeed in a new endeavor. Subsequently, Schorling constructed a new park, with an initial seating capacity of nine thousand, at the former White Sox grounds. "The finest semi-pro park in the world," as Foster referred to it, was situated in the heart of Chicago and proved readily accessible by streetcar. The wooden structure boasted the dimensions of a major league park: the left and right field foul lines were positioned some 350 feet from home plate, and dead center was located at least 400 feet away.[1]

Comiskey, by all accounts, sought to convince both his son-in-law and Foster that a new black baseball team in Chicago could not succeed if it scheduled games when the hometown White Sox were in town. Foster ignored Comiskey's advice, and the newly named Chicago American Giants thrived. Ponying up 50 cents for admission entitled patrons to free ice water when they flocked to Schorling Park to watch black baseball's premier team. On more than one occasion, attendance at Schorling Park reportedly exceeded that at Comiskey Park or the Cubs' ball field. One Sunday afternoon in 1911, an overflow crowd of 11,000 congregated to watch the American Giants; at nearby Comiskey Park, 9,000 had shown up to see the White Sox; across town, only 6,000 were attending a Cubs' game.[2]

Relying on a fast-paced, thinking-man's brand of baseball, Foster now proceeded to establish a dynasty that held its own against first-rate competition throughout the country. Like his earlier teams, Foster's American Giants—which he billed immodestly but not unreasonably as "The Greatest Aggregation of Colored Baseball Players in the World"—toured widely, in the fashion of other leading blackball squads. The American Giants did so perhaps the most extensively, traveling throughout the South and all the way to the Pacific Coast. Fans eagerly awaited the arrival of black baseball's most-celebrated team and its most-heralded figure. Word of the American Giants was spread by black newspapers in the Midwest, especially the *Chicago Defender* and the *Indianapolis Freeman*; porters on the Illinois Central Railroad could regularly be seen hawking copies of the *Defender*. As the American Giants engaged in their far-flung travels, Foster kept an eye out for new talent, ready to grab unknown players in the hinterlands or to raid stars on other top units.[3]

The initial version of the American Giants took the Palm Beach Hotel championship, captured the Chicago city title, and compiled a 78-27 record in claiming the first of four successive western crowns. John Henry Lloyd, Pete Booker, and Home Run Johnson had departed for the New York Lincoln Giants, thereby breaking up the Leland Giants' great 1910 squad. Jess McMahon's new Lincoln Giants, also featuring pitchers Smokey Joe Williams and Cannonball Dick Redding, center fielder Spot Poles and catcher Louis Santop, won 108 games and lost only 12 in taking the eastern title. Bruce Petway, whose already stellar reputation was merely enhanced by his performance in Cuba against Ty Cobb and the Tigers, remained Foster's superb catcher. Leadoff batter Frank Duncan returned to play left field, Jap Payne was still roaming right field, and Pete Hill was in center. Hill, an all-around star, batted .400 for the season and purportedly hit safely in all but one of the American Giants' contests in 1911, a remarkable feat indeed. Hitting cleanup was second baseman Bill Monroe, who had played with Foster on the championship Philadelphia Giants teams. Replacing Lloyd at short was former utility man Fred Hutchinson. Foster, for his part, was now pitching less frequently than in the past, although his outings drew large crowds and considerable publicity. Left-hander Pat Dougherty and righties Frank Wickware and Bill Lindsay led the American Giants' pitching staff. The team's monthly salary opened at $1,500.[4]

Although the American Giants had proven to be a success on the playing field and at the box office, Foster worried about the state of black baseball. In a lengthy essay appearing in the December 23, 1911, issue of the *Indianapolis Freeman,* he bemoaned the "petty jealousy over prosperity . . . that has sounded the deathknell of Negro baseball." Foster blamed his old boss Frank C. Leland for "the downfall of colored baseball in Chicago and throughout the South." The man, Foster dismissively noted, was "a mere accident in baseball." The quest by Leland "to exterminate me from baseball dug a grave for him in baseball, and he is now a detriment to the game." Foster then warned that "a few seekers after notoriety, who were endowed with more ambition than brains, began to lay secret plans to overthrow the ruling powers [namely, the

Chicago Giants] and thereby corral the spotlight position." Engendering considerable support, "the insurgents" helped to turn Chicago into "a regular hotbed of guerrilla campaign in baseball." The Leland Giants and the Chicago Giants, with "practical baseball men" pitted against the insurgents, battled for supremacy, seeking to win public favor. This resulted in "speculation of the wildcat kind and a financial struggle of the survival of the fittest."[5]

As the battle raged, Foster's team "was torn asunder," with only a small portion of the roster that had helped black baseball to thrive in Chicago remaining with the club. Frank C. Leland and Major Jackson, Foster alleged, had persuaded several of his players to accept "fancy" salary offers and thereby bolt from the Leland Giants. His concerns regarding the best interests of baseball, Foster insisted, compelled him to attempt to reason with his former business associates, warning that their players could similarly be induced to jump to another squad. Determined that black baseball would succeed, Foster had constructed "the best colored club ever gotten together, the only club capable of measuring arms with the big league clubs." He had challenged Leland and Jackson to stack their team against his on the playing field, but they "turned a deaf ear" to his entreaties. Instead, they expressed a determination, "to put me out of business in Chicago." To that end, "they not only refused to play us, but wrote all over the country to other managers, telling them they could not play them if they played me, and also told all the white clubs around Chicago." Foster's Leland Giants proceeded to compete against teams willing to meet them, invariably prevailing, thereby establishing an "enviable reputation" that "opened the eyes of the baseball world." Subsequently, Foster, together with John C. Schorling, had established the American Giants.[6]

In the meantime, Chicago's baseball wars had continued. Eventually, the city "found itself congested with the semi-pro game." Only four ballparks—including only one on the South Side—avoided being boarded up. "The notoriety seekers," accused Foster, "were too busy in the war of extermination to listen to sensible entreaties, and in their haste of planning strategic moves against their colored brothers, they forgot to keep up with the whites and their movements." Indeed, "just how much their life and the strength of their fighting depended upon the other race they failed to compute." Eventually, however, Chicago semipro ball was headed for extinction; furthermore, "the destinies of the Negro were in the hands of a few whites." Schorling got hold of the South Side park, constructed "a palatial plant," and chose "yours truly," Foster noted, "as the best available personage to organize and head a club." That decision perplexed the insurgents, who soon sued for peace. That proved "to be a hoax, pure and simple," he wrote, and a wholesale offensive was undertaken.[7]

After his team had demonstrated its superiority on the playing field, Foster cried, "every cheap, mean, low trick was resorted to for the purpose of not only discrediting my club, but to hamper and ruin the prestige of the owner of the plant, if possible." Who paid the price for this? he asked. "Negro baseball," he exclaimed. It was criminal that "four flushers and notoriety seekers" held sway in baseball. Then he contended, "The wild, reckless scramble under the guise of baseball is keeping us down, and we will always be the underdog until we can successfully employ the methods that have brought success to the great powers that be in baseball of the present era, *organization*."[8]

In Foster's estimation, there were "enough good men" with the financial means for black baseball to flourish. Unfortunately, the same suicidal competitiveness that prevailed in Chicago existed elsewhere as well. Black baseball required organization and participation by businessmen, Foster stated, along with teams located in Chicago, St. Louis, Kansas City, Louisville, Indianapolis, and Detroit. That "would be the best thing yet in baseball." Sufficient capital existed to construct the necessary ballparks, and the league could run the Indianapolis and Louisville franchises. "Then we could all reap the benefit," Foster prophesied. "It will pay." Such a league would result in improved attendance and "a standing in baseball." The pennant winner "could force, by public sentiment, the same as Jack Johnson forced Jeffries, the winners in the white league to meet us for the championship."[9]

Such promises, Foster stated, were not unrealistic. "I am for no wildcat schemes. But I know this to be the best way, and when I say I know, those who know me know I am not guessing. I am willing to co-operate with all in doing anything to uplift Negro baseball."[10]

A bounty of emotions characteristically typified Foster's editorial. Vindictiveness colored his condemnation of Frank C. Leland. So did his casting of blame on former colleagues for engaging in the same kind of player raids he himself had undertaken as both player and manager; that propensity also suggested considerable hypocrisy on his part. Boastfulness was present too in his lauding of the American Giants. Yet present as well was Foster's determined commitment that blackball excel and ultimately prove competitive with organized baseball.

Writing in the *Philadelphia Tribune* in late January 1912, Juli Jones Jr. discussed the racial barriers that black baseball performers still confronted. Desperately seeking to have major league teams return to the island, Cuban baseball tycoons allowed their American counterparts to establish the ground rules. The Cubans promised to cover expenses, but more important, the new contract also precluded them from using black American ballplayers against their white counterparts. Thus, the likes of Pete Hill, Bruce Petway, Walter Ball, and Bill Pettus, who had helped to defeat the 1910 World Champion Philadelphia Athletics, to the chagrin of organized baseball's administrators, could no longer go head-to-head against top major leaguers. A rule shaped by American League president Ban Johnson, designed to avoid further embarrassment, declared that the winner of the World Series could not barnstorm in the off-season. Following defeats suffered by the Athletics, the Detroit Tigers, and the National League's Cincinnati Reds, Johnson determined "that another such performance would surely hurt his league." Already, American League bosses had refused to allow any of their teams to play in Cuba in 1911.[11]

McGraw possessed, Juli Jones noted, "the highest regard for the American colored player." The Giants' skipper had "said he would give anything in the world if Rube Foster was a white man; it was too bad that Walter Ball was colored; that it is a shame that Lloyd [*sic*] could not show the public what he could do; that if he had Petway no money could buy him; that the world was robbed of seeing a more sensational player on account of Monroe's color." Nevertheless, McGraw recognized how much the black ballplayers had contributed to the defeat of major league teams in Cuba. Thus, he insisted that only Cuban-born players could compete against his men. Following the latest series there, McGraw departed from the Caribbean island, declaring that the Cubans had "no baseball brains," in contrast to African American players.[12]

*

In 1912, the American Giants repeated as champions of the Chicago semipro circuit, winning 112 of 132 contests. The Giants' everyday line-up was made up of catcher Petway, first baseman Bill Pierce, second baseman Bill Monroe, shortstop Fred Hutchinson, third sacker Candy Jim Taylor, left fielder Frank Duncan, center fielder Hill, and right fielder Jess Barber. Chicago's pitching staff included Pat Dougherty, Bill Lindsay, spitballer Dicta Johnson, Big Bill Gatewood, and Foster. Hill hit .357 and Taylor batted cleanup.

Scattered box scores and news accounts suggest that Foster remained, at least on occasion, a superb pitcher, with such incomplete records displaying a 6-0-1 record for the year. On June 5, Foster pitched the Giants to a 15-3 victory over the Indianapolis ABCs. He held the Plutos to seven hits on June 21, winning 6-5, contributing a double, striking out four and walking only two. The *Chicago Defender* referred to him as "our idol," who put one bad inning behind him—the third, when he gave up all the opponents' runs—and shut them out the rest of the way. Foster's great appeal to fans of black baseball was suggested by a cartoon in the June 22 issue of the *Indianapolis Freeman* that displayed him, readying to pitch, with a caption proclaiming, "Chief Rube Foster was a big drawing card himself." On June 28, Foster allowed but four hits, struck out one batter and issued only one walk, in beating Pittsburgh's U.S. League team 9-1. Now, the *Defender* called him the "Marquard" of the "colored" ballplayers, referring to the New York Giants' star right-hander Rube Marquard, who was in the midst of establishing an all-time mark for consecutive games won by a major league pitcher.[13]

On August 2, Foster struck out seven, gave up only one walk, and relinquished but five hits, in defeating the Sprudels 7-1. The only run he allowed resulted from an error in the game's opening frame. In the middle of the month, Foster again battled the great Cuban pitcher José Méndez, with the two pitching expertly throughout a twelve-inning 2-2 tie. Pregame stories about the upcoming match had referred to it as "the duel of the decade, and the *Defender* termed the actual contest "one of the greatest baseball struggles in the history of semi-pro ball." The Giants struck first, with two runs in the top of the third, thanks to a hit by Jess Barber, a walk to Bill Lindsay, another hit by Frank Duncan, and a deep sacrifice fly by Candy Jim Taylor. The Cubans bounced back with one run in the bottom half of the inning, on a hit by Pelayo Chacon, a sacrifice by the pitcher, and another hit by Chino Moran. In the seventh, the Cubans knotted the score, after Pierce threw errantly in an attempt to pick off Hector Magrinat, who was seeking to move over on an infield out. Both teams threatened in the ninth. The Giants saw Pierce single but get nailed at first. Jap Payne later produced a double, which undoubtedly would have driven in Pierce had he remained on base. The Cubans threatened again in the bottom of the ninth, but excellent fielding by Barber enabled the game to move into extra innings. The last major threat occurred in the twelfth, when Payne, with one out, slammed a triple. However, Méndez got Foster to pop up and Bruce Petway to ground out. Foster ended up with seven strikeouts and two walks; Méndez struck out five and walked three. "It was a great game," the *Defender* reported, "Foster and Méndez twirling great ball. Foster's performance being the greatest in years."[14]

On August 27, a large crowd gathered at Schorling Park, with "hundreds of the friends of Rube Foster" congregating from throughout the country to pay him tribute. Leading members of the National Negro Business Men's League and society folk were prominently displayed in box seats. The American Giants blanked the U.S. Leaguers 7-0, with Dicta Johnson tossing a five-hitter. After being shut out for the first five innings, the Giants got to Bert Keeley, the former Washington Senators' pitcher, eventually driving him from the box.[15]

The *Defender* reported on September 7 that Foster, who had purportedly "begun to teach his baby boy how to throw a spit-ball," was about to participate in another epic pitching duel. His opponent was former teammate Walter Ball, who was then hurling for the St. Louis Giants. Ball's 1912 record to date was said to be 25-0. The next week, the game unfolded with neither pitcher at the top of his game. Both teams scored single runs in the first inning, with St. Louis adding another in the bottom of the second. Chicago, however, converted six hits and an error into five runs in the top of the third, while Foster shut down his foes until relinquishing lone runs in both the eighth and the ninth. The American Giants managed twelve hits, and the St. Louis ball club knocked out nine. Ball was hurt by a lack of control, but "the great Rube Foster," the *Defender* indicated, proved to be "in good trim," following a rocky start. Foster struck out five and walked four; Ball fanned only one and gave up one free pass.[16]

"A stag" party was planned for Rube Foster, the *Philadelphia Tribune* noted as the 1912 season neared a close. Foster, the paper declared, was "widely known in parts of the country as one of the greatest baseball players of the race." Along with "hundreds of his admirers and fans," luminaries such as Elwood Knox, Phil Brown, Roscoe Simmons, and William D. Neighbors attended the function, as did many leading members of the press.[17]

Calling his ball club the "undisputed colored champions of the world," Foster reported on November 9 that the American Giants were participating in the four-team California Winter League. The other three teams—the McCormicks from Los Angeles, Tuft Lyon's of Pasadena, and San Diego—were made up of players from organized baseball. Those ballplayers included New York Giants catcher Chief Meyers and center fielder Fred Snodgrass, Cleveland Indians shortstop Irv Olson, Boston Red Sox pitcher Charley Hall, St. Louis Browns hurler Earl Hamilton, and Philadelphia Phillies outfielder Gavvy Cravath, along with a host of other major and minor leaguers.[18]

The Giants had arrived in Los Angeles on October 14 and opened play on November 1, when the mayor of Los Angeles tossed out the first ball. Foster's ball club won three "pre-season" contests, defeating the All-Natives of California 7-1 on a three-hitter by Dougherty. Lindsay then shut out the H. Franks 14-0, allowing only two hits. Foster threw another whitewash, giving up seven hits, as Chicago crushed the L.A. Giants 21-0.[19]

By mid-December, the American Giants were tied for the top spot in the California Winter League. Such news, Julius N. Avendouph of the *Chicago Defender* admitted, produced "a great deal of satisfaction," particularly because a number of big leaguers competed in the winter circuit. The American Giants, the *Defender* commented, remained "under the leadership of their peerless leader."[20]

At year's end, Foster took time to examine the state of black baseball, while also discussing the American Giants' performance on the West Coast. Somewhat immodestly, he noted that his team was, once again, topping "the big colored clubs." Some teams had players equally good, Foster declared, but "lacked the pilot at the head to bring results." The outlook had seemed bleak as the past season began, but the American Giants' management and loyal fans had helped usher in Chicago's "most prosperous season." Regular day games, for the first time, had been played in Chicago, which proved more supportive of them than anywhere else in America.[21]

The upcoming season, Foster anticipated, promised to be more successful still, with a number of premier opponents already lined up. His team's motto, Foster revealed, "is to surpass anything attempted by other clubs." In the meantime, the American Giants were performing brilliantly in the California Winter League. Their level of play, Foster suggested, had "opened the eyes of all the big leaguers on the coast." To his delight, his American Giants went on to win the California Winter League championship. Coursing through the Midwest, they had also beaten league teams in Michigan and Wisconsin.[22]

In the February 15, 1913, issue of the *Indianapolis Freeman,* Billy Lewis discussed the need for "a colored league." He declared forthrightly, "The colored brother has been rather slow to take advantage of what is offered by way of baseball opportunity. He could have his league also, just like the white people, if he would." Referring to the American Giants' success in the California Winter League, Lewis described most members of the team as "crack players." Sportswriters in California, Lewis noted, effusively praised the American Giants, comparing them to the very best major leaguers, including Ty Cobb, Johnny Evers, Rube Marquard, and Christy Mathewson. Those journalists said "that those dusky knights of the diamond stood right in their class, and near about the head." Yet such testimonials, Lewis remarked, meant nothing.

> When Old Sol has made the equator in his march from old Capricornius, Rube's fine fellows, the fine bunches in St. Louis, Kansas City, Louisville, Indianapolis and French Lick will not be disturbed by drafts of the higher call. They will be safe from the baseball "pirate" who is so woefully decimating the ranks of the young hopefuls.[23]

Acknowledging that large-scale opposition existed to black players joining white teams, Lewis called for "the next best thing." After all, baseball fans, both white and black, desired "to see the major games, the great games." Thus, "colored leagues" should be formed, even if that were a difficult undertaking. Invariably, larger crowds would result. "A few good baseball towns" for black ballplayers existed within fairly close proximity, Lewis declared; these included St. Louis, both Kansas City municipalities, Louisville, Indianapolis, Cincinnati, Evansville, Memphis, Nashville, and Chicago, of course. Lewis urged a meeting of black baseball managers from those communities. Unfortunately, he admitted, managers desired their autonomy, "wearing a chip on the shoulder sometimes rather than manifesting a disposition to unionize."[24]

As the 1913 season approached, the *Indianapolis Freeman* again celebrated the accomplishments of Rube Foster and his American Giants. Together, the *Freeman* asserted, they had been "making great history for the Negro ball player this winter." But as Foster himself predicted, the upcoming year promised "to eclipse anything ever attempted by this club before." The American Giants had already topped their excellent 1912 campaign with even "more brilliant" play in the winter league. Scheduled to depart from California in mid-March, they were to appear in San Francisco, Oakland, and Sacramento before heading on to Portland and Salt Lake City. Then, after going from Texas to Oklahoma, they would show up in Kansas City, Missouri, and Davenport, Iowa. Their new season would open in Chicago on April 20.[25]

At a banquet held in honor of Foster's ball club, the president of the Good Fellows' Club declared:

> The day . . . the American Giants arrived in Los Angeles should be celebrated as, as great a historical event as the landing of Columbus in America was celebrated in Europe or the celebrating of any important event that happens once in a lifetime.

> Here is a team that not only scintillates with individual stars but shines in its great team work. It is a piece of perfect machinery that can only be put together by a master mind and in this case the master mind is, Mr. Foster, known the world over as "Rube."

> Here is a baseball General who is outclassed by no one and who has humbled all opposing ball teams as Napoleon humbled the mighty powers of Europe.

> The name of the Giants preceded them and they have lived up to all that was expected of them and more. Their conduct on the field has always been the best and they have always acted as gentlemen should act.

Words fail me when I attempt to sing the praises of the American Giants the greatest base ball machine on the continent to-day, and [they] are the greatest aggregation of Base Ball Stars in the world.[26]

Following an 18-2 annihilation of the San Bernardino Stars by the American Giants, the local paper admitted that "it was plainly a case of a great ball club outclassing a good team." Indeed, the performance of the Giants proved "faultless" in execution, including unprecedented slugging, "perfect baserunning and clock-like fielding." One fan exclaimed, "White or black, my hat's off to those boys when it comes to playing ball."[27]

In the midst of the American Giants' visit to Lemoore, the town newspaper saluted them. They are an example that lots of white clubs can take pattern from, as during the time they have been in Lemoore they have not entered a saloon, and are never seen upon the street only when going to and from the park. If they go to the post office or a barber shop they pay strictly to their own business and many of the business men and others have nothing but praise for them. They are gentlemen both on and off the diamond and all the time.[28]

After the Giants nipped the Portland Beavers 8-7, a sportswriter urged that Foster's team not be underestimated: "Don't think for a moment that the American Giants, the colored ball players, do not understand the grand old game of baseball and, what is more to the point, understand how to play it." Another newspaper chortled, "Sakes alive, an, but them brunette gentlemen suttingly 'kin play baseball." Moreover, "if only they could be treated with a coat of permanent whitewash Walter McCredle says he would sign the whole bunch and win the Coast league pennant with such ease that it would probably put the league out of business." With that accomplished, he would next seek a major league title.[29]

Among the fullest accounts were the reports by the *Seattle Post-Intelligencer*'s Portus Baxter of a three-game series between the Seattle Giants and the American Giants. Following a 10-5 pounding of the home team by Foster's squad, Baxter, in a write-up entitled "Colored Giants a Wonderful Team," expressed little surprise that Coast League teams had refused to play the American Giants. "The colored wonders" from Chicago, Baxter related on April 3, made up "a better team than the famous

Cuban Giants. There is not the slightest doubt about their being of major league caliber. They play ball all the time any way you look at it, and their skill had something to do with making our team look 'rotten' several times yesterday." After the second contest, shortened to six innings, the *Post-Intelligencer* rang out, "Colored Phenoms Bat out Victory." But that 5-3 victory was easily surpassed by the final game, a 17-7 affair that saw the American Giants' Hill, Taylor, and Gatewood all smack homers. Baxter reported that some five thousand spectators—half of them women—enjoyed the bout, particularly Chicago's "terrific hitting" and the way in which, as the headline explained, the "Colored Giants Mangle Pitchers."[30]

Bob Brown, owner of the Vancouver ball club, proclaimed Chicago "some team." He too was not surprised that the Coast League teams refused to play them but reasoned it would "do our teams good to buck up against a team that is in first-class condition and of major league caliber." Another analyst now understood why top baseball men insisted "that the black fellows could win the pennant in any minor league in the country and that they would be good for the first division in either of the major leagues." One more observer indicated that "the Negroes are lightning fast, everyone of them." In addition, "every man of them is a splendid thrower; they can all hit and hit hard when they land on [a] fast one, and they are so fast on the bases that they hit and run most of the time."[31]

In his column for the *Chicago Defender*, Julius N. Avendouph declared that no "colored baseball team" had ever duplicated what the American Giants had achieved on their western tour. Cheered for both their athletic performance and "gentlemanly conduct on the ball field," they had competed in the California Winter League "against America's idols." The American Giants, the *Indianapolis Freeman*'s Billy Lewis agreed, "had made a fine impression on the Pacific coast" and had "captured the West." Reading accounts of the Giants' games on their tour, Lewis acknowledged, provided "a thrill of joy."[32]

As the 1913 season readied to open, the *Chicago Defender* again applauded the performance of the American Giants out west, declaring that they had established a "record which any baseball team would be proud to hold." The *Defender* then saluted Foster, asserting that "much credit belongs to the greatest ball player and manager in the business and one of the greatest and headiest men in the business, white or black."[33]

In early May, Foster pitched in an all-star game, which was a benefit for former Leland Giants third baseman Danger Talbert. Foster's side lost 6-0, as he struck out five but walked eight. At the beginning of June, he tossed a five-hitter in beating the Plutos 10-2, with Pete Hill smacking a homer run. The *Indianapolis Freeman* declared that Foster, in his first official appearance of the season, displayed "the old time vigor and craftiness that has made him the 'world's wonder' on the mound." Pitching with but three days' rest, Foster, who drove in the winning run, went ten innings to defeat the Plutos once again, 4-3. The *Defender* indicated that Foster hurled "a fine game" but was touched up for four hits and three runs in the bottom of the second. The Plutos garnered only two other hits off Foster, who recorded eight strikeouts and issued no walks. Foster won yet again in an 11-6 contest against the Cubans, despite being relieved by Gatewood, until then, an extremely rare occurrence.[34]

In August, the American Giants played a best-of-twelve-game series against the Lincoln Giants. The New York–based squad, under the guidance of the great John Henry Lloyd, would win its third straight eastern championship in 1913, producing a 101-6 record. The superlative shortstop and hitter—Lloyd batted over .400 during that three-year reign—had replaced Sol White as manager of the Lincoln Giants during their initial season. Centerfielder Spot Poles, whose batting average during the Lincoln Giants' early championship run surpassed even Lloyd's, had returned to the team after a brief period with the Brooklyn Royal Giants, and had managed three consecutive hits off Philadelphia Phillies ace Pete Alexander during a 1913 exhibition contest. Striking out better than a batter an inning, Smokey Joe Williams put together an 18-3 mark. Cannonball Dick Redding, with his great speed and fine control, also remained on the Lincoln Giants' pitching staff.

Prior to the start of the long-awaited series, the *Chicago Defender* uncharacteristically blasted the American Giants' management for never having "spent a nickel to the support of any race paper" in the metropolitan area. The Lincoln Giants, the *Defender* charged, "have more race pride," regularly advertising in all the black-owned newspapers in New York City and Brooklyn. But after the first nine games, which resulted in four wins apiece and a tie, the *Defender* applauded "the famous Rube" for having accomplished "what no other manager has been able to do." He had, after all, brought the Lincoln Giants to town, relying on a sizable guarantee. The series concluded with the Lincoln Giants winning seven games to claim the title of "the world's colored champions."[35]

Notwithstanding the setback, the *Indianapolis Freeman* continued to praise Foster effusively, particularly lauding him after the signing of a new pitcher who, during his initial outing, allowed only one hit over eight innings. Foster "must be given credit for having brains and being the best baseball manager in the country. He is always on the alert for the very best material. Even Charles A. Comiskey does not eclipse him in this direction." Not surprisingly, then, word of a possible banquet to be held in Foster's honor delighted the *Freeman:* "It is argued that no man in this baseball field has done more to uphold baseball sport among the colored people of this country than Mr. Foster and that a testimonial in the form of a baseball love feast would be a fitting climax to the baseball season." The *Freeman,* along with baseball fans throughout Chicago, cheered the idea because Foster had "put baseball on the map in the Windy City." Alfred Anderson declared "that hundreds of fans would be pleased to sit down to a table with Mr. Foster and tender him the honor that is due him." Jerry Mills exclaimed, "Count me as one to be present whenever it comes off. I am a Foster fan from A to Z." Dr. Gordon Jackson, the American Giants' team physician, added, "I am ready at a moment's notice." The *Chicago Defender* also applauded the idea, stating that it was "but fit and proper that the baseball fans and numerous friends of the celebrated manager" would meet somewhere on the city's South Side to "honor the old Roman with feasting, music and oratory."[36]

In the meantime, Foster's ball club began piling up victories once again. On September 2, Foster gave up twelve hits, but defeated the St. Louis Giants 10-6; he struck out five and walked two batters, while scoring once and collecting a base hit. The *Freeman* suggested that Foster was pitching "with old time form." Pete Hill banged out five hits, a third of the American Giants' total. The following week, Foster went eleven innings to beat the Sprudels, who had tied the game with a pair of runs in the bottom of the ninth, 4-3. Allowing only seven hits, while issuing three walks, he struck out eight to win "a twirling duel." Foster lost his next outing, being pounded by the Chicago Giants in a 9-5 loss. The "grand old pitcher" struck out five and walked four in the bout against his old mentor, later turned antagonist, Frank C. Leland. After giving up seven runs in the first two innings, including six in the second, Foster "pitched some classy ball" but to no avail.[37]

In mid-October, the American Giants played their two hundredth game of that year. This was an unprecedented record, the *Defender* asserted, and one that "any team would be proud of." Foster, the paper revealed, "has given us a club within walking distance and has given us games where there has been more inside baseball played than in the world's series." The record-setting contest, won by the American Giants over Gunther, featured an eight-hit, nine-strikeout, four-walk performance by Foster; his traceable mark for the regular season stood at 6-1.[38]

Buoyed by his team's generally successful season, Foster now delivered a challenge to Johnny Evers, manager of the Chicago Cubs, to repeat the 1909 series that had pitted the Leland Giants against the National League squad. His ballplayers who remained in town, Evers responded, could choose to play the blackball powerhouse. The games were never played.[39]

During the off-season, publications like the *Philadelphia Tribune* again urged formation of a "colored league." Organization, the *Tribune* noted, had enabled baseball, "America's most popular national game," to thrive financially. Consequently, "if we as a people expect to improve our condition in the business and financial world, we have certainly got to follow the precedent that has been established by others who have attained the position we are striving to reach."[40]

SIX

Another Championship

In March 1914, Foster again guided the American Giants out west. His already potent squad, however, was about to become stronger still. Undoubtedly due to the defeat suffered at the hands of the Lincoln Giants, Foster resorted to raiding some of the finest players in black baseball back east, particularly from the very team that had wrested away the crown he considered rightfully the property of his American Giants. Foster had no compunction against taking players from eastern teams, especially those, like the Lincoln Giants, that challenged Chicago's supremacy in blackball. Among the latest additions to his squad were Smokey Joe Williams, pitcher Lee Wade, third baseman Billy Francis, left fielder Jude Gans, and shortstop John Henry Lloyd, all snared from the Lincoln Giants. The *Chicago Defender* wondered if Foster had "wrecked" Jess McMahon's great ball club. As for the American Giants, they appeared more potent than ever. Returning were Bill Monroe at third, outfielders Pete Hill and Jess Barber (Barber moved over to first base), along with pitchers Pat Dougherty, Bill Lindsay, and Foster. While the schedule appeared to be one of the toughest ever for a semipro team, the American Giants, in the *Defender's* estimation, were "absolutely the best team of ball tossers that has ever been gathered together. They will be equal to any team in the big leagues." Thus, Foster's team, the *Defender* suggested, would be as good as the White Sox, the Cubs, the Athletics, or the New York Giants. It would be better than the St. Louis Cardinals or Browns and many others.[1]

Once again, Portus Baxter of the *Seattle Post-Intelligencer* saluted the American Giants, and his newspaper favorably referred to them as the "colored demons." After Smokey Joe Williams shut down Seattle on seven hits, while striking out sixteen batters, in a 2-1 victory on April 3,

Baxter declared that the home team had "played a great game of ball . . . against a great team." He particularly cheered Chicago's newest star, who scored once and smacked two hits, including one in the ninth that advanced the eventual winning run to third base: "All that has been said and printed about Shortstop Lloyd . . . falls short of the truth. He is undoubtedly one of the greatest players ever seen on a ball field." The following day's contest was cancelled because of rain, but the *Post-Intelligencer* continued to feature the American Giants. Heaping additional praise on Lloyd, Baxter termed him "a real giant. He reminds one of 'Homerun' Baker, and the way he hits the ball leaves no doubt that he is in his class as a clouter."[2]

In another article, Rube Foster was quoted extensively about the possibility of the color barrier's demise in the major and minor leagues. "Before another baseball season rolls around," he predicted, "colored ball players, a score of whom are equal in ability to the brightest stars in the big league teams, will be holding down jobs in organized baseball." The creation of the Federal League, whose owners sought to compete with the American and National circuits, demanded it, Foster offered. Baseball experts contended that five members of Foster's present roster—probably Lloyd, Hill, Petway, Williams, and Dougherty—were "as good as any big leaguer of the present day." The pool of good players was already thinned because of the Federal League, Foster suggested, which meant that "the colored ranks" would soon "be invaded." Baseball moguls would surmount racial prejudices to lift "the bars . . . because there is no other way out of it." With Cubans now admitted, Foster asserted, "they'll let us in soon. . . . And when they let the black men in, just watch how many present-day stars lose their positions." Calling Lloyd the greatest player anywhere, Foster chortled, "If you don't believe it, wait until he gets into the big league—then watch the Barrys, the Wagners and the Tinkers sweat to keep their jobs."[3]

The previous year, Foster revealed, the architects of organized baseball had planned to construct "a colored league" to take advantage of the impressive crowds black ballplayers attracted in the East. This league was to have been shepherded by the National Commission, baseball's governing body. The advent of the Federal League, however, caused the plan to become stillborn. Yet, "I would not be surprised," Foster stated, "if the league is organized next year."[4]

Before the start of the next contest between the American Giants and the Seattle Giants, "shadow practice," a form of burlesque, was performed at the Rainier Valley ball park, demonstrating what even the finest teams in black baseball were sometimes compelled to resort to. As the *Post-Intelligencer* reported,

> The comedian of the play—was Monroe, the veteran second baseman, who converted himself into a catcher for the time being. Lloyd did the batting, and the bases were occupied by other members of the team. Lloyd would pick up an imaginary ball, toss it in the air and then club it toward an infielder. The infielder would make an imaginary pick-up, fire to another infielder, who would touch out a man, and then try to knock Monroe off the home plate. It was the fastest, funniest burlesque ever seen on a ball field, Monroe's antics being a scream. The crowd roared with laughter.[5]

In another closely fought battle, waged before a record crowd of more than ten thousand, the American Giants on April 5 nipped the Seattle Giants 1-0, the lone run scoring in the bottom of the ninth. Holding Seattle to a single hit after replacing Pat Dougherty in the top of the first with the bases loaded and just one out, Williams again pitched brilliantly, despite lacking quite the overpowering stuff he had in the first game.[6]

As the American Giants' 1914 West Coast tour continued, record crowds turned out to watch the legendary black baseball squad, and area newspapers provided coverage equal to that afforded the major leagues. After flattening Butte 18-1 to wrap up "their spring training," the Giants had a record of 18-6-1. A number of teams refused to play the Giants because of the "color line," sports columnist Frank A. Young of the *Chicago Defender* suggested. But the white press admitted that "a yellow streak" more fully explained the reluctance to compete against the black baseball team. After all, Foster "has what is the best bunch of ball tossers that was ever brought together." On occasion, Foster himself continued to pitch as well as ever. Near the end of the trip, he was on the mound, shutting his opponents out until the eighth, as the American Giants defeated a group of All-Star locals 8-1 in Lewiston, Colorado.[7]

Arriving in Omaha, Nebraska, on April 26, the American Giants' manager encountered a reporter from the *Chicago Defender*. "We have played all along the line and have met victory on every hand," Foster declared. "Just tell them that my team will be in Chicago on Sunday to play the Giants and we will win." Foster was referred to as "the maker of ball players," who guided "his famous squad."[8]

With their powerful lineup, the American Giants had another brilliant season in 1914, amassing a 126-16 mark. Lee Wade has been credited with a 10-2 mark and Horace Jenkins with a 5-1 record, and Foster produced a 6-3 mark in games whose news accounts have been uncovered. Jude Gans had a relatively poor season at the plate, but several Chicago players batted above .300, including Francis, .396; Monroe, .348; Barber, .314; and Hill, .302. No doubt, Lloyd did so as well, but no compiled records of his batting performance for 1914 can be found.[9]

Opening day on April 28 witnessed the American Giants blanking the Gunthers 4-0 on a five-hitter by Wade, who struck out eight and issued no walks. Automobiles had streamed by Schorling Park for hours before the game began, and "the box office was stormed when it opened." Warming up, the American Giants received sustained applause from the packed crowd "as they pulled time and again big league stuff." Many of the Gunthers had played in organized baseball, but major league moguls, the *Chicago Defender* complained, "have overlooked a team that can beat these men and have utterly failed to recognize such stars as Petway, Lloyd, Hill, Wade and others that the mighty Rube has gathered." The *Defender* then added, "Any one of these would be a drawing card by himself and would bring to the owners much more colored patronage than they now have got." The Federal League, the newspaper hoped, would dilute the talent pool so "that these stars or others of the darker hue will be given a chance to earn some big money honestly along with the Indian, the Chinaman and other races, especially the Cubans, who are much darker in color than some of the race men."[10]

St. Joseph, an independent championship squad from Michigan, faced Foster on May 6 before a substantial crowd. Committing five errors and relinquishing nineteen hits, St. Joe's appeared thoroughly overmatched. Pitching easily, Foster struck out six, walked two, and held a 13-2 lead going into the bottom of the eighth when he gave up four runs. "The mighty Foster," in a hard-fought contest against the Cubans on May 26, replaced Horace Jenkins on the mound. In the eighth, with two out and runners on second and third, Foster attempted to nab the Cubans' Chico

Hernandez at second base. No one was covering the bag, however, and the ball sailed into center field; a poor throw from Pete Hill enabled the Cubans to knot the score. In the last of the tenth, the Cubans scored twice to pin the loss on Foster.[11]

As if turning back the clock, Foster faced only twenty-eight batters in shutting out the Cuban Stars 1-0 on June 2. While striking out five, he gave up a lone hit: a double by Cristobal Torriente that Jude Gans misjudged. The game's sole run scored in the top of the first when Jess Barber opened the game with a double, took third as the Stars second baseman Bobby Villa committed an error, and scored on Frank Duncan's sacrifice fly. The *Indianapolis Freeman* referred to Foster's outing as the best-pitched game at Schorling Park in 1914. Nearly duplicating his performance three days later, he shut out the Indianapolis ABCs, one of the finest units in black baseball, 2-0, giving up only three hits. On June 10, Foster, who struck out four and walked no one, defeated Benton Harbor, despite allowing eight hits. Both teams scored in bunches: the American Giants put four runs across the plate in the top of the first; Benton Harbor tied the score with a big third inning. The winning run scored when Hill, who had doubled, tallied on Lloyd's single. The *Freeman* termed this a "sensational game" won by the "king of ball pitchers," who again displayed "just how much he still 'holds 'em.'"[12]

Foster won his fourth straight game, 6-1, on July 2, limiting the French Lick Plutos to six hits, while striking out five and walking four. A tight pitchers' duel was broken up by the American Giants' scoring four times in the top of the seventh. Beginning on July 4, Foster's team swept a three-game series against the Cuban Stars; fifteen thousand fans showed up on the first two days at Schorling Park. Throwing with only two days' rest in the second contest, Foster gave up nine hits and struck out only two before departing in the seventh inning. The American Giants held on for a 5-4 victory. On July 23, Foster shut out a group of top City League players on two hits before eight thousand fans at his home ballpark; throughout the 8-0 whitewashing, Foster "never was in better form," the *Indianapolis Ledger* reported. Going against the Indianapolis ABCs, however, he was knocked out of the box after striking out only one and walking three, whereupon the ABCs swept to a 5-2 victory.[13]

A week later, Foster contributed a brief note on black baseball batterymates for the *Indianapolis Freeman*. "Our pitchers," he offered, "have brought more renown to our race than the players at any other position. The pitcher is the most important personage upon a ball club." As for their catchers, some, "were they white," Foster contended, "could name their own salaries."[14]

The following week, Cary B. Lewis of the *Freeman* related that the "world's greatest baseball pitcher and manager of the American Giants baseball team" had $600 pilfered from him as he waited at the Northwestern Railroad station. A pickpocket, operating with a pair of accomplices, apparently had targeted Foster on the train in Wisconsin, where the American Giants had performed at a local fairground. Arriving in Chicago from Gary, Indiana, Foster disembarked and, along with his team, headed for a streetcar, which he was the last to board. There, one of the thieves brushed against him and then bolted; two others blocked Foster's pursuit to allow for a successful getaway. Three of the fastest American Giants ran after the first culprit but to no avail.[15]

Matched against the Cuban Stars once more on August 18, Foster's fate proved no happier than during his last outing. The *Freeman* indicated that he "pitched a splendid game," but the Cubans managed nine hits and three walks, and struck out only twice, defeating the American Giants 5-1.[16]

In early September, Foster's team met the eastern champion Brooklyn Royal Giants for "the colored world's series." A record crowd was present for the first game. The powerful American Giants swept the four-game set, with Frank Wickware winning the opener 3-0 by fanning twelve and allowing only three hits. Lee Wade took the second game, again blanking the Royal Giants 7-0, while giving up one less hit than had Wickware. The third game was a contentious affair that Chicago won 7-6, despite a shaky pitching performance by Horace Jenkins. The final game ended with the American Giants on top 3-1, thanks to a fine pitching performance by Jenkins.[17]

Two developments tainted an otherwise superlative performance by the American Giants. The death of pitcher Bill Lindsay was disturbing, to say the least. So too was the near-riot that occurred during game three as the American Giants scored the winning run in the bottom of the ninth. With two outs, Petway, batting for Gans, hit the ball to short right field near the foul line. As two Royal Giants players collided, the ball popped out of second baseman Bill Handy's glove, allowing two runs to score. The infuriated Royal Giants stormed the field, went after umpire Fitzpatrick, but could only watch in frustration as the police carted him away.[18]

Shortly following "the colored world's series," Foster traveled to Louisville and Indianapolis, scouting for talent, providing instructional tips, and undoubtedly discussing the possibility of a black baseball league. As he returned to Chicago, the *Indianapolis Freeman* saluted the "Old Roman" yet again. "There is no doubt in the minds of the most incredulous," the *Freeman* declared, "that he is the great baseball teacher-manager of the age. The race is proud of him and the sporting writers of all papers delight to write about his superior ability."[19]

That winter, Foster took his ball club to Havana. After returning home, as the American Giants readied for another western swing, he reflected on his career in an interview with George E. Mason of the *Chicago Defender*. In contrast to the Philadelphia Athletics' Connie Mack and the Chicago Cubs' Frank Chance, who had constructed powerful ball clubs of their own, Foster lacked the resources of his white counterparts. Yet "our 'Rube,' as he is affectionately called by countless white and colored baseball fans," Mason noted, built powerful black baseball teams nevertheless. The sportswriter proceeded to lay out "the story of his wonderful career—strange enough to be fiction, but not less model than the metaphors handed us at the regular Sunday morning services." When Mason visited Rube's "comfy home" early one afternoon, he was pleasantly surprised to discover none of the expected trappings of a celebrated sports figure, such as flags and pennants. The Foster household, by contrast, could have passed for "the home of one of our most pious ministers." The furniture was neat but modest, with a few pictures, most noticeably "one of 'Lil' Rube and Mr. 'Rube'"—referring to Foster's son, Earl, and the great player-manager himself—adorning the plain walls.[20]

As Mrs. Foster escorted Mason to an upstairs office to see "the real shining light of our sporting world," he heard pounding typewriter keys and then was greeted by Foster. "Sorry, I haven't time, sir; I'm awfully busy," Foster politely indicated. "I am from the *Defender*," Mason answered, "and would like to ask you a few questions." Immediately warming up, Foster agreed to the interview. Over the next few hours, Foster revealed much about his career, the tough times, and the successes, which Mason considered "most inspiring of all." Eventually, of course, Foster had molded the American Giants, now considered "the standard of colored baseball clubs." During his eight-year tenure as manager, he had paid the highest salaries in black baseball and was the lone manager to meet every payroll. He was the first operator in black baseball to take his team on a spring tour through the American South and the only one whose squad always traveled in a private Pullman car. Foster's Chicago American Giants had ventured more widely than any other team and were the sharpest dressed in the business. His players displayed their loyalty to him, and ballplayers in general considered him "the backbone of this profession."[21]

Mason asked Foster, "Have you any favorites among your players?" Foster responded forcefully, "No. I try to pick my players by their ability to play baseball. Real teamwork is necessary to become a winner, so every player must be up to the standard or, in spite of personal friendship or public opinion, I insist on judging my men by their ability to play winning ball."[22]

Near the close of the interview, the journalist posed another but equally revealing type of question. "Does the wife know the game?" Foster answered, "She only has interest in it because I play it. Never saw a game before we married." On the other hand, Mrs. Foster was familiar with the business operations of her husband's ball club.[23]

Believing that he had already taken up a good deal of Foster's "valuable time"—the American Giants were about to undertake another extended baseball journey—Mason prepared to depart. He concluded, "I had satisfied myself that Rube Foster, gentleman, ball player, has made baseball a business as well as a pleasure, opening up a new vocation for our clean-living young men. What is possible in Chicago is also possible in other cities, and it's a paying pleasure. Just think of that 10,000 mile trip."[24]

Throughout their pilgrimage, the American Giants characteristically traveled in style. As the team returned from Havana, a student athlete at New Orleans University by the name of Dave Malarcher encountered Foster and the American Giants for the first time. The Giants were playing another semipro outfit, the New Orleans Eagles. Malarcher recalled that the Giants "had five sets of uniforms and all kinds of equipment and I was very impressed of course in the way they operated."[25]

As for Foster, he now weighed well over 250 pounds but could still pitch like a master, at least on occasion. As Malarcher recalled, "[H]e had one of the most baffling curve balls I ever looked at. And he had a real good fast ball—real good fast ball—and he threw a curve ball that was more what people would call a fadeaway. It looked like that fast ball and it would get there and just flutter, like that, away from you."[26]

The American Giants' odyssey in 1915 began on March 4, when they took a train out of Chicago, bound for training camp in New Orleans. Billy Lewis of the *Indianapolis Freeman* now produced his own write-up of Foster and the American Giants. Baseball was attracting more fans, Lewis noted, thanks to the likes of C. I. Taylor, manager of the Indianapolis ABCs, and Foster. Lewis then celebrated Foster's accomplishments and contribution to the game of baseball:

> Rube Foster, the well known baseball player of Chicago, has almost become another name for baseball. To hear his name mentioned is to think of the great game and at its very best.
>
> Rube, as he is known to all base ball fans, is undoubtedly the greatest player and manager that has yet been produced in base ball among the colored people, and has done more to elevate the game among them than any one person. His efforts have been untiring, and his wonderful success has not come over night, but through years of hard and patient work; he is modest and seldom speaks of his success, although he has had more said about him by the best baseball writers than any other colored player. He is proud of his ball clubs whose records under the circumstances have never been equaled nor are they apt to be surpassed.[27]

Foster's teams, Lewis continued, had been the most carefully devised in black baseball. His players, for their part, "look to him as a child would to its parents." They undoubtedly appreciated their uniforms, the finest in "shadowball," and their mode of travel, private sleepers. They conducted themselves in the manner that Foster expected: as gentlemen. His latest team, the American Giants, was a "great ball club" and served as "the standard of colored base ball." As for Foster, Lewis insisted that he had "brought more prominence to the race," where baseball was concerned, than any other individual.[28]

Rainy weather conditions hampered practice, however, and only a half dozen games were played before the American Giants departed for a spring tour of the West. Once in California, Foster indicated that his team's latest edition, thanks to several new ballplayers, was "equal to if not better than the team of last year." Briefly joining Petway behind the plate was Louis Santop, a powerful left-handed slugger who had batted more than .400 in each of the past four seasons with the New York Lincoln Giants. Light-hitting but slick-fielding second baseman Harry Bauchman was another addition. Hurley McNair was the new rightfielder and cleanup hitter. Rejoining the pitching staff was Frank Wickware, who in 1914 had played for three other teams in addition to the American Giants. A 6'4" right-hander, Big Richard Whitworth, a strikeout artist, was just beginning his career. Reuniting with Foster was old teammate Walter Ball, previously one of the premier pitchers in black baseball. Big Bill Gatewood was yet another former Leland Giant who came on board. One key loss, for the first several months of the season, was John Henry Lloyd, who had returned to the New York Lincoln Giants.[29]

On March 27, the American Giants pounded Stanley Covelskie, later a five-time twenty-game winner and eventual Hall of Famer, in flattening the Portland Beavers 9-1. Included among the Giants' fourteen-hit attack were three doubles and a pair of homers, one each by Barber and pitcher Gatewood; Bauchman produced four hits, including two doubles.[30]

A few days later, as a rainout occurred, Foster spoke with Roscoe Fawcett of the *Oregonian* about the Portland nine, which he viewed as the strongest Beaver squad the Giants had faced in the past three years. The paper referred to Foster as "the black McGraw" who believed that the Federal League would either collapse or meld with the major leagues. It also noted that the American Giants were headed for Tacoma and Seattle.[31]

In their opening game against Pacific League champion Portland on March 25, Chicago won 4-2, behind Ball's six-hitter. After Portland nipped the American Giants 4-1, with a run in the top of the ninth, the team rebounded to take the third contest 11-1, relying on a seventeen-hit attack and the four-hit pitching of Big Bill Gatewood. The next game was won by Portland 1-0 in twelve innings that featured a terrific pitching match pitting Ball against an ailing Dutch

Leonard—who had just established a major league mark for the lowest single-season earned-run average. The Boston Red Sox star gave up ten hits, and Ball allowed only seven, but Portland scored on a walk, a single to right, and a sacrifice fly.[32]

By mid-April, the American Giants' western record stood at 20-6. Foster's squad was backed, the *Chicago Defender* reported, "by a strong bevy of slab artists" who had been playing ball for the past two months. After taking two of three from the Tacoma Giants, the American Giants headed for Butte, Billings, and Denver, before returning to Chicago. When the Giants finally arrived back in the Windy City, they had been away for six and a half months.[33]

SEVEN

The Dynasty Is Interrupted

On April 29, 1915, the "peerless" American Giants opened their season by shutting out the Milwaukee Sox 9-0 on a three-hitter by rookie right-hander Big Richard Whitworth. Six thousand fans gathered at Schorling Park to watch the latest version of the American Giants battle the Lake Shore League champions, whose record stood at 31-10. The Giants' attack was imprinted by Hurley McNair's three safeties. Louis Santop was behind the plate; Jess Barber had moved to first base; second was covered by Harry Bauchman; playing short was Fred Hutchinson; and stationed at third was Billy Francis. The outfield, from left to right, included Pete Hill, Frank Duncan, and McNair.

On May 14, the American Giants, behind Horace Jenkins's six-hitter, topped Kavanaugh's League 8-3. Several former big leaguers could be found on the Kavanaugh roster, including Charles "Silk" Kavanaugh, who briefly had played with the Chicago White Sox; pitcher Herold Juul, who made nine appearances with the Brooklyn Feds; catcher Skipper Roberts, formerly of the St. Louis Cardinals and two Federal League teams; and center fielder Lou Gertenrich, whose major league career was short-lived and had ended a dozen years earlier.[1]

Working the first six innings, Foster held a 3-1 lead over the Gunthers on May 21, before being replaced by Walter Ball; Foster departed, having struck out one and walked four. The American Giants eked out a 3-2 victory. Making an increasingly rare appearance on the field, Foster played first base in a doubleheader against the Roseland Eclipse on June 5, won by the American Giants 2-1 and 3-0; Whitworth and Frank Wickware pitched superbly. The *Indianapolis Ledger* highlighted Foster's defensive play: "He took Barber's place at first base, and the famous ball player did some work that startled the fans. 'Rube' made seven putouts unassisted in the first game, and six in the second. He was in apple-pie form, stopping three red-hot liners and crossing his man at first like a streak of lightning." Half-a-dozen times, on heading for the Giants' bench, Foster was compelled to doff his hat.[2]

As the American Giants continued to shine against the best semipro teams, including top white ones, the *Indianapolis Freeman,* on June 19, produced an essay on race and the national pastime. "The color line drawn so tightly around the major league baseball," the *Freeman* charged, "has barred from major league fields three of the greatest pitchers the game ever has produced." The editorial, quoting from the *Indianapolis Daily Times,* then pinpointed John Donaldson of the All Nations, the American Giants' Frank Wickware, and José Méndez. "If Donaldson were a white man, or if the unwritten law of baseball didn't bar negroes from the major leagues," New York Giants manager John McGraw was quoted as saying, "I would give $50,000 for him—and think I was getting a bargain." Donaldson was reported to have pitched thirty consecutive hitless innings and once had struck out twenty men in a twelve-inning contest. Wickware, the *Freeman* asserted, "was another negro pitcher who would rank with the Walter Johnsons, Joe Wood and Grover Clevelands if he were a white man." The Cuban Méndez was deemed "the Black Matty," a reference to the New York Giants ace Christy Mathewson. Méndez was said to possess "terrific power in his arm. The Cuban negro has a canny brain and he always has used it. He has mixed his fast ball with his slow one, and an assortment of beautiful curves and perfect control."[3]

On June 23, Foster, once considered the finest of all the pitchers in black baseball, reached back in time to hold the Indianapolis ABCs to three hits in an 8-1 game. He whiffed three and walked four, in "pitching an article of ball," the *Freeman* reported, "that still keeps him in the champion class." However, on July 5, Foster gave up three runs in the top of the eighth on a walk, a hit batter, and three safeties, which enabled the Cubans to prevail 4-1; in consecutive games, the Cubans beat Wickware, Foster, and Whitworth. A crowd estimated at ten thousand gathered to celebrate "Rube Foster's holiday," but watched the American Giant player-manager yield ten hits, while striking out four and walking two. Fans, transported in taxis, jitneys, automobiles, and carriages, began appearing well before noon; by the time the game opened, spectators ringed the scoreboard area. Foster threw "a splendid game," the *Freeman* insisted, but a misplayed ball in the outfield and errors proved costly. In a subsequent three-game series against the Cubans, the Giants managed only a tie, a feat accomplished during the contest that Foster pitched. Foster and José Junco started, but neither went the distance and the slugfest ended in a 6-6 tie.[4]

Shortly after the debacle suffered at the hands of the Cubans, a performance so uncharacteristic of one of Foster's teams, the American Giants competed against the Indianapolis ABCs in another long-anticipated set of games. Chicago had recently taken three of five games from the ABCs, so the series was likened to "the battle royal of the season." The *Indianapolis Freeman*'s July 17 edition featured a cartoon entitled "Taylor, the Giant Killer, Welcomes 'Big Chief.'" A small-figured C. I. Taylor, the ABCs' manager and occasional infielder, was shown with an oversized bat that read "the swatting power," greeting the American Giants' boss, who was called "the mighty Rube." Three arrows pointed to Foster, proclaiming "the Cubans did it," while a tiny representation of the now-departed John Henry Lloyd was seen with a question mark. A fan was declaring, "What it takes to kill th' giant C.I. carries it." The sketch contained a caption that stated, "A Hint to the Chicago Bugs— 'If you have tears prepare to shed them now.'"[5]

Some 2,500 "lusty fans" were in attendance on July 18, with each ball club exuding "blood in its eyes"; the Taylor brothers, C. I. and first baseman Ben, had bragged that they would take the opener. Frank Wickware went against William "Dizzy" Dismukes, a submarining right-hander. Pomp and ceremony abounded at Greenlawn Park, home of the Indianapolis Hoo-feds. The visiting American Giants, characteristically attired in their bright white uniforms, were warmly greeted by the spectators. The score stood at 3-2, in favor of the Giants, going into the seventh inning, with "Wick" appearing to be at the top of his game. But as Wickware suddenly began to tire, Foster replaced him with Richard Whitworth. The ABCs' outfielder George "Rabbit" Shively greeted him with a single and then second baseman

Bingo DeMoss walked; Foster yanked Whitworth. Big Bill Gatewood proceeded to issue free passes to both rookie center fielder Oscar Charleston and Ben Taylor, knotting the score.[6]

What occurred next became a matter of heated debate. Just as "things looked dangerous for the 'Old Roman,'" the *Chicago Defender* reported, the two teams headed for home plate, where a fight broke out. Bats were grabbed and Pete Hill squabbled with the umpire, who pulled out a gun and smacked the American Giant outfielder on the nose, supposedly breaking it. A number of other players also were injured as the disturbance unfolded. Finally, the umpire ordered a forfeit in favor of the ABCs. The disgraceful scene, the *Defender* warned, would preclude black baseball teams from competing at the major league park in the future and thereby threatened the game's continued existence in Indianapolis. "There was too great a contrast between the gentlemanly playing of the Federal teams and the riot scenes enacted Sunday. Such games mean that baseball in this city will be reduced to a low ebb and respectable people will not patronize them. It was a bloody chapter. Another one will kill Afro-American ball playing."[7]

The *Indianapolis Ledger* accused "the resourceful Foster" of resorting to "all kinds of stunts" to delay the game, once the ABCs threatened to grab the lead. "Every stall known to the game" was relied on, to cause it to be called because of rain, the *Ledger* claimed. The umpire, however, reportedly refused to allow this and after a succession of heated arguments, declared the forfeit.[8]

The second game, played the next day, went to the ABCs 7-4. Big Bill Gatewood was pounded in the first two innings, and the ABCs jumped out to a 6-2 lead, which they never lost. Foster eventually took to the mound himself. As the *Ledger* put it, Foster "marched out solemnly and offered himself to the slaughter. The old man succeeded in holding the home boys in check," relinquishing only a single run in his five-plus innings of work.[9]

After rain cancelled Tuesday's game in the bottom of the first, the ABCs won yet again, 5-3, with Dismukes once more outpitching Whitworth. Pete Hill smacked homers in the first and second innings, but his heavy hitting went for naught. On Thursday, Indianapolis completed a four-game sweep, defeating the Giants 7-6 in thirteen innings. Hill again contributed a pair of homers, but Wickware proved ineffective and was replaced in the seventh inning by Gatewood.[10]

Following the conclusion of the series, another stunning setback for the American Giants, the *Ledger* insisted that Foster's ball club was disqualified from "the race for the World's Colored championship." The ABCs, the paper announced, now were the top team in the West. Their upcoming five-game clash with the New York Lincoln Stars, the *Ledger* declared, would determine who would wear the black baseball crown.[11]

On July 30, a little more than a week following the Giants-ABCs match-up, Foster issued a letter addressed "To the Base-Ball Public of the United States." After considerable reflection, Foster had decided to discuss "the disgraceful series of games" between Chicago and Indianapolis. In the ABCs' hometown could be found "the most disgraceful scenes yet to be seen in public," he charged, although "the daily riots at West Baden" engaged in by C. I. Taylor might be even worse. Foster uncharitably referred to Taylor as Indianapolis's "stool pigeon."[12]

Foster then explained how the events of July 18 had unfolded. In the bottom of the eighth, the ABCs loaded the bases with nobody out. A windstorm caused a delay in the game because the field was unwatered. With dust blowing so fiercely that the outfielders were not visible, umpire Geisel called time. The Indianapolis management then began to sprinkle the infield's left side. When the umpire informed Foster "that he was not going to be shown up," the American Giants' manager responded he was only concerned that the rest of the infield also be wet down. Then Geisel "told me that it was up to me to see that it was done," Foster stated, but then it began to rain. The ABCs' owner Thomas Bowser ordered the umpire to make the Giants take the field. Foster urged Geisel to compel the ABCs to water the infield between first and second bases because the right fielder could not be seen. The Indianapolis bosses again insisted that Geisel force Chicago to play ball, which he attempted to do. Foster's further implorings proved fruitless, and Geisel declared that no additional delay would be tolerated. Bowser demanded that the Giants be instructed to continue or suffer a forfeit.[13]

Still pleading with the umpire, Foster pointed out "that there was so much money at stake on the result of the game." He pressed for a delay until the field was in shape to play; if it remained unplayable after a half hour, the rules were that the game revert to "even innings," which would result in a declared tie. Once again, Geisel was told by Bowser to make the Giants resume play. Obviously riled, Geisel called four straight balls, thus forcing in the lead run before he announced a forfeit. A stunned Foster remained at home plate. Giants captain Pete Hill raced over to find out what had transpired and, as he did, several of the ABCs and many of their fans poured onto the field, thereby precipitating a riot. Luckily, no injuries ensued, despite the antics of policeman Flemmings, who pulled a gun on one of the Giants players.[14]

The American Giants, Foster admitted, "had deliberately forfeited a game," which was "not a crime"; moreover, it "has often been done by the greatest managers in baseball" and hardly warranted the abuse that the Giants had received in Indianapolis. Actual witnesses, Foster insisted, would agree that he "did not for once, in action or words, question the decisions of the umpire." Even when the forfeit was announced, "I made no demonstration, either by acts or words, but started directly to our bench, and to my surprise, turned and saw the most disgraceful scene I have ever witnessed."[15]

The following day the situation became more intolerable still for Foster; by his account, he suffered "the most complete humiliation" yet. The Giants had tallied two runs in the top of the second and led 3-0 with the ABCs coming to bat. Foster headed for the coach's box alongside third base, and a police sergeant came over. That officer

> called me back, calling me the dirtiest names I had ever had said to me, first asking me who it was that started the argument at Sunday's game. I said I did not know and he said to me, You black son-of-a-B. If you open your mouth, I will blow your brains out. He stood there at least five minutes abusing me and calling me all kinds of names.[16]

That scarcely ended the Giants' troubles. Foster sent Harry Bauchman to coach on the left side of the playing diamond, but his infielder discovered that the base was improperly positioned. After Bauchman nudged it in line with his foot, the ABCs manager C. I. Taylor jumped up from his bench, pushed Bauchman aside, and called out the police, who raced onto the field and began pummeling Bauchman's head. Fans booed and exhorted the Giants to refuse to play. As Foster saw matters, "It was the dirtiest work that I or any one else had ever seen on a ball field. It was a crime and there is no one responsible for it but the owner Bowser, and the ingrate Taylor." After all, a policeman was allowed on the field only at the behest of the umpire, if a fight had broken out, or as requested by team management. In this instance, no squabbles had occurred.[17]

Bowser, Foster charged, was in cahoots with the police and had ordered them onto the field. Foster also castigated manager Taylor, again referring to him as "an ingrate," "one of the lowest kind," whose "low tactics" had "ruined base ball at West Baden."[18]

Ironically, Foster indicated, the ABCs players and Taylor himself, like "all the Colored players," were "indebted" to Foster for helping them out financially. That information was not intended "as a boast, but to prove that all my efforts have always been to try and help, and not tear down, and advance colored ball, as well as players, and I hope the lovers of right, and fair play, will—as in the past—judge me by what they know, and not what they hear."[19]

Foster concluded his letter in sadness:

> The incident was more painful to me than to any that saw or read it. It was the complete humiliation of a life's effort to advance and promote baseball among our people, and I can forgive the many hard words that may have been said, knowing they had been said before you had a chance to learn the facts, and you can rest assured that I have not up until the present, and would not in future do one single thing to hurt baseball, nor stoop low enough to permit or stand to see any ball club or players treated as the American Giants were at Indianapolis—whether they are right or wrong—and even now would not permit the public, players, or police to come on our grounds and beat, abuse, or humiliate the Indianapolis Ball Club.[20]

Challenging Foster's statements, while insisting that he would not, Taylor released personal correspondence between the two men. Denying that Hill or other of Foster's players had been injured in any kind of confrontation, Taylor indicated he had no intention of countering "the many malicious and libelous statements" made by "the self-styled 'greatest manager' the game has produced." Further, he would not "malign anybody or try to destroy the usefulness and life's effort of any individual." Only Bauchman had been hit, and that occurred the day following the purported "great and 'bloody riot.'" Taylor asserted he had not approved of the police officer's treatment of Bauchman or of "the abuse" inflicted on Foster by the police sergeant. Indeed, he was unaware of that development until the game was over.[21]

For the past five years, Taylor remarked—abruptly changing the subject—he had urged formation of a "Negro league" but had encountered surprising opposition. "Baseball is in its infancy among Colored people, and with the nourishment of organization it will grow to be a giant organization such as the entire race will be proud of." Hundreds of young black athletes undoubtedly would join professional teams and thereby acquire enough money to attend college. Each year, Taylor revealed, he had written several times to Foster, urging establishment of "the Negro baseball league," telling him "that he is the rightful leader of us in the organization of the league. . . . I only wanted to act as a lieutenant in helping him accomplish the thing that has been uppermost in my mind and his, too, I suppose, for these many years." Taylor had called for Foster to join him in traveling to the cities where they thought league franchises might be viable. There, they would meet with black businessmen to discuss creation of a league of their own. Thereafter, local committees would send representatives to a general meeting to found the league and elect its president. Taylor admitted to Foster that "he would be the best man for president," while recognizing that Foster would probably choose instead to manage his own team when it joined the league.[22]

Just a year ago, Taylor noted, Foster had argued against organizing, using "as an excuse" the new Federal League and the considerable publicity attending its arrival. Foster had contended the Federals were not likely to survive for long, and blackball moguls would be able to obtain vacant ballparks for their purposes—a rationale that made sense to Taylor. The previous fall, Taylor had again broached the subject of a league, but Foster countered that the finding of "good ball clubs, and managers" was a prerequisite. True enough, Taylor acknowledged, while complaining that Foster never explained how to bring that about. The way to produce such teams and leaders, Taylor now declared, involved "an equalization of strength" and an end to players jumping from one squad to another, which "can only be done by organization. The formation of a league is the only remedy."[23]

Taylor next produced a pair of letters that he had written to Foster in May regarding a black league, in which he said again, "I do not care to be put in the light of the public's eye as the leader in this undertaking at all; as I think the leadership rightly belongs to you." A leader must be recognized, but the opinions of others had to be respected. Taylor expressed concern about Foster's perceived "lukewarmness," a stance that spelled "defeat for the movement. It must have your cooperation if it is to amount to anything." In spite of past differences, the ABCs' manager continued, he stood ready to serve as Foster's "lieutenant." Once that was the case, "you could go ahead with the organization."[24]

In closing, Taylor cautioned that "if some radical change is not made, our future in the game is sure to be disastrous." Still, Taylor had no desire to "to issue any call unless it had the stamp of your approval on it. It would not amount to very much." Moreover, "I cannot see any success in anything that I might put on foot alone, but I think I can see much in what we might inaugurate together and in harmony. . . ."[25]

After an obviously unhappy Foster responded, Taylor warned that "there is entirely too much of the 'Great I Am' among colored people in baseball for us to amount to what we might." Taylor pointedly added, "You will find that it is not in the best interests of you nor anybody else to threaten to wipe somebody off the map in baseball every time somebody happens to ask to have the privilege of having something to say and do with affairs that concern them as well as yourself." In almost all instances where the two disagreed on an issue, Taylor reminded Foster, Foster would threaten "to annihilate me forever from baseball."[26]

In the exchange, the seemingly more dispassionate Taylor came out looking somewhat better than black baseball's greatest figure. Foster, for his part, had referred to his closest rival as a "stool pigeon," an "ingrate," and "one of the lowest kind"; Taylor more deftly called Foster "the rightful leader" of black baseball players. Foster had, in fact, accused both Taylor and Indianapolis owner Thomas Bowser of criminal culpability. Taylor wisely desisted from name calling, although—tongue in cheek—he termed Foster "the self-styled 'greatest manager' the game has produced." Taylor also cleverly focused on a broader imperative: black baseball's need to organize. It was politically skillful to advance Foster as the logical head of an organizational effort while staking a claim as a loyal assistant determined to be his own man. Managing almost entirely to sidestep the abysmal treatment afforded the American Giants and, particularly, Foster in Indianapolis, Taylor pointedly concluded with the revelation that Foster had repeatedly threatened to drive him out of baseball.

The exchange between Foster and Taylor appeared in a number of leading black newspapers, along with pictures of the American Giants manager. In the *Chicago Defender*, a photograph of Foster with glove in hand was entitled "The Only 'Rube.'" The caption read, "The 'Lone Star' in the Baseball World. When This Phenomenal Player Steps upon the Slab the Fan Forgets the 'Color Line,' for the 'Master Pitcher' is on the job." Also displayed was a photograph, "'Rube' Foster's Famous American Giants." The *Indianapolis Ledger* ran photos of Rube seated at his home office, his wife, small son, and the Foster residence in Chicago.[27]

Notwithstanding the twin series' defeats suffered at the hands of the Cubans and the Indianapolis ABCs, the *Defender* billed a spate of games with the New York Lincoln Stars as championship fare. The ten games were split evenly, with Foster pounded in the sixth contest, an 11-4 triumph for the Lincoln Stars. Foster struck out only two, walked three, and gave up ten hits, while suffering the ill effects of four Chicago errors. The Stars were ahead during the fourth inning of the eleventh and deciding contest when it was called.[28]

In late August 1915, more trouble broke out in a game involving the American Giants. This time, the opponents were the Cuban Stars, led by center fielder Cristobal Torriente. In the fourth inning, Torriente was called out while attempting to pilfer third base. Torriente exploded, kicking the umpire; Chicago pitcher Sam Crawford rushed over to belt the Cuban in the jaw. Bats and balls then began to be hurled at Giants players by their opponents. The police finally restored order, and the Giants prevailed 3-1. Following the game, Torriente and Crawford started scuffling outside; Foster, the *Chicago Defender* reported, "went to the rescue" as bricks and stones were being tossed at Cuban Star players.[29]

On August 27, it was announced that John Henry Lloyd and Jude Gans were rejoining the American Giants. Lloyd, the *Defender* proclaimed, "is the greatest shortstop in the country barring none. He is ranked greater than Barry and Wagner." The *Indianapolis Ledger* agreed: "[A]s a shortstop John Henry Lloyd is without a peer in this or any other company"; moreover, his batting was generally on a par with "his sensational fielding. He can throw from any position, and is probably the best example of natural ball player of any man, white or black, in the game today." Gans, for his part, was termed "one of the surest fielders that ever wore a glove." With the addition of these two stars from the New York Lincoln Giants, the *Defender* contended, Foster "will have the strongest team in the country."[30]

As the season wound to a close, Foster challenged Joe Tinker's Chicago Whales, the Federal League champs, to play his American Giants. Foster wanted to meet the Whales in competition, the *Defender* reported, "to prove to them that he has a much superior team." Although Tinker had lined up a number of games against semiprofessionals in the area, he refused to go head-to-head with the black baseball squad. Ironically, Tinker and Whales' owner Charles Weegham complained that the major leagues were not affording them "fair play." But they, in turn, treated the American Giants in the same fashion due to "color prejudice," the *Defender* asserted. Foster had even offered to give all the receipts "to charity on a winner and loser basis—that is, for white and color institutions." The *Defender* charged that Tinker was "scared" to accept the challenge.[31]

"We are getting to be too much of a drawing card," reasoned "the wise old owl," reportedly "much peeved" by the Federals' refusal to face his team. After all, Schorling and Comiskey Parks were virtually neighbors on the South Side of Chicago. In contrast to the White Sox, however, the American Giants received only sparse coverage from area newspapers when they traveled outside the city.[32]

A sorely disappointed Foster, whose own 1915 record stood at a modest 2-2-1, instead led his charges on another western excursion. The trip was scheduled to be the longest yet, with the first games to be played against a group of major and minor leaguers in Omaha. Then, another team of all-stars would be encountered in Denver, before the American Giants headed for the coast. They planned to compete again in the California Winter League, which itself boasted a number of big league ballplayers. When the league ended in late February, Foster hoped to take his team then to Honolulu for a five-week venture. Back on the mainland, the Giants would play in Portland on April 1, before moving on to "Seattle, Vancouver, Walla Walla, Wash., Sand Point, Idaho, Butte, Helena and Missoula, Mont., Denver and Omaha." In addition to many of his regulars, Foster was taking along Indianapolis left fielder Jimmie Lyons; St. Louis Giant hurler Andrew "Stringbean" Williams; St. Louis first baseman Tully McAdoo; Brooklyn Royal Giant catcher Speck Webster; and the ABCs' star pitcher William Dismukes.[33]

On January 7, 1916, with a 3-2 victory over the Pantages in San Diego, Foster's Giants clinched another California Winter League title. After a trip back home, Foster took the Santa Fe Limited bound for California, planning to firm up the Hawaiian trip; that enterprise did not pan out. A caption for a photograph appearing in the *Chicago Defender* referred to him as "The Greatest Baseball Manager of 'Them All,'" with "an Enviable Record." The paper noted that during the upcoming season, Foster would probably place the Giants in two circuits, including the Chicago City League.[34]

The following month, Foster was said to be involved in a plan to purchase a series of Federal League ballparks, as organized baseball readied to become a monopoly yet again. Although a major antitrust suit was still being carried out in Federal Judge Kenesaw Mountain Landis's courtroom in Chicago, the baseball war between the Feds and the majors appeared to be ending. In the meantime, "a wealthy syndicate of Negroes" reportedly was bankrolling a scheme that the *Indianapolis Freeman* declared would enable "the black race" to "have a good-sized major league of its own" in 1916. That league would "compare in importance with the American and National leagues." Foster already had control over a park in Philadelphia, and the syndicate planned to take over Federal League stadiums in St. Louis, Pittsburgh, and Chicago.[35]

The *Freeman* also noted that Foster was then in Havana, where his American Giants were to compete in the Cuban National League. On March 18, the team left Cuba and reached New Orleans three days later. The following day, the Giants began play in Gulfport, Mississippi, before moving on to Mobile, Alabama, for a pair of contests. After two games back in New Orleans, the team headed for Portland and an extended trip along the Pacific coast. Foster pitched one game in Portland, where he displayed something of the form that previously had led many to consider him "the world's greatest pitcher." Giving up only four hits, while striking out three batters and walking the same number, Foster nevertheless suffered the loss as the Giants fell 8-5, with Portland scoring six times in the first three innings.[36]

The midpoint of the trip found the American Giants back in Seattle for a three-game set. After the Chicago team annihilated the Seattle Giants 11-3 in the series opener, the *Seattle Post-Intelligencer*'s Portus Baxter declared that Foster had "a wonderful aggregation" that was "in midsummer shape," having both ventured to Cuba and traveled from their New Orleans training camp. The second game was won by the "colored cracks" 9-6, with Lloyd's fielding acumen displayed to "spectacular effect." As the *Intelligencer* related, "Lloyd made a circus one-hand catch of a liner and completed a double play with another one-hand catch at second. He caught the ball with his one flipper right on the runner, and took the ball on the first side of the bag." The Giants took the final contest as well, after falling behind 2-1 heading into the top of the eighth. A lone run in that frame and two in the ninth concluded the sweep.[37]

Writing out of Nashville on April 10, Charles Crockett posed the question that Foster, C. I. Taylor, and other black baseball leaders had long asked: "Why can't we organize between ourselves and have a real 'Colored League'?" In Chicago, St. Louis, Cincinnati, Evansville, Louisville, and Nashville, Crockett indicated, surely the game would succeed financially. Undoubtedly, Foster would serve as the president of such an organization for "he will know more about who to select to look after these other cities than I do." A league, Crockett asserted, would "make the game more popular with our boys, they would work harder, there would not be baseball going to waste." He added that "many good 'Colored' boys" loved and played the game but had no incentive to pursue it. A league would mean that "you will hear more about our stars, you will know more about them. There would be more money in the game for us." Players, management, and fans would all benefit.[38]

The 1916 American Giants appeared stronger than the previous year's squad, which had been something of a disappointment to Foster. The successes in the California Winter League and along the West Coast boded well for the upcoming season, although that barnstorming team was hardly identical to the one he was about to field. Nevertheless, the additions of John Henry Lloyd and Jude Gans at the end of the 1915 campaign had greatly strengthened Foster's squad, which appeared to be loaded. Its catcher was Bruce Petway, still one of black baseball's finest.

The infield featured first baseman Leroy Grant, second baseman Harry Bauchman, third sacker Billy Francis, with Lloyd at short. The outfield was initially made up of Gans, Pete Hill, and Frank Duncan, but Jess Barber was soon back in the lineup. The Giants pitchers included Richard Whitworth, Frank Wickware, Tom Johnson, and Foster.

Mr. Fan, a sportswriter with the *Chicago Defender*, asserted that Foster possessed "the best team that has ever represented the American Giants." At this early point, "the Giants would make the Chicago White Sox look like a bunch of bush leaguers." The American Giants' preseason travels had covered twenty thousand miles and resulted in a 57-15 record. An estimated six thousand fans gathered to watch the season opener on May 2, as the Giants, behind Johnson's seven-hitter, defeated the West Ends 5-2. On May 16, Foster made one of his increasingly rare appearances on the mound, scattering six hits in beating La Porte 13-1; he struck out four and walked only one. Laughter had rippled through Schorling Park when the battery of Foster and Petway was announced. After "the old master of days gone by" whiffed La Porte's leadoff hitter, however, applause filled the air. Cary B. Lewis of the *Indianapolis Freeman* reported that the wily veteran "still possesses some of the old-time punch and is able to fool the boys with that 'Foster curve,' known the world over."[39]

On August 20, the American Giants were declared winners of "the colored world championship" after defeating the New York Lincoln Giants 17-7 to capture a best-of-seven-games series. Republican Edward R. Litzinger, who was running for a seat on the Chicago Board of Review, promised to give the American Giants a flag, the *Defender* declared, "for winning the championship of the world." Each player was also to receive a gold emblem. Litzinger, a good friend of Foster's, had helped to get his team into the Inter-City League. However, as complaints arose that the white ball clubs had no chance against "Rube and his champion sluggers," the Giants pulled out of the league. At that point, Litzinger promised to produce "a fine flag" for Foster's team if it defeated the New York Lincoln Stars. After the Giants also whipped the Indianapolis ABCs in a series, they were declared the champions of black baseball. As for Foster, the *Defender* included a photograph of him along with the caption "Brainiest Man in Baseball; Close Friend of Mr. Litzinger, and Who Did More to Put Chicago on the Baseball Map Than the Big League

Teams." Another photograph had the Giants lined up beneath the heading "World's Champions."[40]

In early October, the American Giants faced the renowned multiracial All-Nations, from Horton, Kansas, who featured fireballer John Donaldson and José Méndez. Chicago White Sox ace spitballer Ed Walsh watched Donaldson throw against the Giants, who bested the All-Nations twice in a three-game series. Walsh's teammates Ray Schalk, Joe Jackson, and Buck Weaver were in attendance as the American Giants swatted the Magnets.[41]

Later in the month, the American Giants battled the Indianapolis ABCs in another series that was now said to determine "the colored championship of the world." The latest round of games, according to the *Freeman,* was to be paired with the earlier season series in which the American Giants had taken three of four games. Chicago and Indianapolis, the *Freeman* proclaimed, were the finest black baseball clubs to be found. Both had completed superb years, the Giants led as always by the "peer of colored baseball managers," who had previously been considered "the greatest colored pitcher." The series, unlike the earlier one, was to be played in Indianapolis.[42]

The opener was won by the Giants 5-3, as Tom Johnson threw a six-hitter. In a pitchers' duel, Frank Wickware dropped the second contest, when the ABCs scored the only run in the bottom of the eighth. Dizzy Dismukes, who would compile a 17-6 record in 1916, limited the Giants to three hits. The third game, played before only about five hundred fans, proved enormously controversial, thereby fueling the running battle between Foster and ABCs manager C. I. Taylor. The ABCs grabbed a 1-0 lead in the third, with the Giants' Ruby Tyree going against Indianapolis's Dicta Johnson. As the sixth inning concluded, Foster, who was coaching along the first base line, put on a glove, which angered Indianapolis first baseman Ben Taylor. The umpire asked Foster, who thought the official was joking, to take off the glove. Then the ump delivered an ultimatum: "Either take off the glove or get off the coaches' line." Foster, recalling the previous year's incidents, responded by asking if his wearing of the glove violated any baseball rules. The umpire admitted that he didn't know, to which Foster replied, "We will appeal to the umpire in chief." No rule had been abridged, that official informed Foster. Returning to the first base area, Foster was told by the first umpire that Taylor insisted the glove be removed. Foster retorted that he was playing by the rules of baseball, not those Taylor concocted. The umpire then indicated that Foster had to make a choice between removing the glove and removing himself from the field. At that point, Foster sent his players to the bench, and the umpire declared a forfeit victory for the ABCs. However, when the same scenario began to unfold in a subsequent game, the chief umpire declared that Foster could wear the glove.[43]

The *Freeman* again referred to Foster as "the greatest Colored baseball man in the country." Nonetheless, its sportswriter, Young Knox, bemoaned the controversy that had developed: "We are very sorry this happened, as it will in the end hurt the men who are trying to build the game up." Taylor had enabled black baseball to flourish in Indianapolis as nowhere else, Knox insisted, and deserved more than "bulldozing actions." Indeed, "when the umpire told Mr. Foster to leave the field, he should have left without a word."[44]

The series concluded after nine games, with the ABCs taking five, including the disputed contest. The *Freeman* extolled Taylor, now proclaiming him "without a doubt, the greatest Negro baseball manager in the country, barring none." This was the first time, the paper noted, that a western club other than the American Giants had won the championship of black baseball. The immediate aftermath of the series, it appeared, had not been Foster's finest moment. In the *Freeman* account, "It was a pitiful sight to look on Mr. Foster as he slowly withdrew from the field. He smiled, but it was not a good smile. He lectured his men severely, but it was not their fault. The best team won. . . ." Still, Foster was heard to admit, "It was a battle of youth and speed against old age, and the A's are just too good for me, that's all."[45]

Mr. Fan, in an essay that appeared in the November 11, 1916, *Chicago Defender*, challenged the notion that Taylor had captured "the colored world's championship." Of nine games played out between Chicago and Indianapolis, each team had won four and another was concluded "under protest." Still another game had been halted after only three innings, even though enough light existed to continue; on that day, Taylor, "fearing a defeat," had refused to play the second half of a doubleheader, according to Mr. Fan.[46]

In a subsequent letter to the *Freeman*, Foster also denied that the

American Giants' championship run had ended. The series, he pointed out, had been scheduled to go twelve games, but only eight full games had been played. Moreover, the forfeit, Foster insisted, "would never in a thousand years have been awarded . . . under the rules of baseball." His team had refused to play any longer, Foster declared, because the umpire "went outside of the playing rules to humiliate me." Foster did praise Indianapolis as "a wonderful ball club" that displayed tremendous courage in overcoming injuries to sweep the American Giants "off our feet."[47] As for himself, Foster continued,

> I have been the recipient of many honors in baseball the past twenty-two years; have received many demonstrations from fans of all races, have tasted the joy of wonderful achievements, have drunk from the cup of glory that comes with victory, but in all my life never have I felt so happy as at the close of the last game, when the fans rushed on the diamond and asked to shake my hand. I felt even greater in defeat than I was ever made to feel in victory, and it made a lasting impression on me—and I would not return that feeling for all the honors I have received on the diamond.[48]

The *Indianapolis Freeman,* on December 2, carried a cartoon featuring "The Rube" with a bandit mask and a pistol emblazoned with "BLUFF" pointed at C. I. Taylor. Foster was demanding, "Hand me that grip," referring to a suitcase labeled "World's Colored Championship." It was an order that Taylor refused: "I will not, it's mine." The cartoon was entitled "AN ATTEMPTED HOLD-UP."[49]

In this instance, however, not only did Foster appear to be every bit as much an aggrieved party as Indianapolis, which was denied the opportunity to capture the title without benefit of a forfeit, but he responded in a more tempered fashion. He even declared that Indianapolis possessed a terrific team, something that was never easy for him to acknowledge about any ball club other than his own. The Indianapolis press saw matters differently, believing—not unreasonably—that Foster had resorted to trickery once more to avoid coming out second best in a contest his American Giants seemed destined to lose.

EIGHT

Back on Top in Wartime

Although the 1915 and 1916 seasons had hardly been unsuccessful ones for the American Giants, they were certainly not up to Rube Foster's standards. From the time he joined the Cuban X-Giants and helped guide them to the "colored world's championship" in 1902 and 1903, Foster had been involved with a virtually unbroken skein of title-bearing ball clubs, and now his American Giants were about to begin another extended reign as black baseball's preeminent team. Even the loss of key players due to military service, the diminution of skills, and defections proved unable to prevent the Chicago American Giants from regaining their asserted domination of all ball clubs outside organized baseball. Consequently, Foster, who would finally cast aside his own glove, received even greater recognition as blackball's most important figure, one whose baseball wisdom rivaled that of Connie Mack and John McGraw. All the while, Foster, along with other prominent blackball supporters, continued to reflect how baseball's color barrier might be surmounted.

In an essay that appeared in the January 27, 1917, *Indianapolis Freeman*, David Wyatt discussed purported designs to form "a colored baseball league." "The scheme" had first emerged in Dayton, Ohio; however, its principal sponsor wanted his name withheld until it approached closer to fruition. In the meantime, the *Freeman*'s readers were readying "to meet face to face the man who is destined to be the Moses, to lead the baseball children out of the wilderness." Articles of incorporation had already been taken out in Dayton and elsewhere. It was clear, Wyatt revealed, that some highly placed baseball people were advising the founders. A number of well-known veterans of black baseball appeared determined to head the league's prospective teams. Names bandied about included Sol White, Home Run Johnson, Charlie Grant, and

Chappie Johnson—all former teammates of Foster's—along with Will Binga, earlier one of black baseball's top third basemen. Teams were slated for a number of municipalities, including Columbus, Cincinnati, and either Toledo or Cleveland, as well as Detroit.[1]

Significantly, the league's franchises were projected to own stadiums, hold guaranteed leases, or wield "complete control of their grounds." Moreover, Wyatt wrote,

> No white men are to have anything pertaining to a controlling interest. The white man who now and has in the past secured grounds and induced some one in the role of the "good old Nigger" to gather a lot of athletes and then used circus methods to drag a bunch of our best citizens out only to undergo humiliation, with all kinds of indignities flaunted in their faces, while he sits back and grows rich off a percentage of the proceeds.

It was white businessmen who had opposed formation of a "colored league," who had realized, after all, that greater profits were available "through methods that degrade and make beggars and make bums of the athletes and then blind the public with the immoral aspect of the players."[2]

The proposed league, Wyatt continued, would enable African Americans to benefit commercially, and to that end, the presence of "colored umpires, score keepers, reporters, special writers" and men experienced in baseball's business operations was a must. Knowing little about such enterprises, the African American "has proven an easy victim to the schemes of the other fellows." He concluded, "When we reach the stage where we can quit clipping his goods, but can ignore it, by producing a brand of original and superior goods, not until then will the colored people be able to acquire a standard that will give them a base or means of comparison in baseball, with the other race."[3]

A former scorekeeper, Wyatt soon expressed concerns about another problem confronting black baseball: the dearth of adequate statistics to measure player performances. Consequently, ballplayers were denied, Wyatt declared, their "most valuable possession," and managers and owners lacked information on which to determine salaries. In a sport so dependent on numerical indices, the absence of the same could prove all but fatal. It also left little in the way of a verifiable, historical record, which repeatedly returned to haunt veterans of black baseball.[4]

*

During the winter months, the American Giants had traveled widely yet again, journeying through the South into Texas. Once more, they captured the championship in Palm Beach and, as the *Chicago Defender* reported, were "royally entertained in every town they have played." As the Giants began their 1917 season on Chicago's South Side grounds at 39th and Wentworth Avenue, the New Orleans Jazz Band provided a blues backdrop.[5]

Foster's latest lineup was another powerful one, easily his strongest since the 1914 unit. The infield included Leroy Grant, Bingo DeMoss, Billy Francis, and John Henry Lloyd; Bruce Petway was behind the plate, and Frank Duncan, Pete Hill, and Jess Barber were in the outfield. That deadball season, Grant batted .268; DeMoss hit .258 and was a constant base-stealing threat; Francis added only a .207; Lloyd hit a mere .266; and Petway notched but a .208 average. Duncan hit .230, and Barber, .205. The pitching staff was led by Cannonball Dick Redding, for whom an incomplete 13-3 win-loss record was compiled, and by Tom Williams, who went 10-2. Leftie Luis Padron, Richard Whitworth, and Frank Wickware were also on the American Giants' roster for part of the 1917 season.

Foster, David Wyatt wrote, planned "to give everybody a crack at his bunch, in hopes that he can uncover something, either individually or collectively that can show ability to hold their own or completely outclass the gang which he calls his property." A large financial bounty, Wyatt believed, awaited the manager who could ensure that the American Giants were "both decisively beaten and outclassed, without any doubt or strings attached to the performance." At Schorling Park, however, a "nerve-racking ordeal" portended, with as many as "fifteen thousand howling, raving, enthusiastic bugs and buglettes" sometimes present.[6]

The American Giants easily took the season series from the Indianapolis ABCs in 1917, precluding any additional controversy between the two squads, at least for the time being. The Giants also defeated a group of white semiprofessional teams that included former major leaguers. This record led Wyatt to conclude on August 4, "There is not a wise semi-pro manager in the country who believes he has a chance against this gang." The squad from Beloit, Wisconsin, had beaten the Giants in their match-up; in a later game, however, Redding won convincingly, 8-1. The Norwoods from Cincinnati, made up of a bundle of former big leaguers, attempted to intimidate Foster with a side bet. He, in turn, offered to play for as much as $5,000, but the Norwoods declined. Foster then called for a winner-take-all contest because the Norwoods drew huge crowds. After watching the Giants trounce the ABCs, however, the Norwoods turned him down. The American Giants did pummel the champions of South Carolina in two straight games, 8-0 and 25-0.[7]

The leaders of organized baseball viewed with increasing disfavor barnstorming encounters that pitted major or minor leaguers against blackball's finest. Wyatt, for his part, advised against the kinds of facile comparisons often drawn by well-intentioned supporters of black baseball; similar comparisons later would be presented by historians of blackball. "All this high false praise of the Negro baseball player," Wyatt bristled, only served to keep "the Negro athlete down in the rut." He wondered how American League president Ban Johnson and the upper echelons in organized baseball, who had invested millions in the major leagues, looked upon the easy generalizations regarding the supposed superiority of black players.[8]

Partially to ward off such analyses, Wyatt charged, the National Commission had mandated that major league ball clubs in uniform not participate in postseason exhibition contests. The National Commission had precluded pennant-winning teams from performing in such contests unless agreed to by baseball's high court. Wyatt saw as a possible next move a campaign to prevent black baseball or semipro squads from appearing in major league parks.[9] The pattern in the making was unfortunate: "Our side of the game has been going along nice and running smooth. We have been given a grand opportunity to get ourselves understood; in hopes that we may eventually be able to work up enough interest amongst our own people;—something that never has been in the history of baseball."[10]

Large crowds continued to watch the American Giants at Schorling Park. On September 23, 1917, broader political currents enveloped the stadium as military regiments—one white, one black—marched in honor of American participation in the war that had already consumed large parts of Europe. "A monster crowd" had gathered to watch the pomp and ceremony. When the game proceeded, the Giants blanked the Central

League Stars, a collection of white ballplayers, 7-0, behind Tom Williams's six-hitter.[11]

Baseball, Wyatt affirmed, was demonstrating its support for the U.S. war effort in a manner surpassed by no other large commercial enterprise. "It can be truly said that the baseball diamond had been the big melting pot of patriotism and where all creeds kinds and gender have been molten and molded into one belief." Moreover, "baseball has given up its full quota of sinew, bone and brawn; yes the flower of American youth and real manhood goes with the rank and file of our athletes upon the diamond." Wyatt acknowledged that "the exact status of the Negro in the present world's struggle, is likened [to] much of the same race's standing in base ball. It is uncertain."[12]

As the 1917 season continued to unfold, the American Giants' supremacy among black baseball teams and throughout semiprofessional ball became still more apparent. Having been throttled by Chicago during the campaign, ABCs manager C. I. Taylor sent a gracious letter to the *Indianapolis Freeman* conceding as much: "Rube Foster has the greatest Colored aggregation in the business, and every true sport ought to give him the praise. . . . Foster's club is truly the World's Colored Champions for 1917. . . . All honor to him and his magnificent ball club."[13]

Wyatt's column of October 20 dwelt on black baseball's greatest manager.

> You know Foster is away past the stage in wanting glory, that yearns for the framed up stuff; his theory is, dig, down into the parts of the fray that the unschooled are most likely to overlook; the Chief is foxy and is over there with tech; so don't for a minute think you can pull the boners and alibis past your Uncle Ruben; nay, nay.[14]

In a letter that appeared in the same issue of the *Indianapolis Freeman*, Foster declared that the American Giants had just concluded "the greatest record in their history." They had soundly beaten "all the big Colored clubs that had the nerve to play them," winning thirty of thirty-four games against "crack clubs" outside Chicago—including the Indianapolis ABCs, the Cuban Stars, the Bacharach Giants, the Chicago Giants, and the Philadelphia All-Stars, composed of top eastern ballplayers. After being shut out by the ABCs in an away game, the American

Giants beat them eleven straight times and ended the season series with a 17-2-2 record.[15]

The *Freeman*'s Billy Lewis, nevertheless, felt compelled to call C. I. Taylor "in some respects . . . the greatest baseball man the Negro race has produced up until this time." Foster, by contrast, "has prestige because of what he has done, but he had greatness almost thrust upon him"; he had come to Chicago, which boasted great ballplayers and where fans were already plentiful. In essence, Taylor had to create the game in Indianapolis and was deserving of the accolade "baseball genius."[16]

As 1917 wound to a close, David Wyatt selected an all-star list for the year he deemed black baseball's finest in the past eight, one that had more stellar performers than any other. Wyatt's team was dominated, not surprisingly, by American Giants, including catcher Bruce Petway, second baseman Bingo DeMoss, third baseman Billy Francis, shortstop John Henry Lloyd, utility infielder Jess Barber, outfielder Pete Hill, and pitcher Dick Redding. The rest of the regular lineup featured Dallas All Star first baseman Edgar Wesley and outfielders Cristobal Torriente of the All Nations and Oscar Charleston of the ABCs; the utility outfielder was Bernardo Baro of the Cuban Stars. Other pitchers included the Cuban Stars' Luis Padron, the Lincoln Giants' Joe Williams, and the All Nations' John Donaldson. Wyatt called Hill "our greatest player"; Torriente, "the greatest batter in all of Cuba"; and Charleston "a big, powerful fellow . . . as fast as any of the so-called speed artists in the big leagues; he is a remarkable ground coverer and his drives are very much SPEAKER-like."[17] Charleston was being compared to the Cleveland Indians' great center fielder Tris Speaker.

Looking ahead, Foster promised that 1918 would be "the greatest year in Colored baseball." In late October, he announced that he would visit Cincinnati, Pittsburgh, Atlantic City, New York, and Detroit, where he had been invited to help organize ball clubs. The next month, Wyatt discussed whether the war might derail Foster's promise. Several top ballplayers, Wyatt noted, were eligible for the draft. Further, a new war tax would add a 10 percent surcharge to the prices of tickets to sporting events. Baseball, as "a gigantic industry," was entitled to be treated as were other large industries, yet baseball, Wyatt insisted, was unique: "It is a mental relaxation and a tonic," an essential diversion, particularly for businessmen and workers. This need "should give our national pastime a firm hold upon all at this time." Wyatt went on to assert that "baseball is peculiarly a sailors' and soldiers' game. Every unit of our army which follows the flag on foreign fields is officered by and equipped by graduates of the diamond. Few men who enter our country's service but are interested in professional baseball," for virtually all, as civilians, had regularly gone to baseball games.[18]

Wyatt, then, also apparently believed that 1918 would "be a banner season." He contended, in fact, that the upcoming campaign would be like "the good old days of long ago, when Negro baseball overnight took root, sprouted and bloomed into most gratifying splendor." Several large and small cities that had had ball clubs now expressed a desire to establish them again. With the draft primed to decimate major league baseball, and with numerous minor league franchises about to fold, many major leaguers readied themselves to head over to the semipro game.[19]

In the *Defender*, W. T. B. Williams of Hampton Institute seemingly afforded other opportunities for black players and blacks generally. Improved wages, employment in manufacturing plants, fuller educational access, easier participation in political processes, greater access to transportation facilities, and better living conditions awaited migrants from the Jim Crow South. The war was transforming the lot of the black in other ways as well. It showcased his patrotism, his economic worth as a laborer, and his combat skills. Additionally, service in the military had "awakened feelings of brotherhood" as common goals were sought and the "common danger" was encountered. Black soldiers, Williams asserted, "carry a great responsibility"; even the *Chicago Tribune* had editorialized, "If they prove themselves the equal of the white race, in point of discipline, self-restraint and courage, they will do a lot toward diminishing race prejudice." Williams exhorted *Defender* readers in his conclusion: "We are on trial. All must stand behind the black soldiers, to hearten and encourage them. Through loyalty and the 'last full measure of devotion' we hope to win, not only freedom for America, but full and unquestioned citizenship for ourselves."[20]

Pitcher Lawrence "Slick" Simpson, a member of the Chicago Union Giants in 1916, had volunteered for active duty months before the celebrated decision by the Boston Braves' Hank Gowdy to do so. Gowdy was acclaimed as the first major leaguer to serve in the U.S. expeditionary forces in Europe. But in contrast to Gowdy and other big leaguers who joined the Allies' fight across the Atlantic, Simpson and his black baseball fellows received no promise from their employers that a pension awaited their kin should death or disability befall them. As David Wyatt conceded, "Baseball, amongst our people, is not conducted in a manner that would permit of a pensioning."[21]

The champion American Giants, C. D. Marshall predicted on January 26, 1918, might be the black baseball team hardest hit by conscription: "Foxy old Ruben" faced the loss of any number of "great players." Even so, when the Giants went to Palm Beach in late January to compete against players selected from the Lincoln Giants and the Cuban Stars, it was the bulk of his 1917 squad that accompanied Foster. Foster had turned down another offer, for the club to play in Havana. Foster's team included catchers Bruce Petway and George "Tubby" Dixon, infielders Leroy Grant, Bingo DeMoss, Billy Francis, and Bobby Williams, and outfielders Pete Hill, Frank Duncan, and Jess Barber. The light-hitting Williams replaced John Henry Lloyd, who had opted not to join the team for the trip down south. Pitchers Dick Redding, Richard Whitworth, Tom Williams, and Frank Wickware were also present. Outfielder Jude Gans was among those expected to arrive shortly.[22]

As the regular season approached, Foster made it known that a series of changes lay ahead for the American Giants. Lloyd would not be returning to the team—Foster had been riled by Lloyd's unwillingness to join the Giants in Palm Beach—and other roster moves were likely. Foster had wanted to rebuild the ball club for some time, but its very success had precluded that possibility. In Palm Beach, the players had demonstrated, in Foster's estimation, "a better brand of the great American pastime than he has ever seen them play." And Foster, the *Chicago Defender*'s Mr. Fan reflected, was more astute than any other baseball manager in evaluating talent: "The owners of the big league clubs used to come to him and do yet to find how such and such a white player worked against his club. If Foster thought he was O.K. against such a strong club as the American Giants, that was enough." Indeed, "many a player in the big leagues today . . . owes his existence there to Andrew Rube Foster, and there are a bunch of them from the coast."[23]

Now facing the possibility that as many as eight of his ballplayers could be drafted, Foster began looking for replacements, while striving to "maintain the same standard that he has in former years." This would undoubtedly occur, Mr. Fan said, because "there is no task in baseball that is too great for him to accomplish, once he . . . makes up his mind to do so." Chicago fans were appreciative of Foster's acumen, rewarding him with the largest attendance figures outside the major league realm. Further, on the road the American Giants remained "the biggest drawing card" across the nation, outside organized baseball.[24]

Just prior to the season, Foster released Tom "Schoolboy" Williams, one of his pitching aces, for having violated team rules regarding alcohol. When an obviously inebriated Williams prepared to board the team train departing from Montgomery, Alabama, Foster had asked him if he was drunk. After Williams confessed that he was, Foster declared "that whisky and the American Giants uniform didn't go together," then ordered Williams to turn in his uniform. Reports suggested that Williams had been chastised repeatedly for the same breach.[25]

Having won the Palm Beach championship and after defeating leading southern teams as well, the new-look American Giants opened the season against the West Ends, a top white semipro Chicago team. Grant, Williams, Redding, Gans, and Dixon all remained draft-eligible, and Tom Johnson, seeking a commission, was already at Camp Grant. Even so, the *Chicago Defender* declared that Foster retained "the foundation . . . of the best ball club in the country." Hill, Duncan, and Barber were "the greatest run-getting outfield in the country." Whitworth, who hadn't dropped a game all winter, was "today the best Colored pitcher. . . ."[26]

By mid-July, Foster had lost pitchers Johnson and Redding, shortstop Lloyd, and his replacement Williams, with all these players but the great John Henry serving in the U.S. military. Still, the *Defender* asserted, the team appeared stronger than the previous year's edition. Although sorry that Williams had been drafted, Foster declared that "war is no respecter of feelings or persons." He was "proud that such a man as Williams can be of some service to his country."[27]

Later that month, the American Giants encountered what the *Defender* called "the hardest and most crucial series in their career." They prepared to play, on consecutive days, the 86th Division's Camp Grand squad, made up of big league ballplayers, and the Fairbanks-Morse nine from Beloit, which also had major leaguers in the dugout. Camp Grand's roster included Tom McGuire, who had pitched for the Chicago Whales of the Federal League, and William Marriott, who had briefly occupied a spot in the Chicago Cubs' 1917 lineup. Foster, the *Defender* wrote, "is considered to be the brainiest man in modern baseball; his color alone keeps him from piloting any of the big league teams." While many called for games between Charles Comiskey's Chicago White Sox and the American Giants, "the color prejudice that exists in the big leagues makes this impossible." Wartime developments, however, had produced "a great change." Many major leaguers, deferring to Secretary of War Newton Baker's "work or fight" edict, had entered shipbuilding yards or steel plants, but they could still play ball on the weekends.[28]

As the American Giants, despite a beautifully pitched game by Whitworth, dropped a doubleheader to Beloit—said to be the first twin killing in the franchise's history—Foster received word that more of his key players were about to be drafted: Leroy Grant, Jude Gans, and Frank Wickware were all called up. To the *Defender*, this was doubly unfortunate, as the Giants, under Foster's "able management," had "given to the public of Chicago the best baseball that has been given in the last few years." Notwithstanding the considerable losses, Foster promised to return "just as strong a ball club." The *Defender* reported, "Every one knows Foster. His aim is to give to the generous public the best that can be had."[29]

Foster's "shipwrecked" squad went east to play the Indianapolis ABCs in Cincinnati, Pittsburgh, and Washington, before battling the Bacharach Giants in Atlantic City and the Pennsylvania Red Caps in the nation's capital. The American Giants then revisited Atlantic City for a three-game set, headed to Philadelphia to play Hilldale, went to Detroit to meet the ABCs, and returned to Chicago to confront the Red Caps at Schorling Park on August 18. Near the end of the trip, "the Big Chief" ventured to New York to scout out hurlers for his now pitcher-poor team.[30]

The American Giants' roster underwent additional changes as the team returned home and readied itself to face top semipro teams: the Fairbanks-Morse Beloits and the Joliet Standards. Added to Foster's squad were José Méndez, formerly a great pitcher with the Cuban Stars and All Nations who had experienced arm trouble. Méndez was now a light-hitting shortstop, who would bat a mere .189 for Chicago.

Another addition was hard-hitting first baseman Edgar Wesley, who was just beginning a brilliant career. A control pitcher, Gunboat Thompson, was another temporary replacement.

In the midst of training for overseas duties, Wickware, Williams, Grant, and Gans received permission to rejoin the American Giants for a spell. Foster, the *Chicago Defender* conjectured, was

> at present in a mighty tough struggle to save his head; yes, that head or needle has reigned supreme over all managers from time immemorial; is up for the trial of its natural life; and the manner in which the paleface clubs are filling up their rosters with big league players and the hurried and certain manner in which Uncle Sam is shearing Ruben of his star actors [are] just about to turn that old bald pate of your Uncle Rube gray.

Still, the American Giants were hardly "soft picking." Their "General Foster" continued to feature a potent defense, with Petway behind the plate, Grant and Bobby Williams back in the infield, and Wickware prepared to pitch better than ever. Indeed, in late August, Chicago garnered a measure of revenge in sweeping a doubleheader from Beloit, defeating right-hander Dickie Kerr in one contest; Kerr would later star with the Chicago White Sox.[31]

The *Defender*'s September 7 edition contained a photograph of a now quite portly Foster taken after he had just delivered a pitch. The caption indicated that Foster, notwithstanding "many handicaps," was leading the American Giants to another championship. Chicago's arch rivals, the Indianapolis ABCs, had won only three of twelve matches. Despite the loss of "stars of the first magnitude," Foster reputedly had "eclipsed his former club in brilliant playing." Foster, the *Defender* said, "has wonderful business ability, [is] a great leader of men; as to baseball brains he has no superior."[32]

As the Giants prepared to meet the Joliets in mid-September, sportswriter David Wyatt termed the encounter "perhaps . . . the acid test in the season's career of our one best bet in baseball." A key question would be addressed: "How do the Colored fellows size up with the leaguers of established class?" Despite the stellar record of the former against all-star teams, many among the public refused to believe that "the colored fellows" measured up. Others, in light of "the great battles" waged recently by the American Giants against white ball clubs, held that there was no guarantee that major league teams would win even one or two games in a series against the Giants. Playing with the Joliets were Chicago White Sox pitchers Joe Benz and Jack Quinn—a twenty-six-game winner with the 1914 Baltimore Terrapins of the Federal League—and substitute catcher Otto Jacobs, along with Cleveland Indian outfielder Braggo Roth.[33]

Still, Wyatt acknowledged something that Foster had long recognized. Without official ties to organized baseball, there was no bona fide way to compare the respective ability of blackballers and their major league counterparts. Contests against semipro teams, Wyatt acknowledged, hardly involved the white professional world's finest. By now, Foster also found it hard to take victories over such squads very seriously.[34]

Nevertheless, Wyatt closely watched the American Giants–Beloits series. The presence of any number of former major and minor leaguers at Schorling Park added considerable prestige to the contests being waged there. Baseball was operating "as a leveler of the races"; the sport, like war, made "strange bed-fellows." Numerous baseball fans had long assumed that blacks were no match for white ballplayers, but, Wyatt declared, careful students of the national pastime recognized that

> a few of our folks . . . can compare with the very best in the land. Big men in baseball are not backward in their praise of "Rube" Foster as a manager; many are just about inclined to the belief that Hill and Lloyd, in their day, were as good as they come; Petway also gets a conspicuous rating. There have been half a dozen or more pitchers who could wear the big leaguers' crown, and a large number of the big leaguers have made a close study of Torriente to see how he measures up with Cobb and Speaker.

In the same fashion, "the high class of skill and play" of the American Giants was favorably regarded.[35]

After nipping the Joliets in the series, the American Giants now had to confront the Fairbanks-Morse Beloits once again. The Beloits, according to the *Defender*, were "coming to win." Added to their roster was Buck Weaver, the White Sox' fiery third baseman, who was viewed as the American League's finest at his position. The Beloits, led by Weaver, again swept a doubleheader from the Giants. Weaver, "the first genuine big leaguer still working regularly in the big show," produced "one of the grandest exhibitions of fielding, throwing and batting" witnessed in a semipro park for some time.[36]

The following month, the American Giants rebounded to capture a series against an all-star team that included several former minor and major leaguers. However, in one essay, the *Defender* acknowledged that the Giants had difficulty handling pitchers from organized baseball. That pointed to a weakness experienced by semipro ball: the scarcity of first-class pitching competition.[37]

In early October 1918, Foster received a request from J. B. McCabe, who shaped athletic programs for the U.S. military based in Puerto Rico, to help organize baseball teams among French and American troops. Suffering from an apparent case of influenza, Foster, however, was unable to accede to the request. The outbreak of the disease also resulted in the closure of Schorling Park, which prevented the American Giants from facing Chicago Cubs ace Hippo Vaughn, the National League's best that year, in a scheduled contest.[38]

Wartime exigencies had proved a mixed blessing for Rube Foster's American Giants. The team had regained its status at the top of black baseball, even though conscription had removed several of its best players from the roster. The 1918 version of the Giants, consequently, was not nearly as potent as that of the previous year and could hardly compare with those soon to come. The war, crippling organized baseball as it did blackball, led to wholesale defections from the major and minor leagues. Many ballplayers, seeking to avoid possible combat in Europe, headed for steelyards and shipping plants, where they joined company teams. They also competed against top black baseball units, like the American Giants, whose performance in those affairs in 1918 was, at best, mixed. Thus, Foster finally had the opportunity he long sought against big league ballplayers, but the squad he sent into the field to face such competition was hardly his strongest.

Nevertheless, the relative success of the 1918 American Giants demonstrated, perhaps more fully than ever before, how artfully Foster steered his club. He lost one of his longtime pitching aces, Frank Wickware, but managed to hold on to Richard Whitworth, whose recognized 16-4 win-loss mark led a decimated staff; Whitworth, in 1918, was probably black baseball's outstanding pitcher, but undoubtedly he was heavily overworked because of the absence of Dick Redding and Tom Williams for much of the season. Chicago's bats appeared no more potent in 1918 than in the previous year. Continuing a slide, Petway hit only .200, and Dixon batted an even .300. In their shortened individual campaigns, Grant hit .290; Gans, .245; and Bobby Williams, .224. DeMoss added a .201 mark; Francis, .242; Duncan, .222; and Barber, .235.

The *Chicago Defender,* on November 2, credited Foster for the American Giants' 77-27 mark: "For a club to make a record against odds as did the Giants," the *Defender* claimed,

> there has to be at the head a leader of great ability. The Giants were fortunate to have Foster, as he is without doubt one of the greatest leaders in baseball, and if he had twenty-five men, as the big leagues, all trained with experience before they come to him, there is no league pennant he would not have a monopoly on.

The newspaper then compared Foster with other black baseball leaders:

> Those who meet Foster with that everyday pleasant smile do not know that he does more work in one season than all the Colored managers combined. First he has the White Sox within four blocks of him as a competitor, which in itself is some task to compete with, yet his following is so great we do not know the Sox are here so far as a handicap to him. He has to book all attractions for the Giants, arrange the dates for all the other big cities, often financing them; also arranging it so that they will be able to continue in the game; has to superintend the [Schorling Park], and many times when the Giants are in need of his advice he is sent for to straighten out some dissatisfied patron or to help keep the crowds back, yet manage and direct the Giants. Even with all this on his shoulders he is the most successful Colored man in baseball, the only one that has made it a business.[39]

The *Defender* piece included that recent photo shot of him pitching, and another caption sang his praise. Foster was not only "a brainy leader" but "a genius in the baseball game." Overcoming the loss of some of his finest ballplayers, he had enjoyed "the best season of his career," while Schorling Park experienced its largest crowds to date. Foster, the *Defender* summed up, "is a genius."[40]

NINE

Rube Ball

The same article in the *Defender* that proclaimed Rube Foster "a genius" also lauded his system. It was a system that afforded him absolute control of the American Giants' operations, from the signing of players to the carving out of a schedule. And that system, Foster insisted, enabled his team to remain on top. In 1918, he lost several key players and released John Henry Lloyd, still perhaps black baseball's finest. Those departures would have proved fatal, he held, "if we had not perfected this system. In so doing we again won the championship, defeated all comers and played better ball this season than the season before. . . . I cannot get away from the system."[1]

By the time the decade neared an end, Foster had honed that system to near perfection. It had enabled the American Giants to follow the path carved out by the Foster-led Leland Giants in being acclaimed the greatest team in black baseball. That very success, of course, continued the championship run Foster had been associated with since he became the ace pitcher for the Cuban X-Giants and the Philadelphia Giants. He, more than any other man in baseball, whether of the blackball or major league brand, was used to winning. Indeed, he was consumed by it. Very seldom a gracious loser, Foster took defeat hard, so it was fortunate that he rarely had to suffer it. As black baseball's top pitcher during the first decade of the century, Foster had compiled an amazing record, although statistics for his games remain fragmentary. Still a fine pitcher for several additional years into the following decade, Foster's win-loss pitching mark from 1903 to 1916 stood at a verifiable 152-24-8. He tossed at least four no-hitters, struck out seventeen and eighteen batters respectively in two 1904 games, and amassed an 8-0 record in "colored world championship" contests. In addition, playing in the Cuban winter league, Foster produced an 18-11 record, with his .621 win-loss percentage bettering Frank Wickware's .600 and Smokey Joe Williams's .595 figures. Impressive too were the twenty-four complete games, including a league-leading fifteen in 1906, that Foster pitched in the winter circuit. His 170 wins in black baseball and Cuban League competition surpassed the recorded victory totals of his half brother William Foster and Satchel Paige. And that number of wins was undoubtedly no more than half the amount Rube Foster had actually achieved.

Although he was one of the greatest pitchers in the annals of black baseball, Foster's stewardship of the Leland Giants and Chicago American Giants had proven still more impressive. Through the 1918 season, his teams had either been acclaimed the "colored world's" titlists or been bested in championship series by squads that were. Both he and others attributed that very success to the Foster system, a top-down approach to guiding his ball clubs that resulted in no brooking of dissent. The players benefited in their own fashion from being part of legendary black baseball teams: they drew the largest salaries among their compatriots, could boast of the sharpest uniforms, traveled in style, and stayed in first-class hotels.

During his years with the American Giants, Foster had the good fortune of a unique relationship with owner John Schorling. Each man had such faith in the other that no written contract was ever necessary. As Dave Malarcher, Foster's eventual successor as the Giants' manager, suggested, "Both must have felt that they would live forever, and that they would need each other as long as they lived." "they had an easy working arrangement": Foster attended to the team's needs; Schorling handled matters pertaining to the ballpark.[2]

The great manager devised a kind of "self-perpetuating" booking agency, a necessity in Malarcher's eyes, because "Rube Foster and Chicago were the life blood of all the teams of the West," and also "contributed to the success of those Eastern teams which traveled West." The American Giants and Chicago, Malarcher pointed out, were "the greatest attractions outside of the major leagues." More important, without them, "the other Negro teams and independent teams could not have survived," for "they lived on Rube's operations of the American Giants and the great drawing [power] of the city of Chicago, the greatest baseball city in independent baseball. The American Giants were the greatest attraction on the road, and Chicago, the greatest drawing city when at home." Thus, owners in Kansas City, St. Louis, Indianapolis, Birmingham, and Memphis supposedly were delighted to visit Schorling Park, often more than once a season. "Even the independent white teams catered to Rube's booking the American Giants in their parks and their teams as visitors in his park at 39th and Wentworth Avenue, Chicago." Virtually every Sunday during the baseball season, the Giants hosted a game or two at Schorling Park. Generally, the only exception to that modus operandi involved a trip to Kansas City to play the Monarchs.[3]

Foster and Indianapolis manager C. I. Taylor, Malarcher said, "were the real and foremost and leading promoters, developers, and expansioners of Negro Baseball. They were the master team organizers, trainers, managers of the playing and business phases of our teams. The credit is due them in any account of the history thereof." Foster, Taylor, and their contemporaries barnstormed against one another and other semipro magnates, sometimes appearing in major and minor league parks. Most significant, according to Malarcher, "[T]hese are the men whose money, patience, time and energy kept Negro baseball developing until the day of entering the promised land of opportunity and equality for the Negro baseball player."[4]

It was Foster and Taylor, Malarcher declared, who "made the greatest contributions to the development and preparedness of the pioneers and forerunners of our present successful players in the major leagues and all organized baseball." But although the two men were blackball's greatest promoters, Foster was "first" in "developing and expanding Negro baseball."[5]

The manager's major responsibility, in Malarcher's opinion, was "to increase the playing ability of his players, to mold them into an efficient, daring, and effective playing machine"—all of which Foster and Taylor did. "By giving them the best of living conditions as a team in order to be able to stand the hard and prolonged drilling of body and mind, their players were developed into [experts]. . . ."[6]

Malarcher called both men just. They paid their players very well, provided for their physical care, and arranged for private Pullman cars on the fastest trains. Foster saw to it that the American Giants were afforded comfort and escape from a good many Jim Crow edicts.[7]

On one occasion—undoubtedly a not altogether isolated event—

while the Giants were traveling through the South, an incident occurred that demonstrated the potency of both segregation and Foster's reputation. His team, in typical fashion, was traveling in a private car that somehow got moved off the main track. A brakeman, spotting large black men pouring out of the Pullman, bellowed out, "Hey there, hey there, what are you Negroes doing getting out of Mr. Rube Foster's car?" The worker had obviously heard of Foster but was unaware that he was black. To the brakeman's astonishment, a voice rang out, "I just happen to be Mr. Rube Foster."[8]

Frank Forbes, a one-time competitor in black baseball ranks and later an umpire and promoter for the Negro National League, applauded Foster as "a mastermind," even as he called him "a thieving son of a bitch." Foster built his team on speed, Forbes recalled. Consequently, "We'd got out there to play those son of a bitches—excuse me—and you know what he does? We don't wise up until the end of the ball game, but he had drowned the goddamn infield the night before. Those suckers lay down a bunt, it rolls nine feet and stops." Foster, in league with the umpires, Forbes charged, used frozen baseballs that even a power hitter like Louis Santop could barely rap out of the infield. When that occurred in a game against the New York Lincoln Giants, owner Jess McMahon demanded to know why the ball did not bounce. In Forbes's words, "Come to find out it was those damn balls. You could feel them. If you held one long enough, your fingers stuck to the ball."[9]

James "Cool Papa" Bell claimed that Foster, relying on the speed that characterized his team, built up the foul lines so bunts would stay fair. In one celebrated Fourth of July contest, as the American Giants trailed the Indianapolis ABCs 18-0, Foster instructed eleven consecutive batters to bunt; undoubtedly, he directed the players through smoke coming out of his corncob pipe. Those safeties, paired with grand slam homers by Cristobal Torriente and Jim Brown, somehow enabled Chicago to tie the score. When nightfall approached, the American Giants walked away with the game knotted up.[10]

In relying on his team's great speed, Foster acted as a master psychologist too. In one game, the opposing third baseman was Oliver Marcelle, considered by some the finest in black baseball history. No matter, Foster sauntered over to Marcelle and declared, "They tell me you're a great third baseman." Marcelle responded, "Well, I do the best I can." Foster came back with "Well, we'll find out today. I got some racehorses out there; we'll lay down some bunts, see if you can field them." After Marcelle muffed the first one, Foster chortled, "I told you so." Jelly Gardner related similar tales. "He'd holler and tell the pitcher that the next fellow was going to bunt and they didn't believe him. But that's what would happen. Or he'd tell the third baseman, 'Get ready to pick this one up.' Well the third baseman wouldn't believe it and sure enough there comes the bunt."[11]

Tellingly, Malarcher discussed the approach to the game by the manager of the American Giants.

> Now one of the things Rube taught was this, that you win the ball game in one or two innings; you don't win it over a long period. Once in a while, you'll see a game when they make one or two runs in the first innings, two more later, and so forth, but in most cases the game is won in one rally. That means that when you get an opportunity to win it, you'd better win it now, and not throw it away by doing the wrong thing. Here's what Rube said: "*Now* is the time." Rube used to say this—and I followed it when I became a manager—you don't have to get three hits every day for me. You don't have to get two—but I want *one* at the right time."[12]

Thus, Foster taught Malarcher about "scientific baseball." Foster was determined, Malarcher recalled, to "let you know what to do." He made clear that "under certain circumstances you do certain things. You just don't play the game like the other fella expects it to come to him. You give it to him in a different way."[13]

Malarcher acquired something else from both Foster and Taylor. In the fashion of those two great managers, Malarcher indicated, he treated his players equally. They, in turn, appreciated being part of the American Giants' "great success on the diamond." As did Foster, Malarcher strove to polish ballplayers who were flawed in various ways.[14]

Arthur Hardy, who had pitched for Foster's Leland Giants, reflected on Foster's management style.

> I wouldn't call him reserved, but he wasn't free and easy. You see, Rube was a natural psychologist. Now he didn't know what psychology was and he probably couldn't spell it, but he realized that he couldn't fraternize and still maintain discipline. Rube was a strict disciplinarian. He wasn't

harsh, but he was strict. His dictums were not unreasonable, but if you broke one he'd clamp down on you. If he stuck a fine on you, you paid it—there was no appeal from it. He was dictatorial in that sense.[15]

Jelly Gardner, who played for Foster in the early twenties, related how he handled free-spirited ballplayers: "Rube was a nice manager, an even-tempered man. Rube never told me what to do after I left the ball park. You can do what you want to do, but when you came to the ball park he wanted you to play or he'd fine you." If a player suffered from a hangover, Foster would bluntly state, "If you can't play, go back to your hotel."[16]

In his excellent study of black baseball, Robert Peterson, who conducted a series of interviews with Malarcher, quoted from him to demonstrate how subtly Foster operated. If a player were giving less than his all, Foster would spin a small tale:

> Once there was a donkey and an ox that were teamed to work on a farm. They worked hard, and one day the ox decided to stay in his stall and take a rest. So he did. When the donkey came back to the barn that night after work, the ox asked, "What did the boss say about me?" "Didn't say nothing," the donkey replied. So the next day the ox decided he'd stay in his stall all day again and eat, and he did. When the donkey came back that night, the ox asked again, "What did the boss say?" "Didn't say anything," the donkey answered, "but he visited the butcher." Well, the next day the ox came out bright and early and backed right into the traces. The farmer told him, "You might as well stay in the stall." "Oh, no," said the ox, "I'm ready to go today." And the farmer said, "You might as well stay, because I've sold you to the butcher."[17]

Deftly directed by Foster and Taylor, the Chicago American Giants and Indianapolis ABCs became, in Malarcher's words, "the greatest and foremost of all Negro baseball teams in its history." Morever, "they were managed by the two greatest managers and organizers of baseball teams in the Negro race." Only the American Giants and the ABCs barnstormed so widely and played in the Cuban Winter League as virtually intact units.[18]

TEN

Black Baseball and the
Segregated Community

Just prior to the war's close, few anticipated that brighter days lay in store for the national pastime, whether involving organized baseball or the blackball variety that Rube Foster seemingly had perfected. With sportswriters questioning the fate of the major and minor leagues, it was hardly surprising that they wondered about the viability of black baseball. F. C. Lane, the editor of *Baseball Magazine*, in an article written before the Armistice, asked, "Where, or where, have the colored ball clubs gone? What has become of the dusky entertainers whose antics—and genuine playing skill—erstwhile sent thrills of joy through the breasts of both white and negro gatherings?" For a good while, Lane acknowledged, black teams had "played some of the best ball anyone could ask to see." Moreover, African American fans reportedly were even more fervently supportive of their favorites than their lighter-skinned countrymen. Thus, "the whole game, as conducted African-fashion," had "been richly enjoyable for many reasons." "But where," Lane inquired, "are the colored players now?"[1]

Lane noted that the best squads—an obvious reference to the Chicago American Giants, the Indianapolis ABCs, and a few others—"had attained eminent distinction." Undertaking a lengthier schedule than big league teams, they performed from early April through October and then headed to Cuba. There, "the agile coons," Lane noted, played on through March. At that point, they returned to the mainland to start another season. In such fashion, teams might participate in more than two hundred games in a year.[2]

The finest black baseball players, Lane argued, "have been as good as their white rivals, but credit has never been given them for their skill." Among the brightest stars was José Méndez, likened by big leaguers who faced him in Cuba to Christy Mathewson and Pete Alexander; Alexander was a great pitcher with the Philadelphia Phillies who had been sold to the Chicago Cubs shortly before his induction into the U.S. military. "Numerous American negroes," Lane continued, "have for years been ranked as topnotchers." Major leaguers had acknowledged as much when they declared that "only the color-line kept these men from standing at the summit of their profession."[3]

Lane voiced high praise for the black athlete, particularly for his temperament.

> The negro ball player has ever "known his place." Cheered by white crowds, given an equal chance against white players 200 times a year, and in fact, receiving far better treatment than 99 per cent of his race, he has never grown fresh or bumptious, never presumed upon his good fortune, never figured in race riots or "black uprisings." His glorious good nature and clean comedy on the ball field, his respectful treatment of white umpires, and his intrinsic merits as a player, have combined to make him popular.[4]

Prior to the 1918 season, black ball clubs traveled extensively and, Lane commented, "made oodles of money." However, this past year, those clubs appeared "to have vanished off the earth." Asking again, "Where are those black boys now?" he attempted to field his own query. Because the black ballplayers were "all great athletes, all in grand condition," they had been welcomed by the U.S. military and were surely playing ball in France. So "why don't we ever hear about their doings?"[5]

Notwithstanding what Lane said, the top black teams had hardly disappeared, and publications like the *Chicago Defender* and the *Indianapolis Freeman* continued to carry news about them.

After the war ended in November Rube Foster anticipated that the next baseball campaign would be even more productive. Any number of black baseball's finest would have returned from overseas. Fans would be eagerly awaiting the opportunity to watch the game once again. Major league baseball did flourish at the turnstiles in 1919, as did the black brand of ball that Foster helped to lead.

During that year, as he made his oft-repeated prediction that this team would be his "greatest" yet, Foster went about developing more ambitious plans to take advantage of changed circumstances. With baseball seeming to be more popular than ever, the time appeared ripe for fuller discussion of whether "a colored league" might be initiated.[6] Organized baseball, like most sectors of American society, remained determinedly segregated. And when black players competed against their white counterparts, they suffered racial invective and threats. Calls of "Nigger!" "Gimme a shine, coon!" and "Go back to the cotton fields, monkey!" rang out from the grandstands.[7]

In Chicago, Rube Foster's American Giants continued to play Jim Crow ball. The city itself, thanks to an influx of blacks from the South, was undergoing dramatic transformations, which proved unsettling to many. During the previous two decades, blacks had fled a region that had proven to be even less hospitable following the demise of Reconstruction. By the tail end of the nineteenth century, the franchise had become all but nonexistent, pseudoscientific nostrums were proclaiming the innate inferiority of dark-skinned folk, and the promises of the Thirteenth, Fourteenth, and Fifteenth Amendments to the Constitution were largely fictions. Slavery had been eradicated, but its vestiges were clearly present, and many whites remained determined to put blacks "back in their place." As the need for field hands lessened, rural blacks were impelled to seek livelihoods elsewhere, but urban centers in the region proved little more inviting.

By contrast, northern and midwestern cities outside the solidly segregated South appeared to beckon to the displaced blacks, offering jobs, education, and a range of opportunities. With the country undergoing a rapid modernization that intensified class chasms, blacks, like many others, underwent trying times in the teeming cities. Even so, multitudes were attracted to Chicago, a leading industrial center that was believed to be an open door to a brighter future. A black middle class in time emerged and soon challenged racial barriers of all types.

Blacks likewise had attained political freedoms. Chicago once had been known as a "nigger-loving town" because of its staunch abolitionists who had challenged the Fugitive Slave Law that required the return of runaways to their owners. Chicagoans subsequently featured their own practices of segregation and disfranchisement in the antebellum period. Still, the Illinois state legislature had repealed its black code in 1865 and within the next five years it guaranteed the right to vote. Four years later, segregation was no longer allowed in the public schools. In 1885, a state civil rights statute was passed. Such measures were enforced infrequently, and racial tensions heightened as black migration to Chicago swelled.[8]

At the same time that blacks were enduring disfranchisement in the South, politicians in Chicago were beginning to pay heed to the African American community in their city. A black political machine associated with the Republican Party helped to elect a pair of African Americans to the state legislature in 1914. In 1915, Oscar De Priest, one of the leaders of that machine, became a city alderman. Appreciative of black support, Republican mayor William "Big Bill" Thompson handed a number of municipal posts to African Americans, condemned racist epithets employed by politicians, and sought more equitable treatment by the city police. Nevertheless, general conditions on the South Side, home to most of the city's African Americans, steadily deteriorated. Between 1910 and the end of the decade, an estimated 50,000 blacks migrated to Chicago; the total number of black residents shot up from 44,000 to almost 110,000. Most settled in the South Side, including in the so-called Black Belt that abutted an industrial and warehouse district.[9]

All the while, blacks continued to endure dismissive racial characterizations and numerous barriers throughout the metropolitan area. The red-light district on the South Side remained a source of contention. A vice commission's report in 1909 had revealed that most employees in the bawdy houses were African Americans and that a goodly number of the most prominent of those establishments could be found in the Black Belt. In fact, many Chicagoans had long associated the black community with illicit operations and unsavory lifestyles. A split opened even among Chicago's blacks as to whether vice should be rooted out or simply segregated. Having accused a white colleague of attempting to push vice activities into the Black Belt, one leading African American minister exclaimed, "The Negro, like the whites, does not care for his wife and daughter to elbow the Red-light denizens."[10]

In 1912, Chicago abolished the red-light district, but prostitutes continued to ply their trade in the Black Belt; equally important, many

Chicagoans still associated the South Side with debauchery. After Booker T. Washington exhorted Chicago's blacks that same year to eradicate vice in their community, one African American responded with the following analysis: "A good deal of the vice in the 'colored belt' is the white man's vice, thrust there by the authorities against the protest of the colored people." He went on to say, "Vice and crime are in large measure the result of idleness, of irregular employment, and even of regular employment that is underpaid and exhausting."[11]

Particularly following the outbreak of war in Europe in 1914, Chicago had begun to expand its industrial operations; a shortage of workers ensued. Recruiters traveled to the South, carrying free train tickets north and promises of well-paying jobs in the factories, including the packinghouses and steel mills. The *Chicago Defender,* a top African American newspaper owned by Robert S. Abbott, did its part, helping to trigger a "Great Northern Drive." The *Defender* benefited at least incidentally from the migration: circulation jumped in two years from 33,000 in 1916 to 125,000. The poet Carl Sandburg said that "the *Defender* more than any other one agency was the big cause of the 'Northern fever' and the big exodus from the South." Dismissing purported attempts by Southerners to reform Jim Crow practices, the *Defender* declared, "We'd like to oblige these unselfish (?) souls and remain slaves in the South, but . . . we . . . have boarded the train singing, 'Good-bye, Dixie Land.'" Participants in the "Great Migration" to the North—undertaken by some half million black Southerners from 1916 to 1919 and by another million during the following decade—left behind, among other things, plummeting cotton prices, floods, food shortages, and boll weevils.[12]

Although urban life proved unsettling for many migrants, others found its vitality appealing. Sections of Chicago, like its South Side, which was soon to be renowned for its jazz artistry, possessed great allure. Remembering his visit to Chicago in 1918, the poet Langston Hughes reflected, "South State Street was in its glory then, a teeming Negro street with crowded theaters, restaurants, and cabarets. And excitement from noon to noon. Midnight was like day. The street was full of workers and gamblers, prostitutes and pimps, church folk and sinners." The *Chicago Whip,* a militant African American newspaper, referred to the South Side as an urban "Bohemia of the Colored folks" and a "Mecca for Pleasure"; there, "lights sparkled, glasses tinkled," and many could be seen strolling along in their finest attire.[13]

Abbott, De Priest, the Reverend Archibald J. Carey of the African Methodist Episcopal Church, and Rube Foster were all part of what later would be referred to as a Black Metropolis. Black newspapermen, politicians, ministers, and entrepreneurs were the leadership core of Chicago's upper-class and middle-class African Americans. By 1915, they had established a host of institutions, many located on the South Side; these included a bank, a hospital, a YMCA, political organizations, clubs, social service networks, newspapers, a wide variety of businesses, and the Chicago American Giants. Social consciousness was not altogether absent. Spurred by black leaders, a protest resulted in the banning of *The Birth of a Nation*, director D. W. Griffith's cinematic adaption of Thomas Dixon's novel *The Clansman*.[14]

A vast array of problems, however, along with a mixed greeting, awaited the unwitting southern blacks who ended up in Chicago during this period. The historian Thomas Philpott declares that "there was probably no Southern city in which blacks were so segregated as they were in Chicago." The *Chicago Tribune* referred to the "peril" posed by the array of diseases, such as tuberculosis, that the new arrivals purportedly brought with them. More telling, the *Tribune* complained that blacks possessed "almost no standard of morals." The city's leading newspaper also highlighted the vice that was said to flourish in the Black Belt.[15]

Although the Illinois state legislature had declared that racial discrimination was not allowed in public schools, accommodations, and municipal services, color barriers remained in place. Goaded by irate white parents, administrators farmed out black children to branch schools. Institutions for African American students occupied the oldest public buildings. Jobs were plentiful, but often blacks were compelled to accept the least desirable ones. Called on as strikebreakers during labor conflicts, they generally were let go after the disputes were settled. The finest chronicler of the Great Migration, James R. Grossman, reports: "Men were likely to work as porters, waiters, servants, janitors, or elevator operators; two-thirds of all employed black women in 1910 were either servants or hand laundresses. . . ." Still, the number of black clerical workers increased fivefold between 1910 and 1920. By the later year more blacks were working in better-paying factories than in service trades. Some, however, endured homelessness; many lacked the fifteen cents that could shelter them for a night at a black hotel like C. K. Smith's.[16]

Housing shortages resulted in "doubling-up and overcrowding" and sharp rent increases. On one lone day in 1917, author Florette Henri notes, nearly seven hundred black families responded to an advertisement listing a mere fifty-three units. Organizations like the Chicago Urban League, the YMCA, and the YWCA, sought to smooth the transition for the migrants and to prevent hostility from building up in the white community. Despite such efforts, fears abounded outside the Black Belt that the strip of land on Chicago's South Side where most African Americans resided would expand—an expansion that did proceed apace. Sensationalistic newspaper accounts, such as the one headlined "HALF A MILLION DARKIES FROM DIXIE SWARM TO THE NORTH TO BETTER THEMSELVES," hardly helped to soothe tensions. Clashes ranging from playground tussles to one of the worst race riots in the nation's history ensued.

Beginning on July 1, 1917, scores of bombs—an average of one every three weeks—were tossed at the homes of blacks and at the homes of realtors willing to sell to African Americans. In passing through white working-class residential areas, black laborers sometimes endured physical abuse. Gangs of white youths decrying racial "contamination" attacked blacks in public parks. Athletic clubs promised to defend neighborhood turf against encroachments by African Americans.[17]

Notwithstanding such unsettling developments, fruitful change appeared to be in store for African Americans, or so Rube Foster imagined. In Chicago, which Foster had adopted as his second home, proud black veterans of Woodrow Wilson's crusade in Europe received a rousing welcome from the South Side's African American inhabitants; these included members of the "Fighting Eighth" Infantry that had fought gallantly during the war. Foster, one of the leading members of the South Side community, contested racial boundaries in his own way. No one, in fact, did more to spread the gospel of black baseball and thereby provide a stage where African American athletes could display their wares.[18]

In the *Half-Century Magazine* on March 1, 1919, Howard A. Phelps presented a biographical sketch of Foster, whose story, Phelps explained, could be likened to "a fairy tale." Foster had become "the greatest Colored athlete of his day," and after years as a superlative pitcher, took on the role of manager of title-bearing black teams. Possessing "all the tricks and arts of the pitching game," he could "impart them to others." Although "many come to him as green as grass, others as rough as boulders . . . when Foster takes them under his surveillance they round out into finished pitchers with little less skill than the old 'fox' himself."[19]

Phelps told his readers that Foster's performance as a ballplayer was unsurpassed: "Foster leaves a record that will stand for generations to come. He won more games than any pitcher who ever pitched. He was a student of the finer points of pitching; at home under any condition; the coolest man under pressure that ever stepped on a field."[20] Foster's managerial record was similarly brilliant, and his administrative skills had transformed black baseball altogether, wrote Phelps. Schorling Park, where the American Giants played, was "the finest semi-professional ball park in the world. It was constructed for Foster's team and he prides himself in that it was expressly built [for] and used only by him."[21]

Phelps concluded his paean with the following observation.

> Foster harbors no envy. He beats the best of the Colored teams and then coaches them as to their mistakes. He has never had his head swollen and is the same good natured, unassuming man, whom I marvelled at years ago, when as a boy one afternoon 10 years ago I saw him laughingly retire to his seat after striking out the last 16 men to face him in a game at the A.B.C. Baseball Park in Indianapolis. Still I wonder at him, not so much as a player now but more for his gentlemanly bearing and conduct.[22]

In early April 1919, a host of blackball veterans and neophytes alike, along with some five hundred fans, appeared at the American Giants' park at 39th and Shields Avenue in south Chicago. Managers Rube Foster and Pete Hill of the Detroit Stars proceeded to divvy up the talent pool. Hill, Foster's star center fielder, slugger, and captain, had taken hold of the Stars in the off-season. His lengthy apprenticeship would pay dividends because Foster was clearly determined to establish a strong team in the Motor City. Undoubtedly, Foster was doing so in anticipation of the league that he had long envisioned. Among those selected to join the new Detroit club were catcher Bruce Petway, outfielder Frank Duncan, pitcher Frank Wickware, and first baseman Edgar Wesley; all, except Wesley, who had joined the American Giants at the tail end of the 1918 season, had played for Foster for several years. Hill soon added strikeout ace John Donaldson to his pitching staff.[23]

"The Big Chief," in turn, retained several ballplayers from his "colored world championship" squad and added others; some of his veterans, like Wickware, were returning from military service. Back with the Giants were catcher George "Tubby" Dixon; first baseman Leroy Grant; second baseman Bingo DeMoss; shortstop Bobby Williams; third baseman Billy Francis; outfielders Jude Gans, Jess Barber, and Cristobal Torriente; and pitchers Richard Whitworth and Tom Johnson. Also beefing up Chicago's roster were outfielder Oscar Charleston and pitcher Jess "Mountain" Hubbard. Charleston and Torriente were black baseball's greatest power hitters during the era, in addition to being outstanding fielders and fine base runners. The light-skinned Hubbard, whom the New York Giants once attempted to pass off as white, was a veteran of both the Brooklyn Royal Giants and the U.S. Army.[24]

After the players had been apportioned, Foster named DeMoss his new captain and paid tribute to Hill, who had served in that capacity for more than a dozen years. On occasion, Hill had been a thousand miles away, the *Chicago Defender* noted, but he always could be relied on to "bring home the bacon." Gans, attired in his soldier's uniform, spun his own tales, sharing overseas exploits; he also indicated that the French, thanks to the *Defender,* were familiar with "the wonderful ball playing of the American Giants."[25]

The Giants, it appeared to the *Defender,* "had not lost any of their old time vim and speed." Fully cognizant of "the rules," they would be apprised of what they didn't know by "their schoolmaster, Chief Foster. . . . All have implicit confidence in him." Foster returned the players' favor: "My men are in fine form and we will make all Chicago proud of us." The paper, for its part, announced that "no one in the world knows better how to pick a player than 'Rube.' As a newspaper man has a 'nose for the news,' so does Mr. Foster have an eye for a good ballplayer." One such performer was southpaw pitcher Dave Brown, who had played for both the Dallas Black Giants and Foster's squad in 1918. Another was catcher Jim Brown, who, like the left-handed pitcher and their manager, came from the Lone Star State. The two Browns "were a whirlwind in Texas."[26]

Appreciating that the American Giants would be making a strong showing, Foster sought in mid-April to expand Schorling Park to accommodate fifteen thousand patrons; he was far more prescient than his major league counterparts, who actually curtailed their 1919 campaigns. In fact, Foster and John Schorling expected as many as twenty thousand spectators to appear at Giant games from June onward; Foster anticipated that the Giants would establish a new attendance mark for black baseball. The expansion of the park was complete by Decoration Day, and a reported twenty thousand fans showed up. Thousands of chairs had been added in the field, and thousands of would-be patrons had been turned away. Benches that would seat two thousand were being built in the outfield. All this demonstrated to the *Defender* that "the drawing powers of the American Giants are greater than any other team in semi-pro baseball," and that Chicago was "the best baseball city in the world."[27]

Chicago's black baseball squad was again in championship form: "Through the leadership of 'Rube' Foster it had 'gone over the top.'" Johnson, Whitworth, Gans, and Brown were pitching superbly; Dixon and Jim Brown were capably handling their assignments behind the plate; DeMoss had eased into his new role as captain; and the team, overall, was pleasing its manager.[28]

Before a packed crowd of fifteen thousand at Schorling Park on June 29, the American Giants, behind Whitworth's three-hitter, shut out the strong Fairbanks-Morse Beloits 4-0. DeMoss, Charleston, and Torriente each produced a pair of hits, with Charleston scoring twice. In "The History of the World's Greatest Colored Pitcher," a story that appeared in the *Chicago Whip,* a new, militant African American newspaper, Whitworth discussed his relationship with Rube Foster, calling him "a square fellow and a good friend even to those who are not deserving." Foster "has given me the benefit of his years of experience, gained by him while pitching. A young pitcher is indeed fortunate to have an experienced pitcher who has the art of fooling the hitters at his finger ends and better still, is always willing to assist you. If I am considered a good pitcher which is my wish, Mr. Foster should have full credit for it."[29]

Later that summer, the American Giants were stationed in Detroit for a full month, where, the *Defender* reported, they battled the Stars before "the largest crowds that ever witnessed semi-pro games." Led by player-manager Pete Hill, Detroit took a key series from the Giants to claim the western title. Because of racial unrest in Chicago, the American Giants headed to the east coast, and played before a crowd of twenty-five thousand at the Dychman Heights grounds in upper Manhattan. A Harlem jazz band, ideal weather, and baseball made for a "perfect day," as did the Giants' doubleheader sweep against the Treat 'Em Roughs. Bingo DeMoss got four hits, Oscar Charleston offered "a hair-raising catch," and Tom Johnson limited his foes to seven hits as the Giants took the opener 2-1. Sam Crawford, entering the game with a man on second and nobody out in the bottom of the ninth, preserved the victory. Crawford then replaced String Bean Williams to take the second contest 7-1.[30]

The loss of home field advantage perhaps explains, at least to some extent, why the American Giants' championship run was interrupted. Racial unrest ravaged Chicago as whites and blacks fought in the streets, leaving thirty-eight dead, upwards of five hundred wounded, and several hundred homeless. Crushed in the process were hopes—held by Rube Foster, among others—that racial divisions could be overcome painlessly or readily.

The nineteen-month period of American involvement in World War I had been instrumental in quickening the migratory process out of the South and in raising still higher the expectations of many blacks. Industrial plants, for the first time, opened their doors to African American workers, including women, while conscription, idealism, and the hope of a better life ahead drew young men into the military. Thus, blacks served with distinction on two fronts: in the plants whose productivity aided the Allied cause and on the battlefields. At war's end, however, it became clear how quixotic were the hopes for a society free of long-standing racial stigmas and stereotypes. Certain veterans of both the nation's industrial centers and its armed forces demonstrated little willingness, however, to continue to accede to their socially assigned second-class status. Resentment built up on both sides of the racial divide and, at times, spilled over into major conflagrations. And now, thanks to the emergence of an African American bourgeoisie, chroniclers of the events came in various shades of black as well as white.

The most violent scenes unfolded in Chicago, then viewed as the

The Reverend Andrew Foster. Courtesy of Doris Foster.

Above opposite: Philadelphia Giants, 1904. Courtesy of NoirTech Research, Inc. *Below opposite:* Philadelphia Giants, 1905. Courtesy of NoirTech Research, Inc. *Above:* Philadelphia Giants, 1906. Courtesy of NoirTech Research, Inc.

Above: Leland Giants, 1909. Courtesy of Doris Foster. *Below:* Chicago American Giants, 1914. Courtesy of NoirTech Research, Inc.

American Giants Base Ball Club

ANDREW (RUBE) FOSTER, CLUB MANAGER

THE GREATEST AGGREGATION OF COLORED
BASE BALL PLAYERS IN THE WORLD

Park Located at 39th St. and Wentworth Ave.

(WHITE SOX OLD GROUNDS)

FINEST SEMI-PRO. PARK IN THE U. S.

OWNED AND OPERATED BY

JOHN M. SCHORLING, OFFICE, 403 WEST 79TH STREET

Chicago 6/26/15_____191_

Mr.J.V.Brasfield,Mgr,

Henry Greys-B.B.Club,

Dear Sir:-

      Your letter confirming the date there-wednesday-July 14-also

accepting the terms-of a gaurantee of Sixty Dollars-(Same to be paid in

case of rain,or no game) received,replying to it-beg to say,I will try

and not play in the Immediate vicinity of Henry-before playing there--

but am trying to fill out a week,around there,so as to make it pay-hence

the terms to you--send me a list of some of the good places around,also

the days that they play---I will pitch the game there for you,providing

I am not sick-or disabled--The terms are with option of Fifty percent

of the gross receipts--   Respectfully Yours-

Andrew Foster

Letter from Rube Foster to J. V. Brasfield, June 26, 1915. Courtesy of Doug Averitt.

Cartoon from the *Indianapolis Freeman*, July 17, 1915.

Cartoon from the *Indianapolis Freeman,* July 24, 1915.

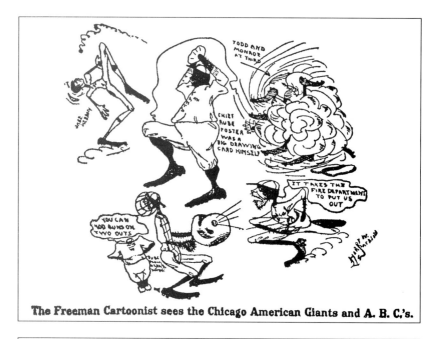

The Freeman Cartoonist sees the Chicago American Giants and A. B. C.'s.

AN ATTEMPTED HOLD-UP.

Above: Cartoon from the *Indianapolis Freeman,* n.d. *Below:* Cartoon from the *Indianapolis Freeman,* December 2, 1916.

Rube Foster, Havana, 1916. Courtesy of
NoirTech Research, Inc.

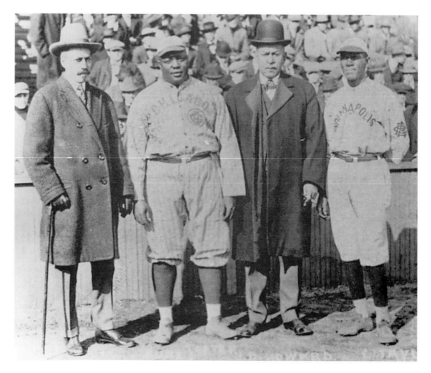

Elwood Knox, Rube Foster, J. D. Howard, and C. I. Taylor, 1916. Knox was the sports editor of the *Indianapolis Freeman*, Howard was the sports editor of the *Indianapolis Ledger*, while Taylor served as manager of the Indianapolis ABCs. Courtesy of NoirTech Research, Inc.

Rube Foster, n.d. Cour-
tesy of NoirTech Re-
search, Inc.

Rube Foster and members
of the Joliet Standards,
circa 1918. Courtesy of
NoirTech Research, Inc.

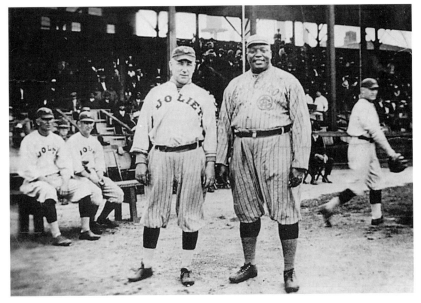

Above: Chicago American Giants, 1919. Courtesy of NoirTech Research, Inc. *Below:* Chicago American Giants, 1920. Courtesy of NoirTech Research, Inc.

Sarah Foster, n.d. Courtesy of Doris Foster.

Grave site of Rube Foster, Chicago, Illinois, December 1930. Courtesy of Doris Foster.

Sarah Foster with Post Commander Colonel Edwin N. Hardy (far right) at Rube Foster
Memorial Field, Fort Huachuca, Arizona, n.d. Courtesy of David Skinner.

Earl Foster with Bowie Kuhn, Commissioner of Major League Baseball, 1981. Courtesy of National Baseball Hall of Fame Library.

country's second greatest metropolis. Yet Chicago was beset by corruption that at times appeared endemic, public services hardly addressed the needs of all inhabitants, and racial tension occasionally seemed palpable. The massive migration from the South exacerbated black-white relationships. The summer of 1918, historian William M. Tuttle Jr. writes, was marked by violence: among other things in June, a number of blacks were attacked in public places; white mobs staked out and murdered African Americans, but no prosecutions followed; gangs wrestled with one another, while promising a final showdown; and Kenwood and Hyde Park Improvement Association members, the *Chicago Whip* charged, had unleashed "the bomb war" against black citizens.[31]

July proved more disturbing. In the evening hours of the twenty-seventh, a race riot broke out next to Lake Michigan. Bands of angry white Chicagoans, headed by gangs, attacked African Americans, who, in turn, formed groups seeking to avenge such treatment. The release of stored-up anger and hostility spilled over into bloodletting that continued for five days, producing large casualty figures and considerable loss of property.[32]

Illinois Governor Lowden declared his intention to form a multiracial committee to determine how "racial segregation" might be accepted by all parties. The *Whip,* under the editorial guidance of William C. Linton, denounced the plan, declaring the paper "uncompromisingly against segregation of any sort." "Any Negro that asserts that he is for separation or segregation on account of color cannot be trusted by either race. He is a traitor and a thief. Under strenuous conditions he would not hesitate to play the role of Benedict Arnold." The editorial staff explained the paper's stance: "The *Whip* is opposed to separation and segregation, first because it is unconstitutional; and it does not believe in violating the organic law of the government." Moreover, "NO SENSIBLE WHITE MAN WANTS IT, OR WOULD STAND FOR IT."[33]

Segregation had failed in Memphis, St. Louis, Springfield, and other metropolitan areas because "it does not effect a cure for the existing social evils, in fact it creates animosity, puts a stigma of primitive savagery upon both races." The *Whip* stated flatly, "THE NEGRO HAS NO COLOR PREJUDICE. BUT HE IS MILITANTLY PREJUDICED AGAINST ANY CONDITION THAT TENDS TO PUT A STAMP OF INFERIORITY UPON HIM OR OBSTRUCT HIS DEVELOPMENT AND PURSUIT OF HAPPINESS."[34]

A commission was not the answer, said the *Whip*, nor was new legislation; an executive with "backbone" to uphold existing measures was required. "We want men in public office that are color and class blind. We want men whose heads are saturated with, and whose acts will subscribe to the principles of the fathers of this great land, 'that all men are created equal.' We want [men] who will not put political expediency above human lives."[35]

The explosions in Chicago, according to the *Whip*, demonstrated the need for new mentors. "As long as the Negro is represented by the cringing, crouching, ignorant, verbose and unscrupulous type of would-be leaders, just so long will mutual and intelligent understanding between races be delayed." African Americans had lacked a genuine leader since the passing of Frederick Douglass. "False leaders" had contended that blacks sought only equality of opportunity. This was "cowardly and hypocritical. The Negro wants everything that is included in the sum total of Americanism." "The time is now ripe for these Old Black Joes and Uncle Toms to go to Mississippi and ally themselves with the cohorts of lynching."[36]

The African American "demands new leadership. Calm, intelligent, unswerving leaders. God, give us Men. Men that are saturated with the true love of life and liberty. Men that love their race and country and know no superior. Men that are rooted and grounded in truth, love and service." The world was watching "the new Negro," who could help "to lead us out of this present pandemonium."[37]

One eyewitness to the riot appeared to second the *Whip*'s reading of race relations. The racial disturbance, he asserted, seemed certain to improve relationships between whites and blacks. African Americans in that great city had displayed "their readiness, willingness, and eagerness to fight the thing through." The riot was likely to produce welcome changes: "It will bring about 'a meeting of the minds' to the effect that the colored man must not be kicked about like a dumb brute." Equally significant, "our white friends, seeing the danger that besets the nation, will become more active in our cause, and the other whites will at least have a decent respect for us based on fear."[38]

W. E. B. Du Bois, editor of *The Crisis* magazine, the organ of the NAACP, declared that African Americans had undertaken a "vast voyage which will lead to Freedom or Death." For three hundred years, black folk had "suffered and cowered" in America, relying on "Passive Resistance and Submission to Evil." Now, "we raise the terrible weapon of Self-Defense. When the murderer comes, he shall not longer strike us in the back. When the armed lynchers gather, we too must gather armed. When the mob moves, we propose to meet it with bricks and clubs and guns." Du Bois praised those who battled white vigilantes: "Honor, endless and undying Honor, to every man, black or white, who in Houston, East St. Louis, Washington and Chicago gave his life for Civilization and Order."[39]

The NAACP's Walter F. White provided his own interpretation of Chicago's racially charged reality: "No city in America," except possibly Philadelphia, he wrote, was so afflicted by "political trickery, chicanery and exploitation"; additionally, the Chicago police were horribly ineffective and frequently criminally negligent. "All of this tended to contribute to open disregard for law and almost contempt for it." In the meantime, "the new spirit aroused in Negroes by their war experiences" had taken hold. Indeed, said White, "One of the greatest surprises to many of those who came down to 'clean out the niggers' is that these same 'niggers' fought back. Colored men saw their own kind being killed, heard of many more and believed that their lives and liberty were at stake. In such a spirit most of the fighting was done."[40]

One reason for African Americans' greater assertiveness, the *Chicago Whip* believed, was the emergence of the heralded New Negro and what that figure represented.

> We are dissatisfied with the treatment we are receiving. We want the existing order of social, economic and political affairs changed. The Negro wants to be treated as a man and consideration on the basis of merit and citizenship. The New Negro is disgusted with lynching and mob violence. He believes in defending his life and his home and all other sacred institutions. For this reason he is radical because the old regime is satisfied with "Uncle Tom" and "Aunt Liza" position.

The "New Negro," of course, went still further, challenging the notion that blacks were innately inferior in any manner.[41]

Three years after the 1919 race riot the Chicago Commission on Race Relations delivered its report on the riot's causes. Acknowledging that no "ready remedy" existed, the commission, in *The Negro in Chicago,* also foresaw no "quick means of assuring harmony between the races." Relying on "the civic conscience of the community," the commission predicted that "progress should begin in a direction steadily away from the disgrace of 1919." In time, "mutual understanding and sympathy between the races will be followed by harmony and co-operation." Certain "solutions" to the race problem that had been tendered were dismissed: "We are convinced by our inquiry . . . that measures involving or approaching deportation or segregation are illegal, impracticable and would not solve, but would accentuate, the race problem and postpone its just and orderly solution by the process of adjustment."[42]

The commission expressed concerns about growing race consciousness in the black community: "While we recognize the propriety and social values of race pride among Negroes . . . thinking and talking too much in terms of race alone are calculated to promote separation of race interests and thereby to interfere with racial adjustment." Needed to be undertaken were educational programs predicated on the belief that "no one, white or Negro, is wholly free from an inheritance of prejudice in feeling and in thinking. . . . Mutual understanding and sympathy . . . can come completely only after the disappearance of prejudice. Thus the remedy is necessarily slow."[43] Not everyone agreed, certainly not the most renowned black figure on Chicago's South Side.

ELEVEN

Organizing Black Baseball

The ferocity of the race riot that ravaged Chicago must have stunned Rube Foster. Having long suffered segregation and discrimination, he nevertheless had optimistically believed that with the passage of time, racial barriers eventually would be surmounted. He had been raised in southeast Texas when Jim Crow practices were intensifying. Then, as a young ballplayer he had skirted the edges of organized baseball, locked out only because of his skin color. For nearly two decades he had been at the summit of the national game's blackened version. As a consequence, he had starkly confronted the racial realities that prevented him first, as black baseball's finest pitcher, and then, as its greatest manager, from competing on a level plane against white counterparts.

In his own fashion, Foster had struck back at the injustice by molding black baseball teams that were in every way the equal of their white counterparts. Foster's hypercompetitiveness sometimes led him to dismiss the accomplishments of fellow black baseball leaders or to minimize setbacks that his seemingly invincible teams occasionally experienced. Still, he strove continually to improve the lot of both his ballplayers and others who were being denied the chance to participate in organized baseball. For more than a decade, he had been involved in various efforts, all eventually aborted, to establish "a colored league" that would afford black baseball players a more visible stage for their mastery and artistry. At the same time, he continued to hope that the national pastime's segregation practices would eventually prove too absurd, embarrassing, and counterproductive, because too many of the game's premier performers were being left on the outside looking in.

The Chicago riot and others that followed must have dashed, however temporarily, hopes that reasonableness, economic considerations, and moral rectitude would soon doom Jim Crow baseball. It must have been such a realization that played a part in Foster's determination to carry through with long unrealized plans for a black baseball league. On July 2, 1919, Foster, in correspondence (with the letterhead "American Giants Base Ball Club, *The Greatest Aggregation of Colored Base Ball Players in the World*") affirmed, "We will have the circuit at last," referring to the next season. Sports columnist Cary B. Lewis of the *Chicago Defender*, on October 4, thought that that season would likely witness "a circuit of western clubs." The just-completed baseball season had proven "so prosperous," fans "so loyal," and attendance "so great" that formation of "a colored league" seemed inevitable. Foster was "the man responsible for the proposed circuit." Indeed, "it has been his dream for years to see men of his Race have a circuit of their own."[1]

One rumor floated that Foster had been asked to move his team to New York City, where a $100,000 stadium would be constructed for it. Foster turned down the offer, believing that Chicago and the West would prove more fertile territory for "a permanent baseball circuit." Every indication suggested that he was diligently planning for the upcoming season and had the backing of "every business man in Chicago." Moreover, Foster possessed "the confidence and respect of the press and fans," Lewis related. "[N]o man in baseball has more influence than 'Rube' Foster."[2]

The peerless shortstop John Henry Lloyd was another figure who seemingly loomed large in the formation of the new league. It was anticipated that he would end up in Kansas City or Indianapolis, two other leading venues for black baseball. The Dayton (Ohio) Marcos, who had defeated the American Giants during the past season, were expected to join the league. So were Cleveland's Tate Stars, the Detroit Stars, and the Cuban Stars, who would be a road team. Charles Mills stood ready to head a club in St. Louis.[3]

The *Defender*'s Lewis considered it noteworthy that the league "will be owned and controlled by Race men." Baseball had proven to be a good investment for black entrepreneurs; now, well-heeled individuals in all the projected circuit sites appeared ready to finance the operations. Thanks to the stewardship of figures like Foster, Pete Hill, and John Henry Lloyd, "the game among us has gone up 100 per cent."[4]

The league's eight teams, sportswriter Lewis asserted, "will have first class attractions" while boasting "the best baseball players that money can buy." Weekday games, it was anticipated, would draw 3000 to 5000 fans; Sunday games, 10,000 to 25,000. It was clear to Lewis "that baseball in the West will pay." Thus, "Mr. Foster has a good reason to remain here rather than going to New York City." The pennant winner would travel east and compete against the best black baseball clubs there. In the meantime, the western league would require more African American scribes and umpires. Ultimately, "it would give a number of our men work and confine a lot of money in the pockets of men of the Race that is now going daily into the pockets of the other fellows." The *Defender* planned to have a sportswriter in every league city and the grandest baseball column anywhere to be found.[5]

In late November 1919, Foster began a column in the *Defender* under the rubric "Pitfalls of Baseball," in which he incisively discussed blackball's need to change. On November 29, he asserted that only one "Colored Club"—a clear reference to his American Giants—had turned a $1,000 profit annually. Even owners whose teams had been in business for years suffered financial losses, but how long they would continue to do so was "questionable." Indeed, without changes, Foster predicted, "next season will see the end." Because of heightened attendance, players would demand large salary increases, yet at present no black team "knows of ten games it will play next season." Further, "[T]hey have never known, nor will they until they are organized."[6]

Only Sunday baseball was proving profitable because expenses associated with materials, ballparks, and administrative costs, continued to mount. Foster pointed to Schorling Park, "the finest, largest and best equipped" black diamond in the country; its patronage was the largest of any "club of color." When idle, it cost $945 weekly; when used three times a week, $1,346. Visiting clubs had to be paid, necessitating hefty attendance figures. Three Sunday rainouts would result in a losing season financially. Even well-connected individuals, like John W. Connors and Nat Strong of the Brooklyn Royal Giants, Slick Schlichter of the Philadelphia Giants, and E. B. Lamar Jr. of the Cuban X-Giants had been compelled "to give it up." C. I. Taylor, too, had fallen "in line" more recently.[7]

What baseball "among our people" required, Foster told readers of his next column, was "a very strong leader, and this leader to be successful must have able lieutenants, all of whom have the confidence of the public"—an obvious reference to himself. He was now more certain than before that "something firm must be done, and done quickly." Foster acknowledged that some eastern magnates and many players had charged that he failed to pay players salaries commensurate with their worth, yet during the past season, those expenses had increased to $450 weekly and another $575 had been expended to pay for additional players once the campaign began. He calculated that the monthly bill would rise to $2,000 in 1920, surpassing any amount expended by eastern teams.[8]

The most poorly compensated American Giant, Foster offered, received a salary equal to that of a postal carrier, clerk, or public school teacher. The players were required to put in only some twenty hours a month and could "sleep all day," he remarked, but they complained about being "underpaid." In fact, some illiterate players received larger checks than did school principals. Such athletes, along with their teammates, were paid more than those who toiled for the government, railroad lines, oil companies, including Standard Oil, and steel combines. It is striking how Foster, at times, referred to players so disparagingly, even while seeking to improve their lot.[9]

"Tried" leadership, Foster insisted, must be turned to. He, quicker than anyone, would follow the man who displayed such ability. Foster then again castigated his fellow moguls, who seemed more inclined to "tear down" than to work together constructively.

> Present-day promoters are blind to many facts. They do not realize that to have the best ball club in the world and no one able to compete with it will lose more money on the season than those that are evenly matched. The majority do not know a ball player when they see one. They have paid big prices for many lemons, thinking that if the man was a success with Foster we will work wonders with him. They forget that I have been a player, whose intellect and brains of the game have drawn more comment from leading baseball critics than all the Colored players combined, and that I am a student of the game. They do not know, as I do, that there are not five players nor three owners among the clubs who know the playing rules.[10]

Foster's third column charged that black baseball as operated was "a disgrace to the name of good, honest sportsmanship." To succeed, many questionable practices by other owners had to be ignored. A more businesslike approach to the game was essential. The raiding of other teams' players had to end; the upcoming campaign would be the "worst" yet in that regard. Greater organization of black baseball, he reasoned, could curb such practices. Then Foster proved unable to avoid a dig at his old rival, Indianapolis ABCs boss C. I. Taylor, whom he again mistakenly asserted was retiring from baseball: the "little success" that Taylor had achieved "was made by the writer."[11]

Wrapping up the year, Foster's fourth column urged a transformation of black baseball and included obvious peace feelers to other magnates. All businessmen who had run black baseball teams, Foster acknowledged, had been well intentioned, but the antics of various players had invariably disillusioned them. He admired J. W. Connors, who was "very ambitious" and wanted "nothing but the best." Major Jackson and Frank Leland were, Foster now said, "fine men. Everything that they did was from their heart. They were honest and their dealings above suspicion." Foster even had a few good words for Taylor, describing him as "an able lieutenant" with "many good qualities; he is full of fire and needs only patience."[12]

As for himself, Foster proclaimed he was "willing to let bygones be bygones." He called for the owners in the West and East to meet to select an arbitration board, a board of experienced businessmen who would draft a constitution that black baseball leaders could accept. Those who promised to do so would deposit $500 as a show of good faith that they would adhere to the agreement.[13]

Foster was not asking that players be swapped; rather, each team would retain its own pool of ballplayers while solidifying "a relationship in working for the organized good of baseball." That plan would replicate organized baseball's and eventuate in a meeting between the eastern and western winners, "a real world's championship." That in turn would ultimately lead to a face-to-face encounter with the holder of the major league title. "This is more than possible," Foster asserted. "Only in uniform strength is there permanent success." Hence, "I invite all owners to write for information on this proposition. It is open to all."[14]

In the column of January 3, 1920, Foster again condemned the player raids that so divided black magnates. The practice had become "so bad" that "managers do not trust players, nor do the players trust the managers." Its effect was still more corrosive: the aggrieved manager often warned colleagues if they competed against the team that had taken on the player, "I will not play you." Many clubs refused to take the field against one another.[15]

Organized baseball, Foster observed, handled things far differently; the reserve clause bound a player to a team until it released or traded him. Major league teams, Foster somewhat naively wrote, refused to tamper with athletes on other squads. "Our club owners laugh at such protection and have year after year done just the opposite." Black ballplayers were also opposed to the idea of organization, fearing that their salaries would suffer. In reality, they could make far more money, Foster countered. Several major leaguers made more in one season than the complete rosters of any three black teams. If investments were protected by means of organization, then more money would be expended on ballparks and player development.[16]

Black baseball could not continue, Foster argued, without organization. Whites would "naturally" support such an effort, although eventually protest against it would lead to profits not accruing to African Americans. "Yet we will be the ones at fault." Current salaries could readily triple, an adequate number of ballparks could appear, and hundreds of black ballplayers could receive employment. The status quo, by contrast, could not last because park rentals had escalated and existing leases were subject to termination at any time. Several African Americans with the financial means, Foster related, had sought to enter black baseball, but "they want it patterned after the way leagues are conducted."[17]

Foster then announced:

> This will be the last time I will ever try and interest Colored club owners to get together on some working basis. I have so often been refused the necessary capital, not desiring to give to others the chance of monopolizing Colored baseball, but they are not going to continue to wait on me with their money. They can do so and leave me where I am. I have made the effort; it's now up to the ones that expect to permanently figure in baseball to get together.[18]

A week passed with little interest expressed in Foster's call for black baseball leagues. Foster deemed his plan "the salvation of baseball" that would have warranted the continued patronage of black fans, "based solely on their loyalty to the Race." A black league had a built-in level of support, Foster declared, because the African American population in the proposed league cities ranged from 50,000 to 150,000. Those urban blacks "would rally around any progressive move."[19]

Foster knew that most teams lacked any capital investment, including some of the finest ball clubs like the Hilldale Royal Giants, the Indianapolis ABCs, the Kansas City Monarchs, the Detroit Stars, the Chicago Giants, and the Dayton Marcos. Only the Lincoln Giants, the St. Louis Stars, and the Chicago American Giants possessed tangible assets. Moreover, those of his team exceeded "all the Colored parks combined."[20]

The black moguls who had refused to join his campaign, Foster warned, would soon be eased from the game altogether. As the cost of constructing a ballpark approached $100,000, many would prove incapable of amassing such a sum, and even if they could, city codes often precluded blacks from obtaining necessary permits. All this was unfortunate.

> I have fought against delivering Colored baseball into the control of whites, thinking that with a show of patronage from the fans we would get together. The get-together effort has been a failure. In justice to myself and the many players that will eventually benefit by ownership with system money and parks, admitting that I cannot prevent it much longer, as in the past, I had better see that the snow does not stay in my yard after these many hard years of effort.[21]

In the final "Pitfalls of Baseball" column, in the January 17, 1920, edition of the *Defender,* Foster again chided those who stood in the way of a blackball league. Western magnates frequently disagreed with one another but would ultimately resolve their differences for the good of the game. Their eastern counterparts behaved differently, as acknowledged by Nat C. Strong, a leading booking agent, who said they were "an IMPOSSIBILITY." "[T]here were several owners, managers and players [the agency] would never do business with again."[22]

As things stood, Foster wrote, the top clubs in the East refused to compete against one another or any of the leading western teams; the latter, who played one another, would not do battle on the diamond with their eastern peers. "If you have taken your club east, win many games, the owners try to take the men away from you, bring about dissatisfaction between you and your men; so much so, you avoid going there." Meanwhile, the eastern ball clubs continued their internecine squabbles, engaging in a kind of "survival of the fittest. You kill my dog. I will kill your dog." This was dumbfounding. "One would not think such IGNORANCE existed in the MODERN AGE."[23]

For Foster, the players were also to blame for having "no respect for their word, contracts or moral obligations." Still, they were far less culpable than the owners, who pirated players by goading them into switching ball clubs: "You had better get it while getting is good." The players never realized, Foster concluded, that their decision to jump to another team made black baseball as an enterprise economically tenuous.[24]

Charles D. Marshall, writing in the *Indianapolis Freeman*, declared that "organized baseball is on and Andrew (Rube) Foster is at the helm. Or, we might say that this great captain of the national game has started the ball to rolling . . . [and] I think the forming of a Colored baseball league may be the outcome." The plan "seems a most plausible one," and virtually all fans were backing "this brilliant idea." If implemented, black baseball would surely acquire a greater following. Marshall agreed that black baseball's appeal would slacken if organization were not forthcoming. Thus, "when a great leader like Rube Foster offers to share his knowledge and costly experience for the betterment of each and every owner . . . I think that there should be an enthusiastic rally to the support of the idea."[25]

In the pages of the *Competitor*, the Indianapolis ABCs' C. I. Taylor also urged formation of a black league. The upcoming season promised to be baseball's "greatest." The sport was every bit as much the national game of blacks as it was of whites because "it is above all things an AMERICAN game. It abides deep in the sport loving natures of all Americans regardless of their creed or color." Then why was baseball as a business enterprise "in such a chaotic condition with the colored people?" "We produce splendid players, men of brilliant talents, many of whom could play rings around the average ball players in the white leagues if they were given the opportunity." Blackball teams were excellent, notwithstanding reliance on facilities far inferior to those in organized baseball. A puzzled Taylor queried, why, in spite of good players and teams, did black baseball "grow so slowly?"[26]

The answer for Taylor: "[L]ack of organization!" Blacks possessed "the goods" but couldn't deliver them. It was necessary to devise a means "to profitably present baseball on the diamond." His nearly-two-decade-long tenure in baseball led him to conclude that only organization would bring that about. Indeed, he had plugged it for some time, doubting that "any other living colored man has carried on such an extensive correspondence in the interest of the sport"; the reference was obviously to arch-rival Rube Foster. Generally, however, his advocacy was fruitless and he himself at times was tagged a "dreamer."[27]

Taylor was delighted "that the very men" who had earlier opposed plans of one kind or another to organize had come to see that organization "is the only hope, if we are to make anything out of baseball for the black Americans. Organization is the intelligent beginning of all things, and the sooner we as a race recognize this fact, the quicker will we be acknowledged by other peoples; and the greater will be our strides in the game of life."[28]

Near the end of his article Taylor mentioned a letter he had written earlier to Foster, saying, "You are the man of the hour to strike the blow which will weld into one harmonious organization, the colored baseball clubs of this country." It was essential to construct "a Negro league . . . to keep alive the great sport among us, for it has been fully shown that we are barred from organized baseball as it exists today in this country." Notwithstanding their ability and numerous allies, black players had been excluded from organized baseball due to "sentiment alone"; "an organization of our own is the speediest and most effective remedy."[29]

Then Taylor added this accolade:

> I say in view of your superior knowledge, executive ability and thorough knowledge of baseball, your national reputation as the greatest organizer the game has produced coupled with the confidence of the baseball public throughout the country would have in an organization headed by yourself, you are particularly fitted to set this wheel in motion.[30]

On February 7, 1920, the *Chicago Defender* indicated that the long-sought meeting of blackball magnates would occur the following week in Kansas City, Missouri. Scheduled to appear were C. I. Taylor, Indianapolis ABCs; John Matthews, Dayton Marcos; John "Tenny" Blount, Detroit Stars; J. L. Wilkinson, Kansas City Monarchs; Charlie Mills, St. Louis Giants; Joe Green, Chicago Giants; and Rube Foster, American Giants. Foster also held the Cuban Stars' proxy. Others attending the session included leading black sportswriters such as David Wyatt of the *Indianapolis Ledger,* Charles Marshall of the *Indianapolis Freeman,* A. D. Williams of the *Indianapolis Ledger,* and Cary B. Lewis of the *Chicago Defender.*[31]

For some time now, the *Defender* declared, it had pressed for just such a meeting. No one had been more supportive of the idea "than the Chicago 'chief.'" In Kansas City a prospective schedule was to be devised, along with "a working agreement." The meeting itself, it was anticipated, would lead to the actual establishment of a black league.[32]

The first session of Foster's conclave took place on Friday, February 13, with virtually all the expected parties and additional ones, too, showing up at the YMCA. Alongside those listed above were W. A. Kelly of Washington, D.C.; Lorenzo S. Cobb, St. Louis Giants' secretary; attorney Elisha Scott of Topeka; and Elwood C. Knox of the *Freeman.* Nominated by Tenny Blount, Foster was chosen "temporary president"; Lewis was selected as secretary. The enthusiastic gathering predicted that 1921 would be baseball's greatest year yet. Those in attendance were taken aback when Foster—who, in the estimation of the *Freeman,* possibly had "more at stake than any fifty men in baseball that could be named"—delivered a bombshell: "Gentlemen, the assets of the baseball club which I represent is more than all the Negro baseball clubs in existence, still if it pleases you all I am willing to throw all these assets upon the mercy of the decision of this body of newspaper men who are present." Foster also revealed that he had obtained a corporate charter "for a National Negro Baseball League." The participants were purportedly astounded when Foster produced the actual document, which proved to be a masterstroke. The league, it turned out, was already incorporated in Illinois, Michigan, Ohio, Pennsylvania, New York, and Maryland.[33]

All potentially contentious issues, including the allocation of players and the crafting of a league constitution, Foster stated, would be handled by attorney Scott and the journalists in attendance. Wyatt, Knox, Lewis, and Scott worked through the evening and into the early morning hours to shape a "baseball bill of rights" for the new league. They presented the preamble and constitution Saturday noon; each magnate signed the governing instrument and purportedly submitted a $500 deposit; stories circulated later that Foster had posted that amount for several of his colleagues. John Matthews of the Dayton Marcos, unable to attend because of the flu, sent a special delivery message indicating his full support of whatever would take place at the meeting. Various road teams also reportedly paid their fees, and Nat C. Strong wrote that he was prepared "to do anything that would promote the best interests of baseball all over the country."[34]

The plan was to open league play in April 1921, so as to allow each team sufficient time to acquire rights to a ballpark, through either ownership or a long-term lease. Following the successful operation of the western circuit, Foster intended to call for a meeting "of a National Baseball League" that would include representatives from the large eastern cities.[35]

Player rosters for the Western League—later, the Negro National League—were chosen to create balance. The Detroit Stars opted for Pete Hill, Bruce Petway, Edgar Wesley, Richard Whitworth, and Jimmie Lyons, among others; all were former American Giants, except for Lyons, who had once barnstormed on the West Coast with Foster. The Kansas City Monarchs featured John Donaldson, José Méndez, and Wilbur "Bullet" Rogan, with his blazing fastball and excellent curve. The St. Louis Giants included first baseman Tully McAdoo and catcher Dan Kennard. The Chicago Giants received Walter Ball and infielder John Beckwith. C. I. Taylor's Indianapolis ABCs obtained Oscar Charleston and William Dismukes. Foster's American Giants remained formidable: James Brown, Leroy Grant, Bingo DeMoss, Thomas Williams, Christopher Torriente, Jude Gans, and new third baseman David Malarcher.[36]

Ira F. Lewis, in an extended article in the *Competitor*, referred to the Kansas City roundtable as "perhaps the most singular and noteworthy meeting ever held in the interest of our sport life." Basically accepting C. I. Taylor's version of previous events, he argued that "the effort all along"—recalling earlier calls for "a colored league"—had only required "Mr. Foster's aid to make the try a success." Now, however, Lewis was willing to applaud Foster's efforts at the historic gathering:

And to his undying credit let it be said that he has made the biggest sacrifice of anyone. For be it known that his position in the world of colored baseball was reasonably secure, inasmuch as he controlled the situation pretty much not only in Chicago, where baseball is the fourth meal of the day, but in the Middle West. With ideal park location, and supported by unlimited backing both in money and patronage, Mr. Foster could have defied organization for many years. But, happily, he has seen the light,— the light of wisdom and the spirit of service to the public. From now on he will begin to be the really big man in baseball, he should be, by virtue of his knowledge of the game from both the playing and business ends.

For Lewis, it was unquestionable that Foster, who offered "his storehouse of knowledge, experience, position and money," should be credited with helping to lay the foundation for a black league.[37]

Establishing player rosters of relatively equal merit, Lewis stated, was particularly wise and would "appeal most keenly to the baseball loving population of the race." To remain competitive, moreover, teams would be compelled to develop new talent, young ballplayers who would turn "into Petways, Grants, Hills, Reddings, Williamses, Charlestons, Taylors, etc.," and who would demonstrate "unstinted loyalty and a 100 per cent effort. . . ." "The ballplayer has the chance he has longed for and is up to him to deliver the goods."[38]

The chance arose much earlier than anticipated. A mere two weeks following the Kansas City summit, the *Freeman*'s Charles D. Marshall reported that the new league, containing eight western teams and characterized by a more genuine professionalism, would begin play on May 1, 1920. Salary caps were expected, a playing schedule was being devised, admission prices were to be posted, and most important, perhaps, the impression was to be fostered that tickets were being purchased "for professional major league ball playing and not outlaw or semi-professional pastime." The most astute move to date was the selection of Rube Foster as league president: "This wily old master of the great game is best suited for guiding the organization safely past all of the pitfalls and loopholes that it is certain to encounter in baseball." Players should be afforded a square deal, Marshall stressed, to invalidate the stereotype of the "tramp ball tosser." "Give us more men like C. I. Taylor, 'Tenny' [*sic*] Blount, Foster and Wilkinson [*sic*] who urge the playing of clean ball."[39]

Less than a month following the Kansas City meet, Foster appeared at a meeting in Atlanta, where he sought to help organize a southern circuit. Representatives were present from Nashville; Birmingham; Knoxville; Chattanooga; Greenville, South Carolina; Atlanta; Jacksonville; Montgomery; Pensacola; and New Orleans. Foster, along with *Chicago Defender* sportswriters David Wyatt and Cary B. Lewis, served as mentors for the proposed league. *The Indianapolis Freeman* indicated that the southern circuit would likely join Foster's new organization in 1921.[40]

Foster's old friend David Wyatt, writing in the *Competitor,* discussed the Negro National League's impending inaugural season. A recent trip of Foster's to Detroit, Wyatt declared, was an early highlight. Foster "not only impressed the fans as being the congenial, business-like kind of a man who should be at the head of the new circuit, but he left behind him an impression that baseball is something more than a mere recreation and pastime institution." Wyatt then analyzed each of the league teams, concluding with a look at the American Giants, who appeared stronger than the previous year. He was putting together a "winning" team, Foster told Wyatt, that would be designed "along safe and sane principles. I am not going to try any new-fangled systems." The game, he remarked, had changed little from "when I was in the limelight as a player." At a minimum, Wyatt agreed that the Giants promised "to play fast ball, keep things stirred up, and even as a loser, will make the other fellows work their very hardest to beat them."[41]

Meantime, Foster continued laying the foundation for the Negro National League, whose motto was "We Are The Ship, All Else The Sea." To that end, he was willing to make considerable sacrifices, relinquishing some of his top players and reducing his team's take for away games. The wily master, at the same time, undoubtedly was determined to redo his ball club, which had failed to take the western title the previous season. Making up the American Giants team were catchers Jim Brown and Tubby Dixon, first baseman Leroy Grant, second sacker Bingo DeMoss, shortstop Bobby Williams, and third baseman Dave Malarcher. In the outfield were Jude Gans, Cristobal Torriente, Chaney White, and Johnny Reese; White and Reese, both fast ballplayers, were additions from the Hilldale Daisies, one of the top eastern clubs. The Giants' pitchers included Tom Johnson, Dave Brown, Frank Wickware,

Tom Williams, and Andrew "String Bean" Williams; Tom Williams had pitched for Hilldale in 1919, and String Bean Williams had ended the season with the Dayton Marcos. Foster lost his ace, Richard Whitworth, and third baseman Billy Francis to the same Hilldale Daisies that he had raided. Veteran Jess Barber joined the Atlantic City Bacharach Giants.[42]

Foster had initially attempted to assign Whitworth to the ABCs. That effort, along with the transfer of Oscar Charleston to the Detroit Stars, caused many to applaud his willingness to sacrifice for the good of the new league. As the *Defender* noted, Whitworth and Charleston were viewed as "the two greatest stars in the profession" and were "both idolized by the fans and great drawing cards." At the same time, Whitworth had been a holdout for a month during the previous season, before returning to lead Chicago with a 10-1 record. Even the presence of the fiery Charleston, on the other hand, had not enabled Foster to win another championship in 1919. Blount also was cheered for shipping Donaldson and Méndez to Kansas City, and Mills was saluted for sending Jimmie Lyons to Detroit.[43]

Wyatt saluted Foster's moves, and the *Chicago Whip* agreed that the American Giants manager had acted "for the good of the game" in making the new league more competitive. Wyatt's praise of Foster was unstinting: throughout his tenure as a baseball leader, he "has been the chief benefactor to a few hundred players and promoters" alike; he had generously reshuffled "one of the greatest playing machines of all time." He "has been the rock against which many a wave of adversity has been dashed to nothingness. He has weathered the storm of fierce criticism; he has sailed smoothly over the many obstacles that the combined power of his adversaries had placed in his path." Now, he was experiencing "his greatest triumph, a realization of a life's dream." And yes, his former adversaries were happily following his lead, but would fans support "good, fast, clean baseball" and help to determine the new league's fate?[44]

In mid-April, the American Giants opened their 1920 season as 4,500 fans came to Schorling Park to watch the home team battle Roger Park. The write-up in the *Chicago Whip* demonstrated the nearly-larger-than-life stature that Rube Foster had attained in certain circles: "Mr. Foster gave orders with the confidence of a Master Mind, and the rapidity of a German Machine Gun."[45]

Of far greater note, of course, was the first game played under the Negro National League's auspices. On May 7, more than eight thousand spectators followed the inaugural contest between the Indianapolis ABCs and the visiting Chicago Giants. The ABCs prevailed 4-2, with Huck Rile, a strapping 210-pound second-year man, scattering seven hits to beat Walter Ball. Some viewed the game as the start, David Wyatt noted, of "the most important and far-reaching step ever negotiated by the baseball promoters of our Race."[46]

An estimated crowd of ten thousand at Schorling Park in early June saw the American Giants, behind Tom Williams's four-hitter, defeat the Cubans 4-1. By the end of the month, Foster's team, in compiling an 18-2 record, had thoroughly outclassed its competition. In second place were the Detroit Stars, with a 12-4 total, four full games back. The only other team above the .500 mark was Indianapolis, which stood at 13-11.[47]

The Negro National League, the *Competitor* said, was "making wonderful progress" in its initial year of operation, despite many obstacles along the way. Not surprisingly, the journal indicated, the league lead had been grabbed by the American Giants and their "indomitable leader." Of little help, however, had been "the unsportsmanlike, unbusinesslike and weak-kneed support" afforded the league by midwestern black newspapers.[48]

By the end of July, the 32-5 American Giants had widened their lead, with the Detroit Stars now stationed at 18-14, eleven and a half games back. The ABCs and the Kansas City Monarchs were also playing winning baseball; the Marcos Daytons and Chicago Giants were league doormats. In late August, Foster's ball club was at 42-12, twelve games ahead of the Detroit Stars, thirteen in front of the Monarchs, and thirteen and a half up on the ABCs.[49]

As the Negro National League's first season ended in late September, it was proclaimed a resounding success. If so, that was thanks largely to the stellar performance of the American Giants, both on the playing field and at the box office. Although no official standings were produced, Foster's squad easily ended up on top, with the Stars, Monarchs, and ABCs also making a respectable showing. The American Giants had won season series against all league opponents and against the best eastern team, the Bacharach Giants. A five-game set with Rogers Park of the Chicago

City League, on the other hand, had been curtailed, with the American Giants taking but one of three contests waged. Throughout the Negro National League, the American Giants had shattered attendance marks, setting black baseball records at Kansas City's American Association Park, Indianapolis Park, Detroit's Navin Field, and in St. Louis. Some 200,000 spectators, approximately a third of the league total, had shown up at Schorling Park.[50]

Dave Brown, Dave Malarcher, and Cristobal Torriente were three of the new league's brightest stars in 1920. In league competition, Brown posted a 10-2 mark and Tom Williams went 9-1, both among the circuit's top marks. The American Giants' attack was triggered by Torriente, who hit .411; Malarcher batted .344, DeMoss .286, and Dixon .222. Torriente bested Jimmie Lyons, who hit .386, for the batting title, although the Detroit star—who had jumped to the Bacharach Giants in August—led the league in steals with twenty-two. The Stars' Edgar Wesley was the home-run king with eleven round-trippers, and Detroit's Bill Holland put together a 17-2 win-loss record.

On September 20, the American Giants opened a southern trip in Nashville. After five days in Knoxville, they played in New Orleans. A jaunt to Birmingham, Alabama, followed, and then another clash with the Knoxville Giants, the southern champs. A bout with the Knoxville squad in Chattanooga preceded the opening of a series against the Bacharach Giants. That five-game set ended inconclusively with each team having won twice. The final game, which would have decided the title of "world's colored champion," was never carried out, supposedly due to "some disruptive tactics on the part of an irate female fan."[51]

On December 3, 1920, representatives of the National Association of Colored Professional Base Ball Clubs, which operated the Negro National League, gathered in Indianapolis for the circuit's second annual meeting; the *Indianapolis Freeman* termed this "the most important gathering in baseball of all time." Once again, Rube Foster was unanimously elected league president and secretary. Hilldale, previously considered outside the pale as an "outlaw" ball club, was admitted to the league, and the Dayton franchise was moved to Columbus. There, Sol White assumed control of team operations. A new league constitution mandated the fining of managers or owners who engaged in "ungentlemanly actions that would hurt the game." A reserve clause, akin to that which prevailed in organized baseball, was henceforth to be included in player contracts. Teams were authorized to refuse to take the field against clubs outside the National Association that had pirated players.[52]

TWELVE

Czar of Black Baseball

Starting with the Negro National League's initial campaign, Rube Foster added another series of titles to his already illustrious record. The American Giants garnered the new circuit's first three championships before beginning something of a slide engendered by diminishing skills and, perhaps, the plentitude of responsibilities its manager-owner and league president now carried. Even in 1921 and 1922, the gap between the American Giants and other top Negro National League teams narrowed. Nevertheless, Foster captured two additional pennants, thus enabling him to claim, with considerable credibility, sixteen black baseball titles in the past twenty-one years; the final eleven occurred while Foster, first as a pitcher, then as a player-manager, and finally as a manager alone, guided ball clubs in Chicago, after he had led the Cuban X-Giants and the Philadelphia Giants to an initial handful of championships. No other figure in baseball history could equal Foster's record, which he contended was still more remarkable. Strikingly, only once had he even acknowledged that his team had lost its crown to another.

Heading into 1921, Foster predicted, as he so often did, that the American Giants were beefed up. The addition of outfielder Jimmie Lyons from the Bacharach Giants had boosted Foster's already considerable confidence. The year opened with Foster's ball club heading for Palm Beach to compete against the New York Royal Giants; in Palm Beach, the American Giants represented the Royal Poinciana Hotel, and the Royal Giants were sponsored by the Breakers. Foster's arrival from Hot Springs, Arkansas, caused "quite a bustle and stir among the local diamond gods." Accompanying the American Giants to Florida were John Beckwith, the powerful shortstop–third baseman with the Chicago Giants; and Frank "the Weasel" Warfield, the Detroit Stars' second baseman. Joining the American Giants' official roster was Otis "Lefty" Stark, who, in 1920, had fanned Babe Ruth three straight times in an exhibition contest.[1]

The Royal Giants, like Foster's team, drew from other ball clubs, including the Lincoln Giants, the Hilldale Daisies, and the Bacharach Giants. The Breakers' lineup contained such stalwarts—all of whom had played for Foster at one time—as Jess Barber, Billy Francis, Louis Santop, John Henry Lloyd, and Joe Williams. No matter, the American Giants took the Winter League championship and were acclaimed by the *Chicago Whip* as "the idol of the baseball fans throughout the entire world." Foster's teams, proclaimed the *Whip*—which featured a photograph of Foster entitled "The Peerless Leader"—were "generally recognized as globe trotters" for they traveled widely. This latest edition, the paper declared, surpassed "all the various great aggregations that in the past have upheld the Foster tradition." During the past year, the American Giants had taken six championships: the "Three Eye League, Chicago Ball League, National Negro League, Southern League, World's Championship . . . and Florida Winter League Championship." On March 19, the American Giants left the Royal Poinciana Hotel and coursed through the South on their way back to Chicago.[2]

As the Negro National League prepared for its second campaign, Ira F. Lewis lauded the circuit head: "Rube Foster . . . is slowly but effectually working towards an ideal. Mr. Foster has seen through the periscope of his uncanny vision and foresight the possibilities of colored baseball, as a business venture which almost staggers the imagination of the man who looks upon the sport as a plaything." Foster was seeking to establish "a real major league" or perhaps two of them, concentrated in major eastern and midwestern cities. Under such a plan, Foster could strive to bring "practically the entire country and especially the South, into a general plan of ORGANIZED COLORED BASEBALL."[3]

That second season proved far more competitive, with the 43-22 American Giants besting the 42-30 St. Louis Giants by four and a half games; the 53-38 Kansas City Monarchs finished third. Chicago's .662 winning percentage easily surpassed the .583 and .562 marks of St. Louis and Kansas City, respectively. Other than slugger Cristobal Torriente, who again topped the lineup with a .338 batting average, the American Giants proved to be virtually a "team of hitless wonders." Brown batted

.288; DeMoss, .261; and Malarcher, only .235. An excellent pitching staff was led by the 11-3 Dave Brown and the 12-7 Tom Williams. St. Louis captured league individual honors, with Charles Blackwell hitting .448, Oscar Charleston belting fifteen home runs, and Bill Drake producing a 20-10 record.[4]

The *Chicago Defender* believed that "from a playing standpoint," the Negro National League's second campaign had proven "a wonderful success." Unfortunately, inclement weather and an economic downturn had contributed to a 25 percent drop in attendance. Columbus, Detroit, St. Louis, and Indianapolis particularly were hard hit. Only the American Giants maintained their fan appeal and profitability.[5]

The American Giants' success on the playing field and at the box office, however, was overshadowed for Foster by the death of his twelve-year-old daughter Sarah and by accusations of financial impropriety. While traveling in his private railroad compartment through Atlanta in the late afternoon of November 12, Foster was confronted by policemen. At the behest of attorney Roy C. Drennan, the district attorney had Foster arrested and charged him with "cheating and swindling" certain ballplayers. Drennan represented Ben Harris, who alleged that Foster had failed to pay him and other players $125 monthly salaries, along with expenses and a percentage of gate receipts, as had been agreed to the previous summer. Released on bond, Foster professed his innocence, asserting that "personal feelings" were at the root of the complaint. As if in denial of his recent troubles, Foster maintained his often harried schedule, meeting with businessmen in various communities who had expressed interest in taking over financially troubled franchises; there was need for personnel changes to place the league on a firmer financial footing. Perhaps disingenuously, Foster also expressed a desire to relinquish the league presidency, professedly wishing to remain in control only of business operations.[6]

In December, Foster contributed four essays to the *Chicago Defender,* analyzing the problems still afflicting black baseball. His reflections, Foster suggested in the first, should be heeded because "I have dealt practically with the subject longer, made a greater success and have been the only man of Color to remain continuously in the game for such a length of time." Black baseball had experienced "many up and downs," largely due to two factors. One derived from the ignorance of many of the respectable, who, in class-conscious fashion, viewed baseball unfavorably. By his making baseball both "a profession" and "a business," Foster had helped to change their attitude. Now, various religious and educational leaders were his "staunchest friends. Their homes are open to me and my home is to them." The other factor now was the dearth of financial backing. More middle-class and wealthy individuals needed to invest in the game.[7]

In the second essay, Foster explained why his managerial methods, unlike those of others, had been successful. "Managing . . . requires brains, patience, endurance and an open mind to deal with all the players on a baseball club squarely." He had "yet to find a player that is hard to manage." To be perfectly blunt, Foster admitted,

> all of my players play baseball as if they had no mind of their own or did not know what to do. I have sent them to do things, take chances when conditions were such that it appeared like suicide to take the chance, yet they have gone willingly, without fear and nine times out of ten it brought them success.[8]

Rigorous training was required before a season began. "All of the men go over every detail, discuss it from every imaginable angle. We sometimes spend two weeks discussing plays without reaching a decision." If an accepted player proposal seemed wrong-headed, Foster would gently explain why. If a proposal seemed promising, Foster would ask which proposal should be implemented. The players would always respond, "The way you suggested." This approach built player confidence. Also helpful was his even-handed to managing and coaching.[9]

Intimate knowledge of his players, Foster wrote, was also instrumental to team success:

> I associate with my players. I go into their homes, study their dispositions and habits, find out the things that appeal to them most. If the places they frequent are bad, I go there with them, make a habit of frequenting places of this sort regularly. When they go to a place and find out I have been there if it is not the proper place they discontinue going. In this way I have broken up many of their bad habits. If they like whisky I buy it for them and after they have taken one or two I say, "Don't let this ruin you." I further inform them that but few men can drink and think accurately, that I hope they won't let it interfere with my work.[10]

His approach, Foster believed, had not diminished the esteem in which he was held by the players or their affection for him.

> I know of no man who has the respect of their men that will surpass the respect I receive from the ball players. If they have any bad association and they come in contact with me, whether it is in a saloon, cabaret or on the street, they go to their company and say: "Look out, here comes Rube; be careful how you act and what you say." They either call me "Rube," "Chief," or "Jock."

Others would do well, Foster insisted, to follow his example.[11]

In the final essays, Foster bemoaned players' lack of vision and the absence of "race" umpires. Players were "doing much to ruin" black baseball, breaking contracts and jumping to whichever team dangled the most money. Even as several black baseball teams were experiencing financial shortfalls, they were paying exorbitant salaries. Short-sightedness was also evident in the failure to train "colored umpires." Might it be that players were less apt to question the calls of white officials than those delivered by "race" umpires? Yet Foster declared, "I cannot allow my preference to run away with my business judgment, judgment of what I know to be to our best advantage at this present day and time." Some sixteen months later, the Negro National League hired seven black umpires.[12]

As the Negro National League's third annual meeting kicked off in Chicago on January 26, 1922, David Wyatt produced another paean to Rube Foster. Foster's "life history could be quoted as an interesting lesson, both to the youth of America and the pessimists who are always contending that this country doesn't give a fellow a fair chance." Lacking wealth or influence, Foster achieved eminence thanks to "his good right arm, backed up [by] a good head and unlimited ambition." Eventually, baseball enabled him "to acquire the honorable place that he now occupies in the country's business affairs."[13]

Wyatt quoted Foster: "Frankly, I regard my baseball position as an honor not one bit inferior to those who have a place in the halls of state and nation. Twenty-five years ago the presidency of a baseball league would have seemed a small affair in comparison to many other offices; now it's a position of responsibility and importance." As for himself, "I am proud of my position in the game, and believe me, I am just as proud because for years, I was a private in the ranks."[14]

Changes were in store for Foster's Negro National League. The Pittsburgh Keystones and Cleveland Tate Stars entered the circuit, replacing the Columbus Buckeyes and the Chicago Giants. Black baseball suffered a great loss when forty-seven-year-old C. I. Taylor died on February 23. Thousands of whites and blacks sought to pay their respects to the Taylor family. Foster, along with other league luminaries, attended the funeral.[15]

The 1922 Negro National League campaign was the most closely contested yet. Foster basically operated with what amounted to a pat hand, although his former star pitcher, Richard Whitworth, briefly returned to the American Giants. Cristobal Torriente remained Foster's hitting star, batting .342, and Dave Brown headed the pitching staff with an 8-3 mark. Al Monroe placed Torriente and Bingo DeMoss on his all-star team. Just past the season's halfway point, the American Giants actually trailed the Indianapolis ABCs in the league standings. The ABCs' 25-13 record by mid-July placed them two and a half games ahead of the American Giants' 21-14 mark. Six consecutive victories put Chicago in front of Indianapolis, which split eight games to fall a half game back. At season's end, the 36-23 American Giants captured their third straight Negro National League championship, finishing 28 percentage points ahead of the 46-33 ABCs. Finishing close behind in third and fourth places were the 43-32 Detroit Stars and the 44-33 Kansas City Monarchs.[16]

In late October, the *Cleveland Call* presented a critical perspective on Rube Foster that was reprinted in the *Chicago Whip*. Condemning what it called "Foster's czar-like methods," the *Call* argued that "the Foster reign has proven anything but a benign blessing in the league's performance." Ruling "supreme," Foster had "dictated without a single reckoning and has backed up his 'take it or leave it' with a mailed fist." The *Call* declared, "No single manager is bigger than baseball." Then, "A HEARING," starting "at the very top," was in order.[17]

Anticipating the fourth annual gathering of the Negro National League, scheduled for the Appomattox Club in Chicago on December 7, Foster delivered a state-of-the-league address. Before the circuit's founding, he recalled, there had existed only three black baseball clubs in the West, and their combined salaries added up to no more than $20,000; the three teams in the east had an aggregate player income of $30,000. The total, $50,000, had jumped more than threefold. Yet as expenses soared, Foster was being vilified. The word had got out that "Foster is all to blame; he gets all the money; many picked this out as capital. Foster has made money out of baseball; also has put more into its developments, and gave other players unfortunate, than all the owners combined."[18]

Another challenge sprang up as 1922 wound down, with eastern black baseball moguls announcing the formation of a new league, made up of teams from Cleveland, Hilldale, Pittsburgh, New York, Richmond, Brooklyn, and other cities. Possessing their own ballparks, those clubs appeared primed to compete with the Negro National League. The *Kansas City Call* in late December 1920 indicated that eight teams could hardly cover the territory from Kansas City to New York, and it also asserted that the American Giants seldom visited Kansas City. That scarcity was hardly surprising, the editorial wrongly continued, for "they never travelled much, anywhere, so they don't count." The *Call* then made a pointed observation, "If the League President's own team, with less than half the distance to go, doesn't get out here often, then the far eastern teams can't be expected."[19]

On January 11, 1923, Rube Foster—never one to suffer easily threats to his hegemony—countered the perceived peril with a blistering attack. He referred to the Eastern League as "Nat Strong's Booking Agency." Edward Bolden, owner of the Hilldale Daisies, responded to the man he called "the self-appointed Czar of Negro baseball," by saying Foster was not content "with the unwieldy regime" he had established out west. No, the Negro National League president sought to "extend his autocratic reign" eastward, employing "libelous propaganda" to curry favor with the general public. Criticism of Foster could be every bit as intemperate as that he leveled against others. Bolden denied that his team had ever paid Strong anything for booking purposes, and asked why Foster failed to acknowledge that he himself charged all league teams 5 percent of their total earnings. Further, the western teams, forced to play Sunday games in Chicago, remained dependent on that city's blackball club, which compelled them to "submit to the gouging tactics of the Foster regime that are just as repulsive to them." Bolden also wondered why Foster refused to admit how many league teams had not tendered the required deposit fee.[20]

W. S. Ferrance spoke out in the *Call* on February 9, reporting that Foster had received $11,220 for the 1920 season, derived from the fixed percentage he charged league teams. In contrast, "the supposed league" received nothing. Given the manner in which Foster had reacted, it was "no wonder that any man that voices his opinion is quickly done away with."[21]

In the midst of these charges, Foster headed for New York to conduct "baseball business." He told a reporter that he stood ready to debate both Nat Strong and Edward Bolden before newspapermen in that city. Journalists there could ascertain who was at fault in the controversy.[22]

The American Giants experienced a series of roster changes as they attempted to defend their league title in the upcoming season. Their ace lefthander Dave Brown and "Huck" Ed Rile bolted to the newly formed Eastern Colored League. Eventually, Foster slammed Brown in what was becoming an increasingly characteristic fashion: he viciously referred to Brown's earlier legal troubles. Brown had been convicted of robbery but was paroled to Foster, who had promised the pitcher's mother that he would post a $20,000 bond and take care of him. If he now attempted to revoke the bond, Foster complained, the public would think ill of him.[23]

The 1923 American Giants included longtime stalwarts, along with a batch of newcomers. Among the latter were pitcher Luther Farrell and outfielder Harry C. Kenyon, neither of whom performed spectacularly for Chicago. Dave Malarcher hit .295, Jelly Gardner batted .302, and John Beckwith added a .323 mark. Tom Williams was credited with a 6-1 pitching record. One addition to the Giant pitching staff was lefty Willie Foster, Rube's younger half brother, who spent only part of the season with the team.[24]

By early August, it was clear that the American Giants were unlikely to retain their Negro National League crown. The Kansas City Monarchs headed the race with a 44-24 record, the Detroit Stars were positioned three and a half games back at 32-19, and the American Giants were stationed four and a half behind at 33-22. The preseason trade of first baseman Leroy Grant to the Indianapolis ABCs had foreshadowed a revamping of the team. When pressed later in the 1923 season, Foster admitted, "It is the beginning of the wrecking of the once great machine that represents the American Giants. I hate to part with some of my men, but I have come to the conclusion that I am forced to do it."[25]

When the 1923 campaign ended, the same three teams were positioned at the top of the standings, with the 57-33 Monarchs defeating the 40-27 Stars and the 41-29 Giants. Foster's club, in fact, finished a full six games behind pennant-winning Kansas City. He was angered when reports circulated that some of the American Giants had sent journalists a letter charging they had failed to win because of inadequate salaries. Countering, Foster revealed player contracts that set payments starting at $175 monthly; he also disclosed that for several years he had split pre- and postseason gate receipts with players. On a happier note, Foster, in his official capacity as the western blackball president, declared, "It is a pleasure to me to see the Kansas City Monarchs win the pennant in our league this year, despite the fact that my club finished behind; this in itself proves the sterling quality and ability of the club from the west."[26]

The 1924 season witnessed the revamped American Giants playing better ball; they finished at 49-24, which still left them four full games behind the Kansas City Monarchs, who ended at 55-22. The 37-27 Detroit Stars remained the other elite team, and the St. Louis Stars, with a 40-36 mark, also finished above .500. The Birmingham Black Barons came in fifth, ahead of another newly added ball club, the Memphis Red Sox, who replaced the Indianapolis ABCs. The Cuban Stars and the Cleveland Browns, also a rookie franchise, finished at the bottom of the pack.

"The John McGraw of Colored baseball," the "master mind of baseball," the "great strategist and peer of baseball generals" strove to remake his pitching staff, which had let him down in 1923. George Harney went 9-2; Tom Williams, 9-4; and Luis Padron, 10-5, but alcoholism and age continued to sap the once-unmatched skills of Richard Whitworth. Ed Rile began the season with the American Giants but concluded it with the Homestead Grays. The Giants staff was no match, ultimately, for the Monarch hurlers, including 16-5 Bullet Wilbur Rogan, 10-8 Bill Drake, and 4-0 José Méndez. The still-light-hitting American Giants were headed once again by Cristobal Torriente, who batted .331 and led the league in doubles.[27]

The campaign proved a mixed blessing for Foster in other ways. Once more, bitter criticism came his way, with the *Kansas City Call* urging his withdrawal from the league that he had founded. Foster "may be the best man available to head the Negro National Baseball League, but it's only because of his wide acquaintanceship in the baseball world, and not because of his sportsmanship." The *Call* reminded its readers that it had long contended he "was not the proper person to head the League," because he "was for the American Giants, first, last and always." Further, Foster manipulated umpires and allowed "his gang of roughnecks" free rein. His determination to win at any cost, the paper contended, "is killing the organization which he heads."[28]

Near the end of the regular season, Foster experienced a happier moment when Edward Bolden of the Eastern Colored League agreed to a kind of peace pact. Judge Kenesaw Mountain Landis, commissioner of major league baseball, was slated to preside over the drafting of a document that would resolve player, contractual, and interleague disputes. At the same time, a long-sought goal of Foster's was reached: there was to be a world championship match between the winners of the Negro National League and the Eastern Colored League. Dave Malarcher later recalled, "He was very proud to have the responsibility and privilege and the honor, as president of the league, with Judge Hueston, Commissioner, to be planning this big series. This really put him in the category of Ban Johnson and Judge Landis. He was very proud of the place which he occupied, and the standard to which he had brought baseball" in a relatively short time. In a controversial move, however, Foster scheduled the final three games for Schorling Park.[29]

The championship between the Monarchs and the Hilldale Daisies was not decided until the tenth contest because each team previously had won four games, and one game ended in a tie. Foster spun a story that the Monarchs' playing manager Méndez, now thirty-seven years old and lacking the explosive fastball that had made him a legend in his Cuban homeland, had told him, "I am going to pitch today." Foster responded, "For the first time during the series you are doing the thing I think best." Méndez then asked, "Do you think I will win?" The American Giant boss replied, "I would rather see you lose it than anyone else win it." To which the Cuban answered, "All right. I will pitch." The closely fought championship game was won by the Monarchs, with Méndez hurling a brilliant three-hit shutout. Supposedly, Foster signaled pitches to Méndez throughout the game.[30]

The following year proved more trying still, both on and off the playing field. The league's three-year experiment in hiring black umpires ceased. In an effort to sustain season-long interest, the Negro National League moguls agreed to split the campaign into two fifty-game schedules. The Kansas City Monarchs, with a 31-9 record, swept to the first-half title, defeating the St. Louis Stars by two and a half games. In third place were the 26-20 Detroit Stars, and the 26-22 American Giants ended up in the first division, nine games behind the Monarchs. The season's second half began more auspiciously for the Giants, who took the early lead before faltering, to end up at 28-18, eight games behind the 38-12 St. Louis Stars. The Monarchs were second at 31-11, and the Detroit Stars concluded with a 27-20 record. Kansas City went on to defeat St. Louis four games to three to advance to the championship series against the Eastern Colored League titlist Hilldale. In that rematch, the Daisies prevailed, to the chagrin of league president Foster.[31]

The "chief" continued to dismantle his once-perennial powerhouse. Before the season even began, Ed Rile was transferred to Indianapolis, and unconditional releases were issued to several players, including Jimmie Lyons, Leroy Grant—who had temporarily rejoined the American Giants—pitcher Lewis William Wolfolk, Tom Williams, pitcher Jack Marshall, George "Tubby" Dixon, reserve outfielder W. P. Evans, and Richard Whitworth. Added to the roster were rightfielder Leroy R. Taylor and pitchers Bill McCall, Harold Ross, and Frank Stevens.[32]

The season's most dramatic moment occurred before it officially began when, on May 26, Rube Foster was nearly asphyxiated by a gas leak in his rooming house in Indianapolis around six in the morning as he reportedly attempted to bathe. Some four hours later, a group of Chicago players, who had not seen their manager that morning at the ballpark, went to his room to check on him. When no response was forthcoming, they rammed the door open only to discover no one inside, just Foster's clothes laid out. Heading for the bathroom, they detected the smell of gas. Led by captain Bingo DeMoss, the players battered their way into the room, where Foster lay unconscious against the gas heater. His left arm had been scorched by the still-lighted heater. Rushed by ambulance to Batiste Hospital, Foster regained consciousness in the late afternoon. DeMoss had contacted Mrs. Foster, who heeded his entreaty that "if she wanted to see her husband alive to come at once." The following day, the Fosters departed for Chicago. Interviewed by reporters for the *Chicago Defender,* Foster recalled only having drawn water for his bath. Rumors of his death had to be dispelled.[33]

Foster never fully recovered from that troubling incident; it is possible that carbon monoxide poisoning induced by the gas leak resulted in brain damage. The year ahead would be equally disturbing as his mental faculties began, or perhaps continued, to deteriorate. The proximity of the Indianapolis injury to the dementia that soon overcame him leads one to wonder if the earlier event were accidental. The pressures on Foster, always considerable, had mounted in the past few years. He had attempted to keep his own team at the top rung of the black baseball world while simultaneously serving as president and secretary of a fledgling league. The league, a near-lifelong dream of his, appeared increasingly troubled as the midpoint of the 1920s arrived. At the same time, his American Giants, for the first time, were not the inevitable favorites for the title of the premier black baseball squad, something to which Foster was largely unaccustomed. When his accident occurred, the Giants were an uncharacteristic 12-15, perched just one position from the bottom of the league standings. For more than two decades, as player, manager, and administrator, he had helped to put his team at the apex of the segregated game in which black players were compelled to participate. All the while, he had believed that racial barriers would eventually be overcome, despite all evidence to the contrary. By the mid-twenties, it was increasingly clear that an early end to Jim Crow baseball was not in the offing.[34]

At this stage, Foster's behavior was increasingly erratic. His players initially attributed its inappropriateness to overwork, but eventually, it was evident that something serious was unfolding. On the playing field, Foster had even begun delivering his signals openly, letting opponents know what he was calling for. Even so, the American Giants engineered something of a comeback in closing out the season.[35]

The year 1926 was the unhappiest period yet for Rube Foster. As it opened, reports were that he was determined to reshape his team still more. Bingo DeMoss moved over to Indianapolis to become a player-manager; his spot as team captain was assumed by Dave Malarcher. Shortstop Bobby Williams joined DeMoss in Indianapolis. A largely new Giants lineup featured an infield of first baseman William Ware, second sacker Malarcher, shortstop Charlie Williams, and third baseman John G. Shackleford. Jim Brown and John Hines were the top backstops. The outfield was made up of Jelly Gardner, James "Sandy" Thompson, and Stanford "Jambo" Jackson. Giants pitchers included Rube Curry, George Harney, Webster McDonald, Willie Ernest Powell, and Robert Poindexter. Willie Foster, Rube's younger half brother, joined the team after the conclusion of his school year.[36]

The American Giants floundered during the first half of the season, ending up in third place, with a 28-16 mark, which placed them just ahead of the St. Louis Stars and the Indianapolis ABCs. The Detroit Stars were in second place, and the Kansas City Monarchs, boasting a 35-12 record, were comfortably in first. On June 19, the *Chicago Defender*, sensing that something was amiss with the hometown favorites, asked, "What's wrong with the American Giants?" then added, "[S]omething is radically wrong." It was true that Foster "has been sick and is sick," but even that did not fully explain the Giants' plight.[37]

Illness had indeed afflicted Rube Foster, soon resulting in his departure as both Negro National League president and the American Giants' manager. Notwithstanding the previous year's traumas, he had maintained a typically grueling pace: at his office around 8:30 in the morning, often not departing before midnight. Now, Foster was talking with his friends Ban Johnson, the American League boss, and John McGraw, the New York Giant skipper, at the Chicago Beach Hotel regarding a plan for the American Giants to play big league teams that visited the Windy City to compete against the White Sox or Cubs but had off-days. Commissioner Landis, however, evidently nixed the notion, which must have been a crushing blow to Foster, whose physical and emotional makeup was far more precarious than usual.[38]

Foster's behavior, in the meantime, began to appear still more erratic. Tales were later spun about his antics—which included an increasing number of memory lapses—during this period. Wee Willie Powell, an American Giants pitcher, recalled seeing Foster running up and down the street in front of his house on Michigan Avenue chasing nonexistent fly balls. While driving his roadster, Foster plowed into a female pedestrian. Shortstop Bobby Williams remembered how Foster bolted himself in his office bathroom and refused to leave until someone entered through the window and drew him out. Outfielder-infielder George Sweatt told of an occasion when he was walking home with Foster after a game and the manager began running for no apparent reason. Sweatt, who lived in an apartment above the Fosters, reflected, "The night he went crazy—1926—we were sitting upstairs and his wife hollered, 'Oh no, don't do that!' So I ran down, knocked on the door, and called out, 'Mrs. Foster, is there anything wrong?' She said, 'There's something wrong with Rube, he's just going crazy down here. I'm going to have to call the law.'" Several men were required to subdue Foster. Sarah Foster spoke of her husband's hearing voices that he was going to be called on to pitch in organized baseball's World Series. Then, after he had destroyed furniture in their home, she had asked the police to restrain him. A short time later, Foster, wielding an ice pick, went after a friend; that episode resulted in his arrest. Compelled to appear in Judge Irving L. Weaver's "Psychopathic Court," Foster was deemed insane and subsequently assigned to the Kankakee Asylum. The *Pittsburgh Courier* referred to the passing from the scene of "the once Rock of Gibraltar of colored baseball."[39]

Rube's son, Earl, spoke later of his father's travails. "What his trouble was I don't know, but he was off and he never did get back to normal. It could have been a borderline case. He wasn't dangerous or anything like that, but he couldn't be at home. Sometimes he'd recognize you and sometimes he wouldn't." The family would naturally suffer because of Foster's condition and also because of the lack of a written contract with American Giants' owner John M. Schorling. After Foster's confinement, his family received no financial compensation from the team he had painstakingly built into a black baseball powerhouse.[40]

Ironically, the second half of 1926 proved to be remarkably successful for the American Giants, now under the guidance of Dave Malarcher, who employed the Foster system. The Giants, with an outstanding 29-7 record, beat out Kansas City by four games and St. Louis was another two and a half games back. Only six teams completed the season, with both the Dayton Marcos and the Cleveland Elites, who had won a mere twelve of seventy-four games, falling by the wayside. In a bitterly fought best-of-nine series, the American Giants defeated the Monarchs in the deciding contest. Pitted against the Eastern Colored League champion, the Bacharach Giants, Chicago captured the "colored world's championship." Despite allowing ten hits, Willie Foster, who had been schooled in the art of pitching by Rube, won the finale 1-0.[41]

Prior to the start of the 1927 season, the Negro National League proclaimed Rube Foster and C. I. Taylor days. In announcing the days, the *Pittsburgh Courier* declared that Taylor "was one of the most important figures in baseball and . . . helped to foster the formation of this league." Foster was adjudged "no doubt . . . the greatest individual figure in baseball." That year, the American Giants took the first-half championship; the Birmingham Black Barons, the second half's. Chicago then swept four straight from the Black Barons and went on, once again, to beat Bacharach in the title series. In 1928, the St. Louis Stars and the Chicago American Giants were declared the respective winners of the two halves of the league's season. St. Louis captured the Negro National League championship, winning the deciding contest 9-2 by pounding Willie Foster; Malarcher resigned as manager, to be replaced by Jim Brown.

Malarcher, despite the American Giants' successes on the playing field, was appalled by management changes that the team had undergone. John Schorling had been compelled to sell the team that spring to a group of businessmen, headed by William E. Trimble, who failed, in contrast to Rube Foster, to maintain Chicago as "the hub of the league." Putting the team on the road more and more, Trimble, and later Robert A. Cole, forced their ballplayers to travel in buses, ride all night long, and play ball day after day inadequately fed and insufficiently rested. The grinding pace grew even more onerous after Cole took control of the Giants' operations during Malarcher's second tenure as team manager in the early thirties.[42]

No "colored world series" was played in 1928, for the eastern league had disbanded. The next year, the Kansas City Monarchs took both halves of the season, thus doing away with the need for a playoff. The American Giants' season was literally a tale of two halves; their 22-29 and 26-9 segments resulted in fifth- and second-place finishes, respectively. The next year, in 1929, St. Louis defeated Detroit in the playoff series. By that point, Willie Foster had taken over the reins as Chicago's manager, supplanting Brown. Again, the American Giants' season was curiously divided; its 24-39 and 19-12 totals garnered seventh- and third-place finishes.[43]

By the end of the decade, player raids, declining attendance figures, and soaring transportation costs prevented interleague title contests. Jim "Candy" Taylor, the Memphis Red Sox manager, pointed to another problem for black baseball: "the players don't care enough for the game to stay in condition." To Taylor, they appeared interested only when payday rolled around. Others designated the "rowdyism" that seemed increasingly evident. On April 15, 1930, Negro National League president W. C. Hueston declared that effective within two months, any player who jumped to another ball club would be banished from the black brand of "organized baseball." Nevertheless, clearly lacking was a firm hand at the helm of the black baseball circuit. Absent Rube Foster, the Negro National League seemed rudderless.[44]

THIRTEEN

Rube Foster's Legacy

Shortly after his confinement to the Kankakee sanitarium, Rube Foster's legacy began to be more fully considered by those familiar with the history of black baseball. In his column for the *Pittsburgh Courier*, W. Rollo Wilson, who later served as the commissioner of the Negro National League, spent considerable time in the early months of 1927 wrestling with the question of who the finest black ballplayer had been. He began by asking, "Who was the greatest colored baseball player of all time?" Respondents offered several candidates, among them, Foster. Almost all of the other athletes mentioned had played for Foster at various points in their careers. They included Bill Monroe, the great infielder with the Philadelphia Giants and Chicago American Giants; shortstop John Henry Lloyd, who appeared on the diamond with Foster for the legendary 1910 Leland Giants and later served under him on the American Giants; and Smokey Joe Williams, who had pitched for Foster's outstanding 1914 team. Also, José Méndez, the stellar Cuban pitcher who performed as a light-hitting shortstop for Foster's 1918 championship team; outfielder Oscar Charleston, who was on his 1919 squad; and infielder John Beckwith, who starred for Foster's 1922 Negro National League titlist. Of the group, only Kansas City pitching ace Bullet Joe Rogan and catcher Bizz Mackey had not played for Foster.[1]

Chappie Johnson, who had caught Foster while with the Cuban X-Giants, the Philadelphia Giants, and the Leland Giants, selected his own "All Time team" for Rollo Wilson. Johnson put Mackey, Bruce Petway, and Tubby Dixon—the latter two, longtime catchers for Foster—behind the plate; he placed on the mound George Wilson, a star with the old Page Fence Giants; Nip Winters, long with the Hilldale Daisies; Phil Cockrell, also with Hilldale; Rats Henderson of the Bacharach Giants;

Williams; Rogan; and Foster. The infield was made up of Ray Wilson, who had played with the Cuban X-Giants; Lloyd; the Bacharach Giants' Dick Lundy; and Ollie Marcelle, also of the Bacharach Giants, with Beckwith as the utility man. The outfield featured Pete Hill, Charleston, Jess Barber, and Cristobal Torriente; Hill, Barber, and Torriente each had spent several years on Foster's ball clubs. Such a squad, Johnson chortled, "could clean up the National league, the American league."[2]

John Henry Lloyd on April 2 picked his own team, which included catchers Mackey and Petway, and pitchers Danny McClellan, Dave Brown, Foster, Connie Rector, and Cockrell. The others players selected were first baseman Leroy Grant, second baseman Bingo DeMoss, shortstop Dobie Moore, third sacker Judy Johnson, and outfielders Chaney White, Jelly Gardner, and Charleston. All except Rector, who had played in the Eastern Colored League; Cockrell; the Kansas City Monarchs' Dobie Moore; and Hilldale's Johnson, had played either alongside or for Foster. A week later, Lloyd added the names of Joe Rogan and Nate Harris, the former infielder with the Leland Giants and the Philadelphia Giants.[3]

Another friend of columnist Wilson's, Doc Lambert, chose Mackey and Petway as his catchers, and Rogan, Cockrell, longtime American Giants ace Frank Wickware, Foster, and Nip Winters as his moundsmen. His infielders were Grant, DeMoss, Lloyd, and Marcelle. In the outfield, he called for Hill, Barber, Charleston, and Gardner.[4]

All three men, Wilson noted, had picked Mackey, Petway, Foster, Cockrell, and Charleston. "And I am safe in saying that 99 out of 100 would pick John Henry Lloyd," he informed his readers.[5]

Yet another all-star squad was selected by Ben Taylor, who put Petway and Mackey behind the plate. And for his pitchers, John Taylor, who hurled for Foster in 1913; Dick Redding, an American Giants pitcher during the 1917 and 1918 championship campaigns; Williams; John Donaldson of the All Nations and the Monarchs; and Foster. Ben Taylor's infielders were Grant; Home Run Johnson, a teammate of Foster's on the Cuban X-Giants, the Philadelphia Giants, and the Leland Giants; Lloyd; and Judy Johnson. His outfielders were Hill, Charleston, and Rap Dixon of the Harrisburg Giants; his utility man was Beckwith; and Foster was his manager.[6]

William Dismukes came up with another list, choosing catcher Petway, along with pitchers Foster, Williams, Redding, and Donaldson. His infielders were Taylor, Home Run Johnson, Lloyd, and Candy Jim Taylor, who played for Foster on the Leland Giants and the Chicago American Giants. His outfielders were the New York Lincoln Giants' Spottswood Poles, Hill, and Mike Moore, formerly of the Cuban X-Giants, the Philadelphia Giants, and the Leland Giants.[7]

In the December 29, 1928, issue of the *Pittsburgh Courier*, Dismukes more fully explored two "immortals of Negro baseball": Rube Foster and C. I. Taylor. From the time Foster left the East Coast for Chicago in 1907, Dismukes declared, he "was the recognized czar of the West." By the mid-1910s, his title was challenged by Taylor of the Indianapolis ABCs. Foster, with the good fortune of financial backing, "could lure star players from any club he wished," promising and delivering guaranteed salaries. Taylor, on the other hand, was forced "to pick up anybody who said he could play baseball." Foster ran a top-down operation, issuing "orders . . . as rigid as those of the United States Army." Dismukes saw him as a master psychologist, who believed that competition would be daunted by his ball club's superiority and, inevitably, fold in the clutch. As a tactician, the man excelled, while becoming "the greatest individual drawing card in Negro baseball."[8]

In its twenty-fifth anniversary edition, the *Chicago Defender*, on May 3, 1930, ran a photograph of Rube Foster entitled "Greatest." Attired in the 1909 uniform of the Leland Giants, Foster was shown preparing to pitch. The caption read, in part,

> He was the greatest pitcher our Race has ever known. He ranked with Cy Young, Christy Mathewson, Joe McGinnity, and other greats. He was a mastermind of baseball and was ranked by the daily newspapermen as one of the three greatest managers of the country. The other two were John McGraw of the New York Nationals and Connie Mack of the world champion Philadelphia American Leaguers. Foster was also the brains and the founder of the Negro National Baseball League, and it was due to his long hours and hard work plus the worry of running the league that caused him to lose his health.[9]

Longtime sportswriter for the *Defender* Frank A. Young produced "The Master Mind of Baseball," an ode that appeared in the November 1, 1930, issue of *Abbott's Monthly*. One baseball fan in Chicago, on hearing that Foster had been taken ill, cried, "After him, they ain't no more."

Agreeing with that assessment, Young put Foster, McGraw, and Mack "in a class by themselves." As for Foster, "he knew the national pastime, how to play it, how to make his men play it, and every technicality of the game." When asked about Foster, Joe Williams had recently declared, "Rube was the greatest pitcher and manager we ever had." Foster's renown was immense, said Young: "No other living human, unless perhaps it would be Babe Ruth, has been able to have devoted to him the amount of daily newspaper space that was once given Rube Foster."[10]

Foster's health had been lost, Young reflected, "in an effort to put baseball, as played by our own men, on the same plane as that of the major leagues." That occurred, unfortunately, precisely "when his services were most needed." Young worried that "the years of toil and care that Foster put in, burning the midnight oil that there might be a league, are about to become wasted"; sadly enough, little recognition was forthcoming from the organization he had birthed and nurtured. Although Foster had given "his time, money and health for the upbuilding of the national game among his own people," no Negro League leader had offered benefit games on his behalf.[11]

Young concluded his piece with the following observation: "Rube Foster's name is written in baseball's history so deep that the years cannot erase it. The greatest tribute to the master mind of baseball is what the bleacher fan said: 'After him, they ain't no more.'"[12]

On Tuesday, December 9, 1930, at nine o'clock in the evening, Rube Foster died in the Kankakee sanitarium where, for more than four years, he had been institutionalized. The *Chicago Defender*'s headline exclaimed, "Baseball's Most Colorful Figure Is Called 'Out.'" The paper lyrically declared, "Andrew 'Rube' Foster, the master mind of baseball, perhaps the most colorful figure the game has ever known, was called out by Umpire Father Time" following a lengthy struggle to overcome illness.

> Rube Foster's name is not only written in the baseball history of his Race, but he is known wherever baseball was played between 1900 and today. He knew more big league players and owners than any other individual, and knew perhaps more newspaper men than any of the present-day players with the possible exception of Babe Ruth, who is the only man to have more space devoted to him in the daily newspapers than Mr. Foster. . . . His loss is more than a loss to baseball—it is a loss to mankind.[13]

All day Friday and Saturday, and from ten o'clock in the morning until two in the afternoon on Sunday, Foster's body lay in state at the Washington funeral parlor, located at 47th and St. Lawrence Avenue in Chicago. Thousands came to pay homage to black baseball's greatest figure, one of the most prominent African Americans of his generation. Funeral services, attended by three thousand mourners, were conducted at three o'clock on Sunday afternoon at St. Mark's M. E. Church, located at 50th and Wabash Avenue; a like number stood outside, despite the snow and rain, unable to obtain admission. The white-robed choir sang "Rock of Ages," and tears flowed freely both in the church and outside. The Reverend John B. Redmond presided, and "the North Star lodge no. 1 of Masons and the Stranger lodge No. 26 Knights of Pythias" participated. Dr. Redmond recalled the moment on Sunday morning, November 9, 1924, when he had asked who sought to be converted as the choir sang out, "What a Friend We Have in Jesus." Rube Foster had come down the church aisle, cupped his hand in the minister's and affirmed, "I have reached first base and I want your help and God's help to reach home plate." Now, Redmond declared, "Mr. Foster's loyalty to the church and to his fellow man, and his squareness all ranked far above his ability as a baseball player and manager second to none in the country."[14]

The burial took place the next day at Lincoln Cemetery as church bells tolled the noon hour. Foster was survived by his widow, Sarah; his twenty-year-old son, Earl Mack, who was attending Wilberforce University; two sisters, Geneva T. Foster, a teacher in Sapulpa, Oklahoma, and Mrs. Gertrude Edwards, who lived in Santa Monica, California; and his half brother Will, then the pitcher-manager of the Chicago American Giants. Foster was buried amidst flowers, including "a huge baseball made up of small white chrysanthemums with roses for the seams and weighing over 200 pounds"; that all-too-appropriate wreath had been delivered by Negro National League officials. "A green baseball diamond with white carnations for the paths between the bases, with Mr. Foster's initials, A.R.F., in the center of the diamond," had been provided by the American Giants Boosters Association. Placed above that great floral display "were two crossed bats of white with a baseball, all flowers in between." The Foster family contributed "a huge white heart-shaped design with the words 'Our heart.'"[15]

Foster, the *New York Amsterdam News* asserted, had "done more to develop and promote professional baseball among Negroes than anyone else." The *Pittsburgh Courier* carried a tribute to blackball's "diamond magnate" who had become "a martyr to the game he tried to put on the same plane as that of the major leagues." Foster's life "was a direct slap at the 'inferiority complex' angle so often assumed by Negroes." Believing that semiprofessional baseball was nearing an end, Foster had helped to found the Negro National League and served "as its active, militant, fighting head." The work on behalf of the league, the *Courier* acknowledged, proved costly to him personally.

His efforts to place teams in various towns cost him plenty of money but his Utopian dream of a smooth-working league kept him working day and night. But failing health and the strain of trying to put his league over were too much even for that fine physique which had made him one of the greatest pitchers, black or white, ever to lace a pair of spikes on a foot.

The brain, whose cunning on the diamond had given him a place with Connie Mack and John McGraw as one of the "master minds" of the game, failed to withstand the pressure of constant opposition. His death can be directly attributed to his interest in baseball.

And in death, as in life, "Rube" Foster stands out as the most commanding figure baseball had ever known.[16]

Shortly following Foster's death, Al Monroe, who asserted that he had battled with Foster before becoming a close friend, discussed the plight of black baseball as the Negro National League ground to a halt. Foster was sorely missed; he was "the one man who might have saved a situation that threatened during his reign and arose to alarming proportions immediately after his passing from the scene." Monroe continued, "Frankly, I shall always feel that Rube's ability to thwart baseball's threatening skies was outstanding among the things which made him famous in the game's development." Foster "was a directing genius; an organizer par excellence," but "was not without his faults." As president of the Negro National League, he drew on the deposits owners placed with the league office and, as booking agent, always took 10 percent of the gate. But he would open his wallet, Monroe granted, when needs arose and not worry about repayment. And Foster was generous in advising managers as to which pitchers to use and when. Star hurlers were to be saved, for instance, for large Sunday crowds, not placed on the mound before sparse Saturday offerings. More striking, though, "baseball's Mussolini" could be ruthless, as when he "crushed" Tenny Blount, owner of the Detroit Stars, "financially and spiritually" for having contested his rule. In the end, according to Monroe, Foster did not leave behind "a real league" but "an outfit constructed for personal gain, however beneficial during its run."[17]

The St. Louis Stars were proclaimed winners of both halves of the Negro National League's 1931 season. The Chicago American Giants, the Detroit Stars, and the Indianapolis ABCs were the only other original teams still belonging to the now-six-team circuit. The Cleveland Cubs and Louisville White Sox were the latest entries. But following that campaign, the league closed shop. It reopened in 1933, with the Cole's American Giants claiming the pennant, but league president Gus Greenlee awarded the title to his own team, the Pittsburgh Crawfords. In 1937, the Negro American League emerged, and the two leagues remained in operation through 1948. The American Giants, who had departed from the Negro National League in 1936, joined the rival organization the following year. After that league collapsed in 1950, black baseball's most storied franchise was taken over by Abe Saperstein but soon ended operations altogether. Blackball was unable to long survive, even in the manner it had previously, once the doors to organized baseball opened.

The Great Depression that wreaked economic havoc had helped to cripple and fatally wound the original version of the Negro National League. That experiment in organized black baseball suffered at least as mightily from the lack of vision and administrative acumen once provided by its founder and dominant architect, Rube Foster. Throughout that economically troubled era, black baseball players competed in exhibition contests against major leaguers. Leadership was offered by the Pittsburgh Crawfords' Gus Greenlee and the Homestead Grays' Cum Posey. But no single figure came close to duplicating what Foster had accomplished: once blackball's greatest player, he then became its most brilliant manager, before helping to create and make viable an entire baseball league.

Foster, moreover, helped to lay a bridge between the loosely played and erratically scheduled blackball game of the early twentieth century and the organized brand of athletic competition initiated by the Negro National League. With the exception of the 1932 campaign, blackball magnates were able to support at least one league of their own until Jim Crow barriers in organized baseball were shattered. In the meantime, legendary black players demonstrated their ability to compete with even the most skilled major leaguers. Such a reality, coupled with the challenge to racial stereotypes unfolding during the 1930s and 1940s, allowed for the discarding of the rigid segregation that had precluded Rube Foster, John Henry Lloyd, Oscar Charleston, Joe Williams, and other black superstars from entering baseball's loftiest ranks. Their sheer brilliance on the playing field and the dogged determination of Foster and others off it, however, eventually could not be ignored.

Still, with the passage of time, the legend of Rube Foster appeared to dim. Black baseball veterans, particularly the older ones, could not forget him, of course. Others, especially those associated with organized baseball, hardly seemed to acknowledge the savior of the national game's blackened version and its ballplayers. On occasion, some hearkened back to black baseball's greatest figure, while bemoaning how many others failed to do so. In 1939, Jewel Ens, a coach with the Pittsburgh Pirates, was heard to say, "Foster was a smart, cagey pitcher. He was one of the greatest pitchers I have ever seen, and I've been in baseball almost 25 years. Foster pitched with his brains as well as his arm. He never did the wrong thing. Rube Foster would have been a sensation in the big leagues." Although Ens lauded Satchel Paige, he deemed Foster "the cream of Negro pitchers." Honus Wagner, the former great shortstop who was also coaching for the Pirates, agreed: "Rube Foster was one of the greatest pitchers of all time. He was the smartest pitcher I have ever seen in all my years of baseball." When asked which blackballers were the best, Pirate manager Pie Traynor replied, "I'd name Paige, Grant, 'Cool Papa' Bell, Biz Mackey, Moore, . . . Rogan, Josh Gibson, Mules Suttles and Rube Foster as ball players who could have made the major leagues had they been given a chance."[18]

That same year, Edwin Bancroft Henderson, in *The Negro in Sports,* also extolled Foster's virtues. He had been "the most colorful of Negro ball players, promoters and managers." He had established a pitching record and achieved fame "that will remain as long as baseball is of interest to Negro players." Further, along with C. I. Taylor, "he was the founder of organized professional ball." In addition, Foster "holds high as a strategist, and measures with Connie Mack and McGraw as a manipulator of inside baseball."[19]

In April 1952, the *Pittsburgh Courier* highlighted some of black baseball's most noteworthy participants. Thirty-one individuals, including former blackball stars, owners, managers, sportswriters, and officials, devised an "all-time, All-American baseball" team from outside the ranks of the major and minor leagues. Selected as first baseman was Buck Leonard, whose vote total was double that of Ben Taylor. Stationed at second base was Jackie Robinson, by now a star with the Brooklyn Dodgers; Robinson beat out Foster's old infielder, Bingo DeMoss. John Henry Lloyd was the shortstop, having outranked Willie Wells, Dicky Lundy, and Dobie Moore. The third sacker was Oliver Marcelle, who was picked ahead of Judy Johnson and Ray Dandridge. The left fielder was Monte Irvin, who had just appeared in the 1951 World Series with the New York Giants; Pete Hill was named to the second squad. In center field, the voters chose Oscar Charleston, who more than doubled Cool Papa Bell's vote total. In right, Cristobal Torriente—who was referred to as "Rube Foster's offensive power"—nipped Charles "Cheno" Smith by one lone vote. Two catchers were selected—Josh Gibson and Bizz Mackey—and Roy Campanella and Bruce Petway made the second team. The pitchers were Smokey Joe Williams, Paige, Bullet Rogan, John Donaldson, and Willie Foster; the last three edged out Dave Brown, Cannonball Dick Redding, Nip Winters, Dizzy Dismukes, and Don Newcombe. On a third tier were "the inimitable 'Rube' Foster," Phil Cockrell, Walter Ball, and Frank Wickware, among others; the only surprise was that Foster was not placed on a loftier level. Martin Dihigo was a utility infielder and outfielder; Sam Bankhead was picked as a utility infielder; John Beckwith and Newt Allen were the second team utility infielders; and Clint Thomas was the backup utility outfielder. The manager was Rube Foster, and the coaches were Dismukes and Danny McClellan; the second team included manager Cum Posey, along with coaches C. I. Taylor and Dave Malarcher.[20]

In 1953, A. S. "Doc" Young published *Great Negro Baseball Stars,* which included an analysis of Rube Foster: "first a great pitcher, next a superb manager, and finally an outstanding administrator." Said

Young, "[I]t was he who lost the most by the Jim Crow bar, for it was he who had the most to offer." Foster, who "might have become a great major league hurler, a manager of the stature of McGraw, and an administrator of Johnson's standing," died without having accomplished any of those feats.[21]

In August 1957, Young's "Baseball's Negro Pioneer" appeared in *Hue* magazine. Pointing to the likes of John Henry Lloyd, Oscar Charleston, and Josh Gibson, old-timers declared them superior to Jackie Robinson, Willie Mays, and Roy Campanella. The early-twentieth-century stars, the sportswriter wrote, were depicted "more like a collection of superstars than professional ballplayers." Young admitted that drawing generational comparisons was largely a subjective determination; however, "in the case of Andrew (Rube) Foster," "the old-timers hold an unbeatable ace. When they mention his name, automatically they win any man-for-man baseball debate. . . . Rube still towers over the field of past and present Negro baseball personalities as a giant Sequoia dwarfs a pine."[22]

Young considered Foster "a gate attraction . . . comparable to the latter-day Satchel Paige or Bob Feller." "As a manager, Foster belonged to the McGraw school of wanna-win guys. He was smart and imaginative like Casey Stengel, Leo Durocher, and Joe McCarthy. He learned from the major leagues and they learned from him." He dealt with men like McGraw, Charles Comiskey, and Ban Johnson, as an equal. Many experts, Young wrote, believed that "Rube Foster paid the highest price for being a Negro during baseball's era of intolerance because he had the most to offer. As they have said of other old-time Negro stars, he was born too soon."[23]

FOURTEEN

The Drive to Cooperstown

On May 18, 1968, the *New Courier* discussed organized baseball's repeated failures to acknowledge Rube Foster's contributions to the game. Major league baseball, the paper contended, owed its continued existence to "the imaginative Foster," who "kept 300 Negro players in uniform." Foster "made it possible for the majors to tap a prime source of recruitment." Baseball's Hall of Fame "would be more complete, with Foster's features preserved and polished in a deserved niche in Cooperstown."[1]

In 1968 and 1969, Robert Peterson conducted a series of interviews with Dave Malarcher, in which Foster's old ballplayer and successor as the American Giants' manager persuasively sang Foster's praises. Malarcher, a student of the game for upwards of a half century, believed that "Rube Foster's system of organization, training, management, and directing a baseball team on the field was superior to any system or management ever employed in the major leagues." Foster "was simply above and beyond everybody else in the business of playing and managing and promoting the game." In the end, Foster's American Giants had "won more ball games, traveled more miles, played against a greater number of teams of all kinds, and standards, in a greater number of places throughout the United States, Cuba and Canada than any other baseball team in history."[2]

Peterson's groundbreaking work, *Only the Ball Was White: A History of Legendary Black Players and All-Black Professional Teams,* appeared in 1970 and contained the chapter "Rube from Texas." It opened with the following analysis:

> If the talents of Christy Mathewson, John McGraw, Ban Johnson, and Judge Kenesaw Mountain Landis were combined in a single body, and that

body were enveloped in a black skin, the result would have to be named Andrew (Rube) Foster. As an outstanding pitcher, a colorful and shrewd field manager, and the founder and stern administrator of the first viable Negro League, Foster was the most impressive figure in black baseball history. From about 1911 until 1926, he stood astride Negro baseball in the Midwest with unchallenged power, a friend of major-league leaders, and the best known black man in Chicago. Rube Foster was an unlettered genius who combined generosity and sternness, the superb skills of a dedicated athlete and an unbounded belief in the future of the black baseball player. His life was baseball. Had he chosen otherwise, baseball would have been the poorer.[3]

Starting in 1971 with Satchel Paige's selection by the specially devised committee on Negro leagues, black baseball luminaries began to be ushered into the Hall of Fame. Shortly after Paige's induction, *Black Sports,* which noted that Josh Gibson would likely soon be added to the pantheon, questioned why there was so little mention of Rube Foster. The magazine found this inexplicable.

> Very few people sing the praises of Andrew "Rube" Foster, the man who, for a long period of time, was Negro baseball. As a star pitcher, an outstanding and knowledgeable field manager, and as the founder and top executive of the Negro National League, Rube Foster, many will argue, was *the* outstanding individual in Negro baseball. For approximately two decades, Andrew "Rube" Foster was the power that propelled Negro baseball, and very little about it could move without his say. He was easily the most well known and most famous Black sportsman of his time.[4]

In early 1973, after it was announced that the next inductee into the Hall of Fame who had starred in Jim Crow baseball would be Monte Irvin, A. S. "Doc" Young seconded the notion that Foster's admission to the Hall should be forthcoming. Furthermore, Young argued that Foster should have been the first blackball veteran so honored, or at the very least, he should have been allowed in alongside Paige. Because the Negro Leagues committee failed to select Foster, Young called for disbanding the project as "there is no point in dragging 'this thing' out to infinity." When Cool Papa Bell stood ready to become only the fifth Negro League's honoree the following year, Young angrily protested. "After Cool Papa is inducted, this program should be ended, unless a comprehensive committee is formed, detailed research is done, and then in one final ceremony, the 20 to 25 deserving people who so far have been ignored are inducted in one mass ceremony." Then, "I never dreamed that this project would be dragged out indefinitely and that, each year, one or two blacks would be rehashed. At best, these awards fall within the range of left-handed compliments."[5]

Young found it inconceivable that the Negro Leagues Committee had "persistently failed to pay proper tribute to the man who did more for Negro league baseball than anyone else." The columnist listed his candidate's unmatched credentials:

> Rube Foster was, first, a fine pitcher who established his credentials against black hitters in regular-season games and exhibitions and against white hitters in exhibitions.
>
> Rube Foster was, second, an outstanding manager.
>
> Rube Foster was, third, an outstanding team operator and baseball promoter. . . .
>
> Rube Foster was, fourth, an almost incredible figure as the leader, backbone, czar, commissioner—call him what you will—of a flourishing, perhaps the most prosperous of all time, Negro league.[6]

John Hall of the *Los Angeles Times* agreed with Young's assessment. "To perpetuate and glorify, in bits and dribbles, one of the great American tragedies—the time spanning the first 47 years of this century when blacks weren't allowed in the major leagues—is as disgraceful as the original injustice." As for Young, he complained, "I can see that some people in organized baseball may hold the misconception that the plan brings baseball good publicity. But it is far from what it should be. It's a farce."

> As I have pointed out many times, the first man the committee should have honored is the late Andrew (Rube) Foster. If Rube Foster isn't going to be honored, nobody should be honored. Foster was a great baseball promoter, team operator and league head as well as an outstanding pitcher. If he had been white, he would rank today with John McGraw, Judge Landis, the Comiskeys and Branch Rickey.[7]

Foster and Jackie Robinson, Young asserted, did not "fit the stereotype. Foster was living proof blacks could handle ANY role in baseball, including that of commissioner. He wasn't a hypocritical, Uncle Tom-ming black out there dancing a jig for the entertainment of whites and doing nothing more." For that matter, why was Frank Thompson, a waiter in Long Island "who founded Negro baseball," not in the Hall of Fame? And where were Charleston, Dihigo, Wells, Smokey Joe Williams, Bullet Joe Rogan, and Bingo DeMoss, who should have been allowed in before the others?[8]

Peterson, in an article that appeared in *Sport* magazine in May 1975, termed Foster "the most impressive figure in Negro baseball history." He was "black baseball's best pitcher for nearly a decade," then its most brilliant manager, "a shrewd strategist" who "directed his play-ers with the precision of Bobby Fischer at the chess board—and with comparable success." At the same time, he was "a strict disciplinarian" who "demanded total obedience and delivered swift retribution to the erring."

> As an administrative impresario [Negro National League President], Rube Foster was as much a force—in his time and in his arena—as Ban Johnson, the founding president of the American League. As a pitcher, he best ap-proximated his contemporary, Christy Mathewson. And as a manager, he was on a level with his friend, John McGraw. That Rube Foster has not been elected to baseball's Hall of Fame by the special committee on Negro Leagues, that he has not even been mentioned publicly as a likely candi-date, is—sadly—a measure of how the rich, bittersweet lore of Negro base-ball has faded with the passing years.[9]

One of the staunchest advocates for Foster's admission into the Hall of Fame was Normal "Tweed" Webb, a former ballplayer, sportswriter, and baseball historian. In the U.S. House of Representatives on July 8, 1975, congressman William Clay offered Webb's analysis of the black baseball giants. Writing that the special committee "had better wake up!" Webb listed the reasons that Foster should be recognized: "(1) He was greatest pitcher (up to 1910); (2) he was greatest manager . . . in the class with John McGraw of the New York Giants and Connie Mack of the Philadelphia Athletics."[10]

Amazingly enough, the Negro Leagues Committee, before it dis-banded, failed to target Foster for inclusion into baseball's Valhalla. This obviously stunned Robert Peterson, whose *Only the Ball Was White* in

1970 had piqued interest in blackball. Foster "from 1903 to 1910 was the preeminent black pitcher. From 1910 to 1925, he was generally regarded as the best manager. And, most important, he was the founder of the first *viable* Negro league." With nine players already in the Hall of Fame, Peterson proposed that a manager be named as well.[11]

Finally, on March 12, 1981, William J. Guilfoib, director of public relations at the Hall of Fame, announced that "the best of the Negro league managers" was to receive long overdue recognition in Cooperstown. Foster, prior to his managerial days, was "black baseball's best pitcher for nearly a decade." He headed the great 1910 Leland Giants and then presided over the Chicago American Giants, "the dominant black team in the Midwest," from 1911 to 1926. "A shrewd strategist, he emphasized the steal, the hit-and-run, the bunt and the squeeze play." And "in 1920, as the leading black baseball man in the country, he organized the Negro National League, bringing stability to Negro baseball for the first time."[12]

Seventy-one-year-old Earl Foster spoke on his father's behalf at the induction ceremony in the summer of 1981. In tossing aside his prepared address, Earl received warm applause. "I don't want to take up your time," he declared. "I just want to say 'thank you, thank you, thank you.'" His father, Earl remembered, had not died an embittered man because of his treatment at the hands of organized baseball. "You have to look at it this way. I never heard him say anything when I was young. The only thing I knew was that a few men in baseball said they would let my father's team into baseball but not all the others. They died a few years later, so it never happened."[13]

In the wake of Foster's long-overdue selection, baseball historian John B. Holway wrote,

> The doors of Cooperstown opened at last to one of the most towering figures in the history of American baseball.
>
> White baseball has never seen anyone quite like Rube Foster. He was Christy Mathewson, John McGraw, Connie Mack, Al Spalding and Kenesaw Mountain Landis—great pitcher, manager, owner, league organizer, czar—all rolled into one.[14]

Characterizing Foster as "The Father of Black Baseball," Holway stated, was insufficient.

Throughout much of the long years of baseball apartheid, 1887–1946, Rube Foster was black baseball.

Foster organized one of the first great black teams, the Chicago American Giants. He also saved black baseball from financial destruction. He organized the first black league in 1920, for the first time assuring black players a regular paycheck, and he urged blacks to maintain a high level of play so that when the white doors were open at last, they would be ready. That day came in 1947, and Jackie Robinson, not yet two years old in 1920, was ready. Without Foster, it is fair to say, there might never have been a Robinson—or a Willie Mays or a Hank Aaron, also products of Foster's league. All baseball, both black and white, is in his debt.[15]

In 1987, third baseman Ray Dandridge, another Negro League veteran, was named to the Hall of Fame. Nearly a decade passed before additional blackballers were added, and then, beginning in 1995, the very scenario that Doc Young had so fiercely opposed but that nevertheless had unfolded in the seventies recurred. On an annual basis, one Negro Leaguer was ushered into Cooperstown; the inductees included pitcher Leon Day, Rube's half brother Willie Foster, Willie Wells, Bullet Joe Rogan, Joe Williams, Turkey Stearnes, and Hilton Smith.

At long last, Rube Foster's seminal role in the history of blackball, baseball in general, and twentieth-century American society, has become impossible to ignore. The successful campaign for his admission into the Hall of Fame certainly played a part in that development. Yet sadly and inexplicably, the inclusion of black baseball's greatest and most important figure would likely not have been attained without the determined efforts of individuals like A. S. "Doc" Young, Robert Peterson, Normal "Tweed" Webb, and John Holway. All four men helped to call attention to black baseball's finest, when too few were so inclined. They both agitated in the popular press and painstakingly crafted studies calling attention to Foster and other black baseball legends. As a consequence, when Ken Burns produced his 1994 PBS television series on baseball, he included a highly moving segment on the father of organized blackball while weaving racial themes throughout his television masterpiece. Geoffrey C. Ward, in the companion volume to the series, referred to Foster as "the finest black pitcher of his time" and "black baseball's first great impresario."[16]

Nevertheless, as the twenty-first century begins, other blackball stars are being given short shrift in baseball circles. A. S. "Doc" Young's complaint of nearly thirty years earlier remains valid. Young had criticized the piecemeal manner in which the National Baseball Hall of Fame had come to accept blackball veterans. There remain more than a score of exceptional players, managers, and administrators who, because of the color of their skin have been denied entrance into organized baseball's most elite club. They are still treated, at least to some extent, as outside the pale, with arguments tendered that playing records are virtually non-existent, the level of competition was not first-rate, and many exceptional white players also have not been welcomed into Cooperstown. With the passage of time, a sprinkling of these extraordinary veterans of black baseball will undoubtedly be ushered into the Hall of Fame, but others will not.

Among the most deserving of those who toiled in the shadows of America's national pastime were pitchers Walter Ball, Chet Brewer, Dave Brown, Ray Brown, Phil Cockrell, Dizzy Dismukes, John Donaldson, Danny McClellan, José Méndez, Willie Powell, Cannonball Dick Redding, James Robinson, Big Richard Whitworth, Frank Wickware, and Nip Winters. Bruce Petway, Bizz Mackey, and Louis Santop were black baseball's greatest catchers during the first part of the twentieth century. An infield of the still-excluded cohort includes first basemen Leroy Grant, Mule Suttles, and Ben Taylor; second basemen Bingo DeMoss, Charlie Grant, Frank Grant, and Bill Monroe; shortstops Sam Bankhead, John Beckwith, Bus Clarkson, Home Run Johnson, Dick Lundy, and Dobie Moore; and third sackers Ollie Marcelle, Alec Radcliffe, and Jud Wilson. The outfield includes Jesse Barber, Willard Brown, Pancho Coimbre, Rap Dixon, Jelly Gardner, Pete Hill, Spot Poles, Chino Smith, and Cris-tobal Torriente. With the selection of Rube Foster, the greatest architects of black baseball still among the "outs" are Dave Malarcher, Cum Posey, C. I. Taylor, Sol White, and J. L. Wilkinson.

NOTES

Notes to Chapter 1

1. Lawrence D. Rice, *The Negro in Texas, 1874–1900* (Baton Rouge: Louisiana State University Press, 1971).

2. Mark Ribowsky, *A Complete History of the Negro Leagues, 1884 to 1955* (Secaucus, N.J.: Carol Publishing Group, 1997), p. 55.

3. Howard A. Phelps, "Andrew 'Rube' Foster," *Half-Century Magazine* (March 1, 1919): 8.

4. Robert Peterson, *Only the Ball Was White: A History of Legendary Black Players and All-Black Professional Teams* (New York: Oxford University Press, 1992), pp. 104–105; David Malarcher Notes from tape, p. 7, David Malarcher File, Ashland Collection, National Baseball Hall of Fame Library; "Baseball Hall of Fame," *Sepia* 30 (June 1981): 38.

5. Peterson, *Only the Ball Was White*, p. 105.

6. Ibid.

7. Rube Foster, "Pitfalls of Baseball," *Chicago Defender*, December 13, 1919, p. 11.

8. "Oh! What a Headache! Philadelphia Giants Play Camden To-Day!" *Philadelphia Item*, April 23, 1902, p. 9; Philadelphia Giants–Camden City box score, *Philadelphia Item*, April 23, 1902, p. 9.

9. Foster, "Pitfalls of Baseball," December 13, 1919, p. 11; Penn Park–Cuban X-Giants box score, *Philadelphia Item*, July 17, 1903, p. 4; Penn Park–Cuban X-Giants box score, *Philadelphia Item*, July 18, 1903, p. 7.

10. "Base Ball Gossip," *Philadelphia Item*, September 13, 1907, 12; Sol White, *Sol White's History of Colored Base Ball, with Other Documents on the Early Black Game, 1886–1936* (Lincoln: University of Nebraska Press, 1995), p. 40.

11. Cuban X-Giants–Philadelphia Giants box score, *Philadelphia Item*, September 14, 1903, p. 4; "Base-Ball," *Philadelphia Item*, September 16, 1903, p. 7; Cuban X-Giants–Philadelphia Giants box score, *Philadelphia Item*, September 19, 1903, p. 7; Cuban X-Giants–Philadelphia Giants box score, *Philadelphia Item*, September 26, 1903, p. 7.

12. Ribowsky, *A Complete History of the Negro Leagues*, p. 55.

13. "The Philadelphia Giants will be faster . . . ," *Philadelphia Item,* April 6, 1904, p. 7; White, *Sol White's History of Colored Base Ball,* p. 146.

14. Dennis Clark, "Urban Blacks and Irishmen: Brothers in Prejudice," in *Black Politics in Philadelphia,* ed. Miriam Ershkowitz and Joseph Zikmund II (New York: Basic Books, 1973), pp. 22–23; John T. Emlen, "The Movement for the Betterment of the Negro in Philadelphia," in *Black Politics in Philadelphia,* p. 40; Florette Henri, *Black Migration: Movement North, 1900–1920* (Garden City, N.Y.: Anchor Press, 1975), pp. 92, 102, 105, 108–109, 111–112.

15. Henri, *Black Migration,* pp. 33, 126, 188; W. E. B. Du Bois, "The Black Vote of Philadelphia," in *Black Politics in Philadelphia,* pp. 32, 36–39; Du Bois, *The Philadelphia Negro: A Social Study* (Philadelphia: University of Pennsylvania Press, 1996).

16. Philip A. Klinkner with Rogers M. Smith, *The Unsteady March: The Rise and Decline of Racial Equality in America* (Chicago: University of Chicago Press, 1999), pp. 104–105.

17. Ray Robinson, *Matty: An American Hero* (New York: Oxford University Press, 1993), p. 58.

18. Philadelphia Giants–Murray Hill box score, *Philadelphia Item,* April 4, 1904, p. 7; Philadelphia Giants–Ridgewood box score, *Philadelphia Item,* April 11, 1904, p. 7.

19. Philadelphia Giants–Camden box score, *Philadelphia Item,* April 26, 1904, p. 7; Philadelphia Giants–Camden box score, *Philadelphia Item,* May 3, 1904, p. 7; Philadelphia Giants–Pottstown box score, *Philadelphia Item,* May 6, 1904, p 5; Wilmington A.A.–Philadelphia Giants box score, *Philadelphia Item,* May 10, 1904, p. 5.

20. "The Philadelphia Giants have been . . . ," *Philadelphia Item,* May 26, 1904, p. 5; Camden–Philadelphia Giants box score, *Philadelphia Item,* May 31, 1904, p. 5; Philadelphia Giants–Hoboken box score, *Philadelphia Item,* June 5, 1904, p. 6; Johnstown–Philadelphia Giants box score, *Philadelphia Item,* June 11, 1904, p. 5; Philadelphia Giants–Harrisburg A.C. box score, *Philadelphia Item,* June 15, 1904, p. 4; Philadelphia Giants–Hoboken box score, *Philadelphia Item,* June 20, 1904, p. 4; Murray Hill–Philadelphia Giants box score, *Philadelphia Item,* June 27, 1904, p. 4.

21. Philadelphia Giants–Edgewood Park box score, *Philadelphia Item,* July 1, 1904, p. 4; Williamsport–Philadelphia Giants box score, *Philadelphia Item,* July 5, 1904, p. 7; Mt. Carmel A.A.–Philadelphia Giants box score, *Philadelphia Item,* July 8, 1904, p. 4; "A Great Pitching Feat," *Philadelphia Item,* July 10, 1904, p. 6; Philadelphia Giants–Atlantic City box score, *Philadelphia Item,* July 10, 1904, p. 4; Philadelphia Giants–Pottstown box score, *Philadelphia Item,* July

12, 1904, p. 4; Oxford–Philadelphia Giants box score, *Philadelphia Item,* July 13, 1904, p. 4.

22. Atlantic City–Philadelphia Giants box score, *Philadelphia Item,* July 16, 1904, p. 5; Philadelphia Giants–Hoboken box score, *Philadelphia Item,* July 18, 1904, p. 2; Mt. Carmel A.A.–Philadelphia Giants box score, *Philadelphia Item,* July 22, 1904, p. 4.

23. "Foster, of the Philadelphia Giants . . . ," *Philadelphia Item,* July 26, 1904, p. 4; Trenton YMCA–Philadelphia Giants box score, *Philadelphia Item,* July 26, 1904, p. 4; Atlantic City–Philadelphia Giants box score, *Philadelphia Item,* July 30, 1904, p. 5; "The Philadelphia Giants won . . . ," *Philadelphia Item,* August 2, 1904, p. 4; Pottstown–Philadelphia Giants box score, *Philadelphia Item,* August 2, 1904, p. 4; Philadelphia Giants–Clayton box score, *Philadelphia Item,* August 3, 1904, p. 4. Sol White in his *History of Colored Base Ball* credited Foster with eighteen strikeouts in the Trenton contest.

24. "The Philadelphia Giants won . . . ," *Philadelphia Item,* August 6, 1904, p. 5; Atlantic City–Philadelphia Giants box score, *Philadelphia Item,* August 6, 1904, p. 5; Pottstown–Philadelphia Giants box score, *Philadelphia Item,* August 7, 1904, p. 6; Haddington–Philadelphia Giants box score, *Philadelphia Item,* August 11, 1904, p. 4; "At the St. George Cricket Grounds . . . ," and Philadelphia Giants–Hoboken box score, *Philadelphia Item,* August 15, 1904, p. 4; Atlantic City–Philadelphia Giants box score, *Philadelphia Item,* August 24, 1904, p. 4; Pottstown–Philadelphia Giants box score, *Philadelphia Item,* August 25, 1904, p. 4.

25. "By winning yesterday's game . . . ," *Philadelphia Item,* September 1, 1904, p. 4; White, *Sol White's History of Colored Base Ball,* p. 44.

26. Philadelphia Giants–Cuban X-Giants box score, *Philadelphia Item,* September 2, 1904, p. 4; "In capturing two of the three games . . . ," *Philadelphia Item,* September 2, 1904, p. 4; Frank A. Young, "Rube Foster: The Master Mind of Baseball," *Abbott's Monthly* (November 1, 1930): 43.

27. Philadelphia Giants–Cuban X-Giants box score, *Philadelphia Item,* September 3, 1904, p. 7; Philadelphia Giants–Cuban X-Giants box score, *Philadelphia Item,* September 6, 1904, p. 4; White, *Sol White's History of Colored Base Ball,* p. 46.

28. "In capturing two of the three games . . . ," p. 4.

29. "The Philadelphia Giants, colored Champions of the World . . . ," *Philadelphia Item,* September 21, 1904, p. 5; John Thorn, "Tales of the Hudson Valley League," *Saugerties Old Dutch Post Star,* July 23, 1981.

30. "Efforts are being made for a series . . . ," *Philadelphia Item,* September 30, 1904, p. 4; Frederick North Shorey, "A Historical Account of a Great Game

of Ball: How Rube Foster Cleaned up with one of the Best Teams in the Country," *Indianapolis Freeman,* September 14, 1907, p. 6.

Notes to Chapter 2

1. "The Palm Beach Daily News gives . . . ," *Philadelphia Item,* March 5, 1915, p. 11.

2. Ibid.

3. Philadelphia Giants–Murray Hills box score, *Philadelphia Item,* April 3, 1905, p. 2; Murray Hills–Philadelphia Giants box score, *Philadelphia Item,* April 9, 1905, p. 6; "The third and final game of the series . . . ," *Philadelphia Item,* April 9, 1905, p. 6; Newark–Philadelphia Giants box score, *Philadelphia Item,* April 9, 1905, p. 6; "Philadelphia Giants Win," *Philadelphia Item,* April 23, 1905, p. 6; Philadelphia Giants–Ingersol-Sergeant box score, *Philadelphia Item,* April 23, 1905, p. 6.

4. "The record of the Champion Philadelphia Giants . . . ," *Philadelphia Item,* April 29, 1905, p. 5.

5. "The most remarkable batting aggregation . . . ," *Philadelphia Item,* May 26, 1905, p. 2.

6. "With the Amateurs," *Philadelphia Item,* May 12, 1905, p. 2; Philadelphia Giants–Johnson's Pets box score, *Philadelphia Item,* May 12, 1905, p. 2; Haddington–Philadelphia Giants box score, *Philadelphia Item,* May 14, 1905, p. 9; Philadelphia Giants–Monarch A.C. box score, *Philadelphia Item,* May 20, 1905, p. 5; Philadelphia Giants–Plainfield box score, *Philadelphia Item,* May 21, 1905, p. 6; Philadelphia Giants–Manhattan box score, *Philadelphia Item,* May 23, 1905, p. 5.

7. "The Philadelphia Giants play in Chester . . . ," *Philadelphia Item,* June 6, 1905, p. 5; Chester–Philadelphia Giants box score, *Philadelphia Item,* June 7, 1905, p. 5; Philadelphia Giants–Manhattan box score, *Philadelphia Item,* June 19, 1905, p. 5; "In a six inning game . . . ," *Philadelphia Item,* June 23, 1905, p. 5; Philadelphia Giants–Murray Hill box score, *Philadelphia Item,* June 26, 1905, p. 5; Chester–Philadelphia Giants box score, *Philadelphia Item,* June 29, 1905, p. 5.

8. "Philadelphia Giants Down Haddington," *Philadelphia Item,* July 2, 1905, p. 13; Haddington–Philadelphia Giants box score, *Philadelphia Item,* July 2, 1905, p. 13; Philadelphia Giants–Trenton YMCA box score, *Philadelphia Item,* July 5, 1905, p. 5; Philadelphia Giants–Glassboro box score, *Philadelphia Item,* July 8, 1905, p. 5; Philadelphia Giants–P.R.R. YMCA box score, *Philadelphia Item,* July 16, 1905, p. 13; Hoboken–Philadelphia Giants box score, *Philadelphia Item,* July 17, 1905, p. 5; Royal Giants–Philadelphia Giants box score, *Phil-*

adelphia Item, July 21, 1905, p. 7; Philadelphia Giants–Quakertown box score, *Philadelphia Item,* July 23, 1905, p. 13; "The Philadelphia Giants were defeated yesterday . . . ," *Philadelphia Item,* July 26, 1905, p. 5; "Among the Amateurs," *Philadelphia Item,* July 29, 1905, p. 5; Philadelphia Giants–Walkovers box score, *Philadelphia Item,* July 29, 1905, p. 5.

9. Medford F.C.–Philadelphia Giants box score, *Philadelphia Item,* August 3, 1905, p. 2; Philadelphia Giants–Pottstown box score, *Philadelphia Item,* August 12, 1905, p. 5; "With the Amateurs," *Philadelphia Item,* August 15, 1905, p. 5; Atlantic City–Philadelphia Giants box score, *Philadelphia Item,* August 15, 1905, p. 5.

10. "All records for attendance at Olympic Field . . . ," *Philadelphia Item,* August 28, 1905, p. 2; Manhattan–Philadelphia Giants box score, *Philadelphia Item,* August 28, 1905, p. 2; Atlantic City–Philadelphia Giants box score, *Philadelphia Item,* August 30, 1905, p. 5; Atlantic City–Philadelphia Giants box score, *Philadelphia Item,* August 31, 1905, p. 5; Philadelphia Giants–Manhattan box score, *Philadelphia Item,* September 8, 1905, p. 2; Philadelphia Giants–Allentown box score, *Philadelphia Item,* September 13, 1905, p. 5.

11. "With the Amateurs," *Philadelphia Item,* September 15, 1905, p. 5; Philadelphia Giants–Royal Giants box score, *Philadelphia Item,* September 15, 1905, p. 5; "With the Amateurs," *Philadelphia Item,* September 16, 1905, p. 8; Philadelphia Giants–Royal Giants box score, *Philadelphia Item,* September 16, 1905, p. 8; Philadelphia Giants–Royal Giants box score, *Philadelphia Item,* September 17, 1905, p. 6.

12. Philadelphia Giants–Harrisburg A.C. box score, *Philadelphia Item,* September 19, 1905, p. 5; Manhattan–Philadelphia Giants box score, *Philadelphia Item,* September 25, 1905, p. 5; "With the Amateurs," *Philadelphia Item,* October 1, 1905, p, 6; Philadelphia Giants–Holyoke box score, *Philadelphia Item,* October 1, 1905, p. 6.

13. "Base Ball," *Philadelphia Item,* October 25, 1905, p. 7.

14. "Base Ball," *Philadelphia Item,* October 28, 1905, p. 7; Cuban X-Giants–All Cubans box score, *Philadelphia Item,* October 28, 1905, p. 7.

15. White, *Sol White's History of Colored Base Ball,* p. 33; John L. Footslug, "In the World of Sports," *Indianapolis Freeman,* November 18, 1905, p. 6.

16. Shorey, "A Historical Account of a Great Game of Ball," September 14, 1907, p. 6.

17. David Malarcher Notes from tape, p. 7; Young, "Rube Foster," p. 44.

18. Young, "Rube Foster," p. 44.

19. Ibid.

20. Ibid.

21. "At Brighton oval yesterday . . . ," *Philadelphia Item,* April 2, 1906, p. 7; Brightons–Philadelphia Giants box score, *Philadelphia Item,* April 2, 1906, p. 7; "'Rube' Foster, last year's phenominal [*sic*] pitcher . . . ," *Philadelphia Item,* April 18, 1906, p. 2; "What promises to eclipse . . . ," *Philadelphia Item,* April 6, 1906, p. 5.

22. Altoona–Philadelphia Giants box score, *Philadelphia Item,* April 20, 1906, p. 7; Leland Giants–Philadelphia Giants box score, *Philadelphia Item,* May 20, 1906, p. 5; "The Royal Giants of Brooklyn played . . . ," *Philadelphia Item,* June 1, 1906, p. 7; Philadelphia Giants–Royal Giants box score, *Philadelphia Item,* June 1, 1906, p. 7; Philadelphia Giants–Royal Giants box score, *Philadelphia Item,* June 5, 1906, p. 5; "To-morrow's game for the benefit . . . ," *Philadelphia Item,* June 13, 1906, p. 7; Philadelphia Giants–Hazleton box score, *Philadelphia Item,* June 23, 1906, 7; Philadelphia Giants–Roebling box score, *Philadelphia Item,* June 30, 1906, 6; "On Sunday the Philadelphia Giants defeated . . . ," *Philadelphia Item,* July 10, 1906, 4; Philadelphia Giants–Rockville box score, *Philadelphia Item,* July 19, 1906, p. 7.

23. "The International League has made more changes . . . ," *Philadelphia Item,* July 24, 1906, 4; Peterson, *Only the Ball Was White,* p. 62; "International League Standing," *Philadelphia Item,* August 19, 1906, p. 6; Millville–Philadelphia Giants box score, *Philadelphia Item,* August 24, 1906, p. 5; "A misunderstanding between the managers . . . ," *Philadelphia Item,* September 18, 1906, p. 7; "York, the Tri-State League pennant-winners . . . ," *Philadelphia Item,* September 19, 1906, p. 3; Philadelphia Giants–York box score, *Philadelphia Item,* September 19, 1906, p. 3; "The Philadelphia Giants made a record Sunday . . . ," *Philadelphia Item,* October 2, 1906, p. 4; "The Philadelphia Athletics narrowly escaped . . . ," *Philadelphia Item,* October 13, 1906, p. 7; Philadelphia Athletics–Philadelphia Giants box score, *Philadelphia Item,* October 13, 1906, p. 7.

24. White, *Sol White's History of Colored Base Ball,* p. 49; "A Meeting held Monday afternoon . . . ," *Philadelphia Item,* October 29, 1906, p. 7.

25. "A Meeting held Monday afternoon . . . ," p. 7.

26. Roberto Gonzáles Echevarría, *The Pride of Havana: A History of Cuban Baseball* (New York: Oxford University Press, 1999), pp. 126–127.

27. White, *Sol White's History of Colored Base Ball,* pp. 55–62.

28. Ibid., pp. 110–111.

29. Ibid., pp. 111, 118.

30. Andrew Foster, "How to Pitch," in White, *Sol White's History of Colored Base Ball,* pp. 96, 99.

31. Ibid., p. 99.

32. Ibid., p. 100.

Notes to Chapter 3

1. Peterson, *Only the Ball Was White*, p. 107; George E. Mason, "Rube Foster Chats about His Career," *Chicago Defender*, February 20, 1915, p. 9.

2. Mason, "Rube Foster Chats about His Career," p. 9; Peterson, *Only the Ball Was White*, p. 107.

3. Michael L. Levine, *African Americans and Civil Rights: From 1619 to the Present* (Phoenix: Oryx Press, 1996), p. 123; St. Clair Drake and Horace R. Clayton, *Black Metropolis: A Study of Negro Life in a Northern City*, vol. 1 (New York: Harper & Row, 1962), p. 55; Henri, *Black Migration*, p. 159.

4. Levine, *African Americans and Civil Rights*, p. 135.

5. Footslug, "In the World of Sport," *Indianapolis Freeman*, April 27, 1907, p. 7.

6. Footslug, "In the World of Sport," *Indianapolis Freeman*, August 31, 1907, p. 7.

7. Ibid.; "Giants Take Three-Game Series," *Indianapolis Freeman*, August 31, 1907, p. 7; ABCs–Leland Giants box score, *Indianapolis Freeman*, August 31, 1907, p. 7.

8. Dave Phillips, "Boxing Baseball and Athletics," *Indianapolis Freeman*, August 31, 1907, p. 7.

9. Frederick North Shorey, "A Historical Account of a Great Game of Ball," *Indianapolis Freeman*, September 7, 1907, p. 7.

10. Ibid.

11. Ibid.

12. All-Stars–Leland Giants box score, *Indianapolis Freeman*, September 7, 1907, p. 7.

13. "Giants Win One; Lose One," *Indianapolis Freeman*, September 7, 1907, p. 7.

14. Shorey, "A Historical Account of a Great Game of Ball," *Indianapolis Freeman*, September 14, 1907, p. 7.

15. Ibid.

16. Ibid.

17. Ibid.

18. Ibid.

19. "Bostons Sign a Colored Player," *Indianapolis Freeman*, September 14, 1907, pp. 6–7.

20. David Wyatt, "Baseball: Booker T. Washington or the Fifteenth Amendment," *Indianapolis Freeman*, September 21, 1907, p. 7.

21. Ibid.

22. Ibid.

23. Ibid.

24. Ibid; "'Rube' Foster in Star Role [*sic*]," *Indianapolis Freeman*, September 28, 1907, p. 6.

25. "Last Season Greatest for Baseball," *Indianapolis Freeman*, February 15, 1908, p. 6.

26. Peterson, *Only the Ball Was White*, p. 107.

27. Malarcher to Robert W. Peterson, November 20, 1968, p. 3, David Malarcher File, Ashland Collection, National Baseball Hall of Fame Library.

28. "Growing Interest in Proposed League," *Indianapolis Freeman*, November 16, 1907, p. 6; "Nothing but Success in Sight for League Meeting," *Indianapolis Freeman*, December 7, 1907, p. 6.

29. "League Meeting a Successful One," *Indianapolis Freeman*, December 28, 1907, p. 6.

30. "Rube Foster Saves the Day," *Indianapolis Freeman*, July 25, 1908, p. 5; Leland Giants–Normal box score, *Indianapolis Freeman*, July 25, 1908, p. 5.

31. "Base Hits of Chicago," *Indianapolis Freeman*, July 25, 1908, p. 7.

32. Ibid.

33. "Leland Giants Defeat Spaldings in Ninth," *Indianapolis Freeman*, August 1, 1908, p. 5; Leland Giants–Spaldings box score, *Indianapolis Freeman*, August 1, 1908, p. 5.

34. Frank C. Leland to the editor, *Indianapolis Freeman*, August 1, 1908, p. 7.

35. "Leland Giants Defeat Philadelphia Giants," *Indianapolis Freeman*, August 15, 1908, p. 8; Leland Giants–Philadelphia Giants box score, *Indianapolis Freeman*, August 15, 1908, p. 8; "Giants Win Out in Ninth," *Indianapolis Freeman*, August 8, 1908, p. 5; Leland Giants–West Ends box score, *Indianapolis Freeman*, August 8, 1908, p. 5; "Leland Giants Again Win," *Indianapolis Freeman*, August 8, 1908, p. 5; Leland Giants–Philadelphia Giants box score, *Indianapolis Freeman*, August 8, 1908, p. 5; "Take Third Straight from Leland Giants," *Indianapolis Freeman*, August 15, 1908, p. 5; Logan Squares–Leland Giants box score, *Indianapolis Freeman*, August 15, 1908, p. 5; Foster, "Come, Fans, Rally around the Flag!" *Indianapolis Freeman*, November 13, 1909, p. 7.

36. Phelps, "Andrew 'Rube' Foster," p. 8.

37. "Champion Leland Giants to Go South for Spring Training," *Indianapolis Freeman*, February 20, 1909, p. 7.

38. "Leland Giants Complete a Successful Southern Trip," *Indianapolis Freeman*, May 15, 1909, p. 7.

39. Ibid.

40. Foster, "Come, Fans, Rally around the Flag!" p. 7; "Gophers Win in Hot Finish," *St. Paul Pioneer-Press,* July 27, 1909, p. 7; "Gophers Easy Meat," *St. Paul Pioneer-Press,* July 28, 1909, p. 7; "Tale of a Toe Salad," *St. Paul Pioneer-Press,* July 29, 1909, p. 9; "Gophers Win Out," *St. Paul Pioneer-Press,* July 30, 1909, p. 7; "Gophers Get Bacon," *St. Paul Pioneer-Press,* July 31, 1909, p. 7.

41. "Former World's Champions Defeat Leland Giants," *Indianapolis Freeman,* October 16, 1909, p. 4; "Cubs Beat Leland Giants 4-1," *Chicago Daily Tribune,* October 19, 1909, p. 8; "Cubs' Rally Beats Leland Giants," *Chicago Daily Tribune,* October 22, 1909, p. 12.

42. "Cubs' Rally Beats Leland Giants," p. 12; Frank Albert Young, "The Colored Men in Athletics," *Chicago Defender,* January 25, 1913, p. 7.

43. "Cubs Trim Giants in Final Game, 1-0," *Chicago Daily Tribune,* October 23, 1909, p. 14.

Notes to Chapter 4

1. "Frank C. Leland Resigns," *Indianapolis Freeman,* October 2, 1909, p. 7; Frank C. Leland letter to the editor, *Indianapolis Freeman,* October 2, 1909, p. 7; Ribowsky, *A Complete History of the Negro Leagues, 1884 to 1953,* pp. 71–72.

2. Foster, "Negro Base Ball," *Indianapolis Freeman,* December 23, 1911, p. 16.

3. Foster, "Come, Fans, Rally around the Flag!" p. 7; Foster, "Pitfalls of Baseball," December 13, 1919, p. 11; Harry W. Jackson, "No Club Has Real Claim to Colored Baseball Championship for Season of 1909," *Indianapolis Freeman,* October 9, 1909, p. 7.

4. Foster, "Come, Fans, Rally around the Flag!" p. 7.

5. Ibid.

6. Ibid.

7. David Wyatt, "Baseball War for Chicago," *Indianapolis Freeman,* December 4, 1909, p. 7.

8. Ibid.

9. Ibid.

10. Major R. R. Jackson to the editor, "No Baseball War in Chicago," *Indianapolis Freeman,* December 18, 1909, p. 8.

11. Ibid.

12. David Wyatt, "The Bulls and Bears of the Base Ball Market," *Indianapolis Freeman,* December 25, 1909, p. 13.

13. Ibid.

14. David Wyatt, "Time Now Ripe for Formation of a Colored League," *Indianapolis Freeman*, January 22, 1910, p. 8.

15. "Rube Foster Will Invade the East," *Indianapolis Freeman*, December 25, 1909, p. 7; "Leland Giants to Make Great Southern Tour," *Indianapolis Freeman*, January 15, 1910, p. 7.

16. "Leland Giants to Make Great Southern Tour," p. 7.

17. "Rube Foster Back in Form," *Chicago Defender*, February 5, 1910, p. 1; "What the Royals and Leland Giants Did at Palm Beach," *Indianapolis Freeman Supplement*, April 16, 1910, p. 9.

18. Foster, "Success of the Negro as a Ball Player," *Indianapolis Freeman Supplement*, April 16, 1910, p. 9.

19. Ibid.

20. Ibid.

21. Ibid.

22. David Wyatt, "Season 1910 to Be Banner," *Indianapolis Freeman Supplement*, April 16, 1910, p. 10.

23. Ibid.

24. Thomas I. Florence, "Who I Think Will Win the Championship," *Indianapolis Freeman Supplement*, April 16, 1910, p. 10.

25. Cary B. Lewis, "Gala Day in Baseball at Chicago," *Indianapolis Freeman*, May 21, 1910, p. 4; Leland Giants–Gunthers box score, *Indianapolis Freeman*, May 21, 1910, p. 4.

26. "'Rube' Foster's Day," *Indianapolis Freeman*, May 28, 1910, p. 4; Leland Giants–Stars of Cuba box score, *Indianapolis Freeman*, May 28, 1910, p. 4; "Leland Giants, 14; Gunthers, 8," *Indianapolis Freeman*, June 4, 1910, p. 4.

27. "Lelands Defeated at Last," *Indianapolis Freeman*, June 18, 1910, p. 4; "The Leland Giants will leave soon . . . ," *Indianapolis Freeman*, June 18, 1910, p. 4; "Cubans and Lelands Play to Draw," *Chicago Defender*, July 30, 1910, p. 3; Stars of Cuba–Leland Giants box score, *Chicago Defender*, July 30, 1910, p. 3; "Giants Take Benefit Game," *Chicago Defender*, August 27, 1910, p. 5; Lelands–Gunthers box score, *Chicago Defender*, August 27, 1910, p. 5; "Lelands Make Triple Play," *Chicago Defender*, September 10, 1910, p. 7.

28. Billy Lewis, "The American Giants!" *Indianapolis Freeman*, March 8, 1915, p. 7.

29. Phil Dixon with Patrick J. Hannigan, *The Negro Baseball League: A Photographic History* (Mattituck, N.Y.: Amereon House, 1992), pp. 101–102.

30. Foster, "Pitfalls of Baseball," December 13, 1919, 11; Harold C. McGath, "In the Field of Sport," *Indianapolis Freeman*, January 14, 1911, p. 7.

31. McGath, "In the Field of Sport," p. 7.

32. Ibid.

Notes to Chapter 5

1. Frank Young, "More about Foster's Baseball Team," *Half-Century Magazine* (June 1, 1919): 8; Foster, "Negro Base Ball," p. 16; John B. Holway, "Historically Speaking Bill Foster," *Black Sports* (March 1974): 59.

2. Young, "More about Foster's Baseball Team," p. 8.

3. *The Negro Leagues Book,* ed. Dick Clark and Larry Lester (Cleveland: Society for American Baseball Research, 1994), p. 21.

4. Lewis, "The American Giants!" p. 7; Foster, "Pitfalls of Baseball," December 13, 1919, p. 11.

5. Foster, "Negro Base Ball," p. 16.

6. Ibid.

7. Ibid.

8. Ibid.

9. Ibid.

10. Ibid.

11. Juli Jones Jr., "Baseball in Cuba," *Philadelphia Tribune,* January 27, 1912, p. 7.

12. Ibid.

13. "The Freeman Cartoonist Sees the Chicago American Giants and the A.B.C.'s," *Indianapolis Freeman,* June 22, 1912, p. 7; "Rube Foster and his Giants returned . . . ," *Indianapolis Freeman,* June 22, 1912, p. 7; Young, "In the Sporting World," *Chicago Defender,* June 22, 1912, p. 6; "American Giants," *Chicago Defender,* June 29, 1912, p. 6; American Giants–Pittsburgh box score, *Chicago Defender,* June 22, 1912, p. 6.

14. "Foster Wins His Games," *Indianapolis Freeman,* August 3, 1912, p. 4; Sprudels-Giants box score, *Indianapolis Freeman,* August 3, 1912, p. 4; "The Sporting World," *Chicago Defender,* August 18, 1912, p. 6; Holway, *Blackball Stars: Negro League Pioneers* (New York: Carroll & Graf, 1992), p. 17.

15. "The Sporting World," *Chicago Defender,* August 31, 1912, p. 6; U.S. Leaguers–American Giants box score, *Chicago Defender,* August 31, 1912, p. 6.

16. "Baseball Notes," *Chicago Defender,* September 7, 1912, p. 7; "The Sporting World," *Chicago Defender,* September 14, 1912, p. 7; American Giants–St. Louis Giants box score, *Chicago Defender,* September 14, 1912, p. 7.

17. "Rube Foster to Be Honored with Stag," *Philadelphia Tribune,* September 14, 1912, p. 7.

18. Foster, "The American Giants, Champions—in Los Angeles, Cal.," *Indianapolis Freeman,* November 9, 1912, p. 7; Foster, "'Rube' Foster's Review on Baseball," *Indianapolis Freeman,* December 28, 1912, p. 11.

19. Foster, "The American Giants, Champions—in Los Angeles, Cal.," p. 7;

Chicago American Giants–All-Natives of California box score, *Indianapolis Free-man*, November 9, 1912, p. 7; Chicago American Giants–H. Franks box score, *Indianapolis Freeman*, November 9, 1912, p. 7; L.A. Giants–Chicago American Giants box score, *Indianapolis Freeman*, November 9, 1912, p. 7.

20. Julius N. Avendouph, "'Rube' Foster's Giants Hold Their Own in California," *Chicago Defender*, December 14, 1912, p. 7.

21. Foster, "'Rube' Foster's Review on Baseball," p. 11.

22. Ibid; Young, "The Colored Men in Athletics," p. 7.

23. Billy Lewis, "Baseball Is now the Subject," *Indianapolis Freeman*, February 15, 1913, p. 7.

24. Ibid.

25. The Old Fan, "The Coming Season of Baseball," *Indianapolis Freeman*, March 8, 1913, p. 7.

26. "To the American Giants," *Indianapolis Freeman*, April 5, 1913, p. 7.

27. Billy Lewis, "The American Giants Getting Recognition," *Indianapolis Freeman*, April 12, 1913, p. 7.

28. Julius N. Avendouph, "Local Sports," *Chicago Defender*, April 5, 1913, p. 8.

29. Billy Lewis, "The American Giants Getting Recognition," p. 7.

30. Portus Baxter, "Colored Giants a Wonderful Team," *Seattle Post-Intelligencer*, April 3, 1913, p. 11; Baxter, "Colorful Phenoms Bat out Victory," *Seattle Post-Intelligencer*, April 6, 1913, part 4, p. 11; Baxter, "Colored Giants Mangle Pitchers," *Seattle Post-Intelligencer*, April 7, 1913, p. 4.

31. "The American Giants," *Indianapolis Freeman*, April 19, 1913, p. 7.

32. Julius N. Avendouph, "Rube Foster and His American Giants," *Chicago Defender*, April 5, 1913, p. 8; Billy Lewis, "The American Giants Getting Recognition," p. 7.

33. "Local Sports," *Chicago Defender*, April 26, 1913, p. 8.

34. Frank A. Young, "Sporting," *Chicago Defender*, May 10, 1913, p. 7; American Giants–Plutos box score, *Indianapolis Freeman*, June 7, 1913, p. 4; Cary B. Lewis, "American Giants Take Four of Five in Series from Plutos," *Indianapolis Freeman*, June 7, 1913, p. 4; "Tuesday's Game," *Indianapolis Freeman*, June 7, 1913, p. 4; Young, "The World of Sports," *Chicago Defender*, June 17, 1913, p. 8; "Tuesday's Game with Cubans," *Indianapolis Freeman*, June 21, 1913, p. 4.

35. Frank A. Young, "Sporting," *Chicago Defender*, August 2, 1913, p. 3; Young, "Sporting," *Chicago Defender*, August 9, 1913, p. 7; "Lincolns Win Best Seven out of Twelve Games," *Indianapolis Freeman*, August 23, 1913, p. 4.

36. "Americans Win," *Indianapolis Freeman*, August 30, 1913, p. 4; "The

Foster Banquet," *Indianapolis Freeman*, August 30, 1913, p. 4; Frank A. Young, "Sporting," *Chicago Defender*, October 18, 1913, p. 8.

37. "American Giants Win from St. Louis Giants," *Indianapolis Freeman*, September 6, 1913, p. 4; "Errors Beat Sprudels," *Indianapolis Freeman*, September 13, 1913, p. 4; "Sunday's Game," *Indianapolis Freeman*, September 20, 1913, p. 4; Chicago Giants–American Giants box score, *Indianapolis Freeman*, September 20, 1913, p. 4; Frank A. Young, "Sporting," *Chicago Defender*, September 20, 1913, p. 7.

38. Frank A. Young, "Sporting," *Chicago Defender*, October 18, 1913, p. 8; Frank A. Young, "Base Ball Doings in the Windy City," *Indianapolis Ledger*, October 18, 1913, p. 4; American Giants–Logan Squares box score, *Indianapolis Ledger*, October 18, 1913, p. 4.

39. Young, "Base Ball Doings in the Windy City," p. 4; Frank A. Young, "Sporting," *Chicago Defender*, October 18, 1913, p. 8.

40. "We Should Have an Organized League," *Philadelphia Tribune*, January 10, 1914, p. 7.

Notes to Chapter 6

1. "The Sporting World," *Chicago Defender*, March 21, 1914, p. 6.

2. Portus Baxter, "Colored Demons Play Here Today," *Seattle Post-Intelligencer*, April 3, 1914, p. 11; Baxter, "Seattle Loses a Great Game to a Great Team," *Seattle Post-Intelligencer*, April 4, 1914, p. 11; Baxter, "Two Giant Teams Will Battle This Afternoon," *Seattle Post-Intelligencer*, April 5, 1914, part 3, p. 1.

3. Royal Brougham, "'Rube' Thinks Black Men Will Play in Big Leagues," *Seattle Post-Intelligencer*, April 5, 1914, part 3, p.1.

4. Ibid.

5. Portus Baxter, "Baxter's Sporting Gossip," *Seattle Post-Intelligencer*, April 6, 1914, p. 9.

6. Portus Baxter, "Seattle Loses in Hot Battle 1 to 0," *Seattle Post-Intelligencer*, April 6, 1914, p. 9.

7. Frank A. Young, "The Sporting World," *Chicago Defender*, April 18, 1914, p. 8; Young, "The Sporting World," *Chicago Defender*, April 25, 1914, p. 3; "Giants Victorious," *Chicago Defender*, April 25, 1914, p. 6; Lewiston-Giants box score, *Chicago Defender*, April 25, 1914, p. 6.

8. "American Giants Enroute to Windy City," *Chicago Defender*, April 25, 1914, p. 6.

9. Billy Lewis, "The American Giants!" p. 7.

10. "American Giants Win Opener as Big Crowd Cheers," *Chicago Defender,* May 2, 1914, p. 4; American Giants–Gunthers box score, *Chicago Defender,* May 2, 1914, p. 4.

11. Frank Young, "American Giants Win against St. Joe Team," *Indianapolis Ledger,* May 9, 1914, p. 4; American Giants–St. Joe box score, *Indianapolis Ledger,* May 9, 1914, p. 4; Cary B. Lewis, "American Giants Win," *Indianapolis Freeman,* May 9, 1914, p. 4; American Giants–St. Joe box score, *Indianapolis Freeman,* May 9, 1914, p. 4; "American Giants Meet Tartars," *Chicago Defender,* May 30, 1914, p. 7; Cubans–American Giants box score, *Chicago Defender,* May 30, 1914, p. 7.

12. Cary B. Lewis, "'Young Cy' Young Coming," *Indianapolis Freeman,* May 5, 1914, p. 4; American Giants–Cubans box score, *Indianapolis Freeman,* May 5, 1914, p. 4; "Rube Foster Triumphs," *Chicago Defender,* June 6, 1914, p. 5; "'Rube' Foster Wins Sensational Game," *Indianapolis Freeman,* June 13, 1914, p. 5; American Giants–Benton Harbor box score, *Indianapolis Freeman,* June 13, 1914, p. 5.

13. Cary B. Lewis, "Monday's Game," *Indianapolis Freeman,* July 4, 1914, p. 4; American Giants–Plutos box score, *Indianapolis Freeman,* July 4, 1914, p. 4; Cary B. Lewis, "American Giants Win First Three Games against Cuban Stars," *Indianapolis Freeman,* July 11, 1914, p. 4; American Giants–Cubans box score, *Indianapolis Freeman,* July 11, 1914, p. 4; Tony Langston, "American Giants Trim City Leaguers," *Indianapolis Ledger,* July 25, 1914, p. 4; "Rube Foster Knocked out," *Indianapolis Freeman,* August 1, 1914, p. 4; American Giants–ABCs box score, *Indianapolis Freeman,* August 1, 1914, p. 4.

14. Foster, "Rube Foster Has a Word on Pitchers and Catchers," *Indianapolis Freeman,* August 8, 1914, p. 7.

15. Cary B. Lewis, "'Rube' Robbed of $600.00," *Indianapolis Freeman,* August 15, 1914, p. 4.

16. Cary B. Lewis, "Americans Lose First Game," *Indianapolis Freeman,* August 22, 1914, p. 4.

17. Frank A. Young, "American Giants Take Lead in World's Series," *Chicago Defender,* September 5, 1914, p. 2; Young, "Giants Make Clean Sweep," *Chicago Defender,* September 19, 1914, p. 7.

18. Young, "Giants Make Clean Sweep," p. 7; Young, "American Giants Take Lead in World's Series," p. 4; "A Near Riot at American Giants' Park," *Indianapolis Ledger,* September 5, 1914, p. 4.

19. "Foster Back from Kentucky," *Indianapolis Freeman,* September 19, 1914, p. 4; "'Rube' Foster Praised," *Indianapolis Freeman,* September 26, 1914, p. 1.

20. Mason, "Rube Foster Chats about His Career," p. 9.

21. Ibid.

22. Ibid.

23. Ibid.

24. Ibid.

25. "And then in 1920," transcribed interview with Dave Malarcher, n.d., p. 4, Malarcher Ashland Collection.

26. Malarcher Notes from tape, p. 6.

27. "Colored Giants Improved," *Oregonian*, March 24, 1915, p. 12; Billy Lewis, "The American Giants!" p. 7.

28. Billy Lewis, "The American Giants!" p. 7.

29. "Colored Giants Improved," p. 12.

30. "Covelskie Takes Terrible Beating," *Oregonian*, March 28, 1915, sec. 2, p. 1.

31. Roscoe Fawcett, "Beavers Stronger, Says Rube Foster," *Oregonian*, April 2, 1915, p. 14.

32. "American Giants Beat Portland, P.L. Champions," *Chicago Defender*, April 10, 1915, p. 4.

33. Frank A. Young, "American Giants Clean up along Western Coast," *Chicago Defender*, April 17, 1915, p. 2; "American Giants Win 2 out of 3 in Tacoma Series," *Chicago Defender*, April 24, 1915, p. 7.

Notes to Chapter 7

1. "American Giants Win the Opening Game, 6000 Fans," *Chicago Defender*, May 1, 1915, p. 7; American Giants–Milwaukee Sox box score, *Chicago Defender*, May 1, 1915, p. 7; "American Giants Defeat Former Big Leaguers," *Chicago Defender*, May 15, 1915, p. 7; American Giants–Kavanaugh's League box score, *Chicago Defender*, May 15, 1915, p. 7.

2. "Rube Foster Beats Gunthers 3 to 2," *Chicago Defender*, May 22, 1915, p. 7; American Giants–Gunthers box score, *Chicago Defender*, May 22, 1915, p. 7; "Giants Take Two on Decoration Day," *Indianapolis Ledger*, June 5, 1915, p. 4.

3. "Color Line Has Kept Many a Good Ball Player out of Majors," *Indianapolis Freeman*, June 19, 1915, p. 7.

4. "Rube Wins First Game . . . ," *Indianapolis Freeman*, June 26, 1915, p. 5; American Giants–Indianapolis ABCs box score, *Indianapolis Freeman*, June 26, 1915, p. 5; "Biff! Bang!! Foster Got It!" *Indianapolis Ledger*, July 10, 1915, p. 4; Cubans–American Giants box score, *Indianapolis Ledger*, July 10, 1915, p. 4; "The Cuban Stars Win Three Straight from the American Giants," *Indianapolis Freeman*, July 16, 1915, p. 4; "Cubans Continue to Handle Rube Foster," *Indianapolis Ledger*, July 17, 1915, p. 4.

5. "American Giants in Fierce Riot at Hoosier City," *Chicago Defender,* July 24, 1915, p. 7; "Taylor, the Giant Killer, Welcomes 'Big Chief,'" *Indianapolis Freeman,* July 17, 1915, p. 1.

6. "American Giants in Fierce Riot at Hoosier City," p. 7; "Foster Is Shown up by A.B.C.'s," *Indianapolis Ledger,* July 24, 1915, p. 4.

7. "American Giants in Fierce Riot at Hoosier City," p. 7.

8. "Foster Is Shown up by A.B.C.'s," p. 4.

9. Ibid.

10. Ibid.

11. "Foster's Team Disqualified for World's Championship," *Indianapolis Ledger,* July 24, 1915, p. 4.

12. Foster, "Rube Foster Has His Say," *Indianapolis Ledger,* July 31, 1915, p. 4.

13. Ibid.

14. Ibid.

15. Ibid.

16. Ibid.

17. Ibid.

18. Ibid.

19. Ibid.

20. Ibid.

21. "Taylor Replies to Foster," *Indianapolis Ledger,* August 7, 1915, p. 4.

22. Ibid.

23. Ibid.

24. Ibid.; C. I. Taylor to Foster, May 5, 1915, *Indianapolis Freeman,* August 14, 1915, p. 7.

25. Taylor to Foster, May 17, 1915, *Indianapolis Freeman,* August 14, 1915, p. 7.

26. Ibid.

27. "The Only 'Rube,'" *Chicago Defender,* July 31, 1915, p. 7; "'Rube' Foster's Famous American Giants," *Chicago Defender,* July 31, 1915, p. 7: "This Illustration Shows Andrew ('Rube') Foster Seated at His Desk in His Office, His Wife and Little Son and His Residence at Chicago," *Indianapolis Ledger,* July 31, 1915, p. 4.

28. "American Giants Leading in Lincoln American Series," *Chicago Defender,* August 7, 1915, p. 7; "American Giants on Top in Long Pitchers' Battle," *Chicago Defender,* August 14, 1915, p. 7.

29. "American Giants Beat Cubans Who Start Trouble," *Chicago Defender,* August 28, 1915, p. 7.

30. "Lloyd Joins the American Giants," *Chicago Defender,* August 28, 1915,

p. 7; "Lloyd and Gans Add Strength to Darlings," *Indianapolis Ledger*, September 4, 1915, p. 4.

31. "Rube Foster Challenges Tinker's Feds," *Chicago Defender*, October 2, 1915, p. 7.

32. Ibid.

33. "American Giants Ring down Curtain with a Win," *Chicago Defender*, October 16, 1915, p. 7.

34. "American Giants Win the Pennant," *Chicago Defender*, January 8, 1916, p. 7; "Rube Foster off for the Coast," *Chicago Defender*, January 22, 1916, p. 5.

35. "A Big League of Negro Players," *Indianapolis Freeman*, February 12, 1916, p. 7.

36. Ibid.; Billy Lewis, "Rube Foster Setting the Base Ball Pace," *Indianapolis Freeman*, March 25, 1916, p. 7; "Rube Foster on the Coast," *Indianapolis Freeman*, April 22, 1916, p. 7.

37. Portus Baxter, "Crack Chicago Giants Aggregation Trims Dug's Pets in Uneven Contest," *Seattle Post-Intelligencer*, April 8, 1916, p. 12; Baxter, "Seattle Giants Drop Second to Colored Cracks," *Seattle Post-Intelligencer*, April 9, 1916, part 3, p. 1; Baxter, "Colored Giants Win an Exciting Battle from Seattle in the Ninth," *Seattle Post-Intelligencer*, April 10, 1916, p. 12.

38. Charles Crockett, "Suppose We Had a Colored Baseball League?" *Indianapolis Freeman*, April 22, 1916, p. 7.

39. "American Giants Open To-Day," *Chicago Defender*, April 29, 1916, p. 7; "Rube Foster and His Fast Team," *Indianapolis Freeman*, May 13, 1916, p. 7; American Giants–West Ends box score, *Indianapolis Freeman*, May 13, 1916, p. 7; Mr. Fan, "Rube Foster in Come Back Role," *Chicago Defender*, May 20, 1916, p. 7; Cary B. Lewis, "A Comedy of Errors," *Indianapolis Freeman*, May 20, 1916, p. 7.

40. Cary B. Lewis, "Foster's Giants Capture a Title," *Indianapolis Freeman*, August 26, 1916, p. 4; "Flag Day," *Chicago Defender*, September 6, 1916, p. 6; "Andrew Rube Foster," *Chicago Defender*, September 6, 1916, p. 6; "World's Champions," *Chicago Defender*, September 6, 1916, p. 6.

41. David Wyatt, "American Giants and All Nations Pull Largest Crowd of the Season," *Indianapolis Freeman*, October 7, 1916, p. 7; "White Sox Stars See Giants Win," *Chicago Defender*, October 14, 1916, p. 8; "Foster's Giants to Play Series Here," *Indianapolis Freeman*, October 21, 1916, p. 7.

42. "Foster's Giants to Play Series Here," p. 7; "Andrew 'Rube' Foster," *Indianapolis Freeman*, October 21, 1916, p. 7.

43. Phil Dixon, *The Negro Baseball Leagues: A Photographic History* (Mattituck, N.Y.: Amereon House, 1994), pp. 113–114; Young Knox, "Rube Foster Takes First Game," *Indianapolis Freeman*, October 28, 1916, p. 7; ABCs–American

Giants box score, *Indianapolis Freeman,* October 28, 1916, p. 7; American Giants–ABCs box score (second game), *Indianapolis Freeman,* October 28, 1916, p. 7; American Giants–ABCs box score (third game), *Indianapolis Freeman,* October 28, 1916, p. 7; "Andrew 'Rube' Foster," *Indianapolis Freeman,* October 21, 1916, p. 7. For the American Giants' manager's take on the contested 1916 series between his team and the Indianapolis ABCs, see Mr. Fan, "Rube Foster Tells a Few Things of Interest," *Chicago Defender,* November 11, 1916, p. 10, and "Rube Foster Speaks," *Chicago Defender,* November 18, 1916, p. 9; Foster, "Rube Wants Championship without Fighting for It," *Indianapolis Freeman,* November 11, 1916, p. 7.

44. Knox, "Rube Foster Takes First Game," p. 7.

45. "A.B.C.'s Win World Series," *Indianapolis Freeman,* November 4, 1916, p. 7.

46. Mr. Fan, "Rube Foster Tells a Few Things of Interest," p. 10.

47. Foster, "Rube Wants Championship without Fighting for It," p. 7.

48. Ibid.

49. Ibid.; J. R. Warren cartoon, "An Attempted Hold-Up," *Indianapolis Freeman,* December 2, 1916, p. 7.

Notes to Chapter 8

1. David Wyatt, "The Annual 'Chestnut' Negro Base Ball League," *Indianapolis Freeman,* January 27, 1917, p. 7.

2. Ibid.

3. Ibid.

4. David Wyatt, "Base Ball!" *Indianapolis Freeman,* March 3, 1917, p. 7.

5. Mr. Fan, "American Giants Begin Local Season Sunday," *Chicago Defender,* April 21, 1917, p. 7; "Rube Foster's Team Wins," *Indianapolis Freeman,* March 31, 1917, p. 7.

6. David Wyatt, "Base Ball!" *Indianapolis Freeman,* June 16, 1917, p. 7.

7. David Wyatt, "Base Ball!" *Indianapolis Freeman,* August 4, 1917, p. 7; "A.B.C.'s Caught Napping—Foster's Giants Win by Hair," *Indianapolis Freeman,* August 25, 1917, p. 7; "For Thousands Here's One that Goes Foster One Better," *Indianapolis Freeman,* August 25, 1917, p. 7.

8. David Wyatt, "Base Ball!" *Indianapolis Freeman,* August 18, 1917, p. 11.

9. Ibid.

10. Ibid.

11. David Wyatt, "Base Ball!" *Indianapolis Freeman,* September 29, 1917, p. 7; American Giants–Central League Stars box score, *Indianapolis Freeman,* September 29, 1917, p. 7.

12. Ibid.

13. C. I. Taylor to the Sporting Editor of *Indianapolis Freeman, Indianapolis Freeman,* September 29, 1917, p. 7.

14. David Wyatt, "Base Ball!" *Indianapolis Freeman,* October 20, 1917, p. 7.

15. Foster, "The Season of 1917 Closes. Rube Foster Makes an Observation. The Status of the A.B.C.s of Indianapolis," *Indianapolis Freeman,* October 20, 1917, p. 7.

16. Billy Lewis, "C. I. Taylor, One of the Foremost Men of Baseball," *Indianapolis Freeman,* December 22, 1917, p. 7.

17. David Wyatt, "Dave Wyatt's All-Star Team," *Indianapolis Freeman,* December 22, 1917, p. 17.

18. Foster, "The Season of 1917 Closes," p. 7; David Wyatt, "Base Ball!" *Indianapolis Freeman,* November 17, 1917, p. 7.

19. David Wyatt, "Base Ball!" *Indianapolis Freeman,* December 29, 1917, p. 7; David Wyatt, "Base Ball!" *Indianapolis Freeman,* January 5, 1917, p. 7.

20. W. T. B. Williams, "The World War and the Race," *Chicago Defender,* January 5, 1918, p. 10.

21. David Wyatt, "Base Ball's 'Bit' in the World's War," *Indianapolis Freeman,* February 9, 1918, p. 7.

22. C. D. Marshall, "Taylor's Champs May Win from Foster," *Indianapolis Freeman,* January 26, 1918, p. 7; David Wyatt, "Base Ball!" *Indianapolis Freeman,* January 26, 1918, p. 7; Foster, "American Giants Arrive Safely in South; Turn down Havana Trip," *Chicago Defender,* February 2, 1918, p. 10.

23. Mister Fan, "American Giants to Present New Line-Up for This Season," *Chicago Defender,* March 30, 1918, p. 9.

24. Ibid.

25. "Rube Fires Tom Williams Outright," *Chicago Defender,* April 6, 1918, p. 9.

26. "American Giants Open Baseball Season Sunday," *Chicago Defender,* April 13, 1918, p. 9.

27. "A.B.C.'s Come for Another Series," *Chicago Defender,* July 13, 1918, p. 9.

28. "American Giants Face Hardest Test in History," *Chicago Defender,* July 20, 1918, p. 9.

29. "Giants Lose Both Games to Beloit," *Chicago Defender,* July 27, 1918, p. 9; American Giants–Beloit box score, *Chicago Defender,* July 27, 1918, p. 9; "Draft Hits Rube Foster's Club Hard," *Chicago Defender,* July 27, 1918, p. 9.

30. "Penn Red Caps Are Beaten by Foster's Shipwrecked Crew," *Chicago*

Defender, August 10, 1918, p. 9; "Giants to Go East," *Chicago Defender,* July 13, 1918, p. 9.

31. "Big League Ball Again," *Chicago Defender,* August 24, 1918, p. 9; "Giants Take Double Header," *Chicago Defender,* August 31, 1918, p. 9.

32. "Andrew 'Rube' Foster," *Chicago Defender,* September 7, 1918, p. 9.

33. David Wyatt, "White Sox Players Will Tackle Fosterites," *Chicago Defender,* September 14, 1918, p. 9.

34. Ibid.

35. David Wyatt, "Whitworth's Arm Wins Another Victory, *Chicago Defender,* September 21, 1918, p. 9.

36. "Beloit Returns to Wrest Championship from American Giants," *Chicago Defender,* September 21, 1918, p. 9; "Beloits Take Both Ends of Twin Bill; Giants' Batter off Watch," *Chicago Defender,* September 28, 1918, p. 9; "Beloit Downs American Giants," *Indianapolis Freeman,* September 28, 1918, p. 7.

37. "All Stars Win First Game I Series against the Giants," *Chicago Defender,* October 5, 1918, p. 9; "Am. Giants Win Series from All-Star Team," *Chicago Defender,* October 19, 1918, p. 9.

38. "Am. Giants Win Series from All-Star Team," p. 9; "Andrew Foster Gets Offer for War Services," *Indianapolis Freeman,* October 12, 1918, p. 7; "Influenza Epidemic Closes Baseball Season for American Giants," *Chicago Defender,* November 2, 1918, p. 9.

39. "Influenza Epidemic Closes Baseball Season for American Giants," p. 9.

40. "Rube Foster," *Chicago Defender,* November 2, 1918, p. 9.

Notes to Chapter 9

1. "Influenza Epidemic Closes Baseball Season for American Giants," p. 9.

2. Malarcher to Peterson, March 20, 1969, p. 2, David Malarcher File, Ashland Collection, National Baseball Hall of Fame Library.

3. Malarcher to Peterson, December 16, 1968, p. 1; Malarcher Notes from tape, n.d., p. 8.

4. Malarcher to Peterson, November 20, 1968, pp. 2–3.

5. Ibid., p. 3; Malarcher to Peterson, December 16, 1968, p. 3.

6. Malarcher to Peterson, November 20, 1968, p. 4.

7. Ibid., pp. 2, 5; David Malarcher Notes from tape, David Malarcher File, Ashland Collection, National Baseball Hall of Fame Library. "And then in 1920," pp. 4–5.

8. John Holway, *Blackball Stars: Negro League Pioneers* (New York: Caroll & Graf, 1992), p. 18.

9. Ibid., p. 19.

10. Robert Gardner and Dennis Shortelle, *The Forgotten Players: The Story of Black Baseball in America* (New York: Walker and Company, 1993), pp. 28–29.

11. Ibid.

12. Ibid.

13. Ibid., p. 2.

14. Malarcher to Peterson, November 20, 1968, pp. 4–5.

15. Peterson, *Only the Ball Was White,* pp. 109–110.

16. Holway, *Blackball Stars,* p. 26.

17. Peterson, *Only the Ball Was White,* p. 110.

18. Ibid., p. 5.

Notes to Chapter 10

1. "The Colored Clubs," *Baseball Magazine* (December 1918): 117.

2. Ibid.

3. Ibid.

4. Ibid., pp. 117–118.

5. Ibid., p. 118.

6. Ibid., "Giants' Recruits Work Hard," *Chicago Defender,* April 5, 1919, p. 11; "'Rube' Foster Will Present the Greatest Team of His Career," *Chicago Defender,* April 12, 1919, p. 11.

7. Jack Connelly, "Baseball's Dark Past," p. 68, File Racism, National Baseball Hall of Fame Library.

8. James R. Grossman, *Land of Hope: Chicago, Black Southerners, and the Great Migration* (Chicago: University of Chicago Press, 1989), p. 163.

9. Levine, *African Americans and Civil Rights,* pp. 149–150; Drake and Cayton, *Black Metropolis,* p. 58; Philip Klinkner, *The Unsteady March: The Rise and Decline of Racial Equality in America* (Chicago: University of Chicago Press, 1999), p. 115.

10. Drake and Cayton, *Black Metropolis,* pp. 55–56.

11. Ibid., p. 56.

12. Ibid., pp. 58–60; Klinkner, *The Unsteady March,* p. 115; James R. Grossman, "African-American Migration to Chicago," in *Ethnic Chicago: A Multicultural Portrait,* ed. Melvin G. Holli and Peter d'A. Jones (Grand Rapids, Mich.: William B. Eerdmans Publishing Company, 1995), p. 306; Grossman, *Land of Hope,* p. 79; Henri, *Black Migration,* pp. 63, 167.

13. "State Street the Great White Way," *Chicago Defender,* May 11, 1912, p. 8; Langston Hughes, *Big Sea: An Autobiography* (New York: A. A. Knopf, 1940), p. 33; Grossman, "African-American Migration to Chicago," p. 317;

Geoffrey C. Ward and Ken Burns, *Jazz: A History of America's Music* (New York: Alfred A. Knopf, 2000), p. 87.

14. Grossman, "African-American Migration to Chicago," pp. 322–323; Henri, *Black Migration*, p. 231.

15. Grossman, *Land of Hope*, pp. 169–170.

16. Thomas L. Philpott, *Slum and the Ghetto: Neighborhood Deterioration and Middle-Class Reform, Chicago 1880–1930* (New York: Oxford University Press, 1978), p. 210; Grossman, "African-American Migration to Chicago," pp. 320, 325; Henri, *Black Migration*, pp. 168–169, 181.

17. Drake and Cayton, *Black Metropolis.*, pp. 60–64; Henri, *Black Migration*, p. 105; Klinkner, *The Unsteady March*, p. 115.

18. Grossman, *Land of Hope*, pp. 178–179.

19. Howard A. Phelps, "Andrew 'Rube' Foster," *Half-Century Magazine* (March 1, 1919): 8.

20. Ibid.

21. Ibid.

22. Ibid.

23. Ibid; "Foster Asks Patience," *Chicago Defender*, April 19, 1919, p. 11.

24. "Giants' Recruits Work Hard," p. 11.

25. Ibid.

26. Ibid.

27. "Foster Asks Patience," p. 11; "Giants' Seating Capacity Enlarged," *Chicago Defender*, June 7, 1919, p. 11.

28. "Giants' Seating Capacity Enlarged," p. 11.

29. "American Giants Whitewash Beloit," *Chicago Whip*, July 3, 1919, p. 7; American Giants–Beloit box score, *Chicago Whip*, July 3, 1919, p. 7; Richard Whitworth, "The History of the World's Greatest Colored Pitcher," *Chicago Whip*, July 9, 1919, p. 7.

30. "All Chicago to Welcome American Giants Sunday," *Chicago Defender*, August 23, 1919, p. 11; "25,000 See Am. Giants," *Chicago Defender*, August 30, 1919, p. 11; American Giants–Treat 'em Roughs box score, *Chicago Defender*, August 30, 1919, p. 11.

31. William M. Tuttle Jr., *Race Riot: Chicago in the Red Summer of 1919* (Urbana: University of Illinois Press, 1996); "Breaking the Shell," *Chicago Whip*, June 24, 1919, p. 8.

32. Tuttle, *Race Riot.*

33. "A Dangerous Experiment," *Chicago Whip*, August 9, 1919, p. 8.

34. Ibid.

35. Ibid.

36. "The Passing of Uncle Tom," *Chicago Whip*, August 9, 1919, p. 8.

37. Ibid.

38. "A Report on the Chicago Riot by An Eye-Witness," *Crisis* 18 (September 1919): 11–12.

39. W. E. B. Du Bois, "Let Us Reason Together," *Crisis* 18 (September 1919): 231.

40. Walter F. White, "Chicago and Its Eight Reasons," *Crisis* 18 (October 1919): 293–297.

41. "Radicals and Raids," *Chicago Whip,* January 10, 1920, p. 8; "The Cause of the New Negro," *Chicago Whip,* January 17, 1920, p. 8.

42. Chicago Commission on Race Relations, *The Negro in Chicago* (Chicago: University of Chicago Press, 1922).

43. Ibid.

Notes to Chapter 11

1. Foster to W. T. Smith, July 2, 1919, Rube Foster Officials File, National Baseball Hall of Fame Library; Cary Lewis, "Baseball Circuit for Next Season," *Chicago Defender,* October 4, 1919, p. 11.

2. Cary Lewis, "Baseball Circuit for Next Season," p. 11.

3. Ibid.

4. Ibid.

5. Ibid.

6. Foster, "Pitfalls of Baseball," *Chicago Defender,* November 29, 1919, p. 11.

7. Ibid.

8. Foster, "Pitfalls of Baseball," *Chicago Defender,* December 13, 1919, p. 11.

9. Ibid.

10. Ibid.

11. Foster, "Pitfalls of Baseball," *Chicago Defender,* December 20, 1919, p. 11.

12. Foster, "Pitfalls of Baseball," *Chicago Defender,* December 27, 1919, p. 9.

13. Ibid.

14. Ibid.

15. Foster, "Pitfalls of Baseball," *Chicago Defender,* January 3, 1920, p. 9.

16. Ibid.

17. Ibid.

18. Ibid.

19. Foster, "Pitfalls of Baseball," *Chicago Defender,* January 10, 1920, p. 9.

20. Ibid.

21. Ibid.

22. Foster, "Pitfalls of Baseball," *Chicago Defender,* January 17, 1920, p. 9.

23. Ibid.

24. Ibid.

25. Charles D. Marshall, "Rube Foster Wants 'Get Together' Meet of All Baseball Owners," *Indianapolis Freeman,* January 17, 1920, p. 3.

26. C. I. Taylor, "The Future of Colored Baseball," *Competitor* 1 (February 1920): 76.

27. Ibid.

28. Ibid.

29. Ibid., p. 78.

30. Ibid.

31. "Call for National League Issued," *Chicago Defender,* February 7, 1920, p. 11; "Negro Base Ball League Assured," *Indianapolis Freeman,* February 21, 1920, p. 3.

32. "Call for National League Issued," p. 11.

33. "Baseball Magnates Hold Conference," *Chicago Defender,* February 14, 1920, p. 11; "Baseball Men Write League Constitution," *Chicago Defender,* February 21, 1920, p. 9; "Negro Base Ball League Assured," p. 3.

34. "Baseball Men Write League Constitution," p. 9.

35. Ibid.

36. Ibid.

37. Ira F. Lewis, "National Baseball League Formed," *Competitor* 1 (March 1920): 66.

38. Ibid., p. 67.

39. Charles D. Marshall, "National Negro Baseball League Is Formed," *Indianapolis Freeman,* February 28, 1920, p. 7.

40. "Southern Baseball League Is Formed," *Chicago Defender,* March 6, 1920, p. 12.

41. David Wyatt, "National League of Colored Clubs Prepares for Season's Opening," *Competitor* 1 (April 1920): 73–74.

42. "'Rube' Assigns Players to Giants," *Chicago Defender,* March 20, 1920, p. 9; Foster, "Rube Foster Tells What Baseball Needs to Succeed," *Chicago Defender,* December 10, 1921, p. 10.

43. "'Rube' Assigns Players to Giants," p. 9.

44. David Wyatt, "Success of the League Is up to the Fans," *Chicago Defender,* April 3, 1920, p. 9; "American Giants Open Schorling Park," *Chicago Whip,* March 20, 1920, p. 4.

45. "Foster Raises the Lid," *Chicago Whip,* April 17, 1920, p. 5.

46. Wyatt, "A.B.C. Triumph in First Home Games," *Chicago Defender,* May

8, 1920, p. 9; Chicago Giants–ABCs box score, *Chicago Defender,* May 8, 1920, p. 9.

47. "10,000 Fans See Giants Win 4 to 1," *Chicago Whip,* June 5, 1920, p. 5; American Giants–Cubans box score, *Chicago Whip,* June 5, 1920, p. 5; "Look Here, Fans," *Chicago Defender,* July 3, 1920, p. 9.

48. "Big League Making Progress," *Competitor* 2 (July 1920): 69.

49. "Watching Scoreboard," *Chicago Defender,* July 31, 1920, p. 6; "League Standings," *Chicago Defender,* August 28, 1920, p. 6.

50. David Wyatt, "Foster Team Ends Chicago Season," *Chicago Whip,* September 25, 1920, p. 5.

51. Ibid.; "Foster Vs. Bacharach," *Chicago Defender,* October 9, 1920, p. 6; Holway, *Blackball Stars,* p. 29; "Rube Defeats Bacharachs Twice," *Chicago Defender,* October 23, 1920, p. 6.

52. "Baseball Magnates in Big Harmony Meeting," *Chicago Defender,* December 11, 1920, p. 6; "Annual Meeting of National Association," *Indianapolis Freeman,* November 27, 1920, p. 7; Ira F. Lewis, "Baseball Men Hold Successful Meeting," *Competitor* 3 (January–February 1921): 51, 54.

Notes to Chapter 12

1. David Wyatt, "Baseball Men Face New Year with Optimism," *Chicago Whip,* December 18, 1920, p. 7; "Rube Foster and His Gang to Palm Beach," *Chicago Whip,* January 8, 1921, p. 7; "Base Ball Babble," *Chicago Whip,* January 8, 1921, p. 7; "The Champion American Giants," *Chicago Whip,* January 15, 1921, p. 7.

2. "Winter League Championship Goes to Fosterites," *Chicago Whip,* March 19, 1921, p. 7; "The Peerless Leader," *Chicago Whip,* March 19, 1921, p. 7; "The Champion American Giants," p. 7.

3. Ira F. Lewis, "Big Clubs Ready for Season," *Competitor* 3 (April 1921): 37.

4. "Official Standings of N.N. League Clubs Monday Morning, Oct. 3. The Close of Season," *Chicago Whip,* October 22, 1921, p. 7; "Rube Has Team of Hitless Wonders," *Chicago Whip,* September 17, 1921, p. 7.

5. Mr. Fan, "National League Circuit Will Be Changed at January Meeting," *Chicago Defender,* November 26, 1921, p. 10.

6. Ibid; "Rube Foster Jailed for Fraud," *Chicago Whip,* November 12, 1921, p. 1; "Laughs at Accusers," *Chicago Whip,* November 12, 1921, p. 1.

7. "Rube Foster Tells What Baseball Needs to Succeed," (first article), *Chicago Defender,* December 10, 1921, p. 10.

8. "Rube Foster Tells What Baseball Needs to Succeed," (second article), *Chicago Defender,* December 17, 1921, p. 10.

9. Ibid.

10. Ibid.

11. Ibid.

12. Foster, "Players Prove Serious Drawback to Baseball," *Chicago Defender,* December 24, 1921, p. 10; Foster, "Future of Race Umpires Depends on Men of Today," *Chicago Defender,* December 31, 1921, p. 10; "Seven Colored Umps Signed for League," *Kansas City Call,* April 27, 1923, p. 7.

13. David Wyatt, "Baseball Powers in Big Bow Wow Here," *Chicago Whip,* January 28, 1922, p. 7.

14. Ibid.

15. Wyatt, "Cleveland and Pittsburgh now in N.N. League," *Chicago Whip,* February 4, 1922, p. 7; David Wyatt, "Magnates to Make 1922 Banner Year," *Chicago Whip,* February 18, 1922, p. 7; Arthur Williams, "C. I. Taylor, Veteran Manager and Baseball Club Owner, Dead," *Chicago Defender,* March 4, 1922, p. 10; "Many at Funeral of C. I. Taylor," *Chicago Whip,* March 4, 1922, p. 7.

16. "Monroe's [*sic*] All Star Team," *Chicago Whip,* October 7, 1922, p. 7; "The Standings," *Chicago Whip,* July 15, 1922, p. 7; "The Standings," *Chicago Whip,* July 22, 1922, p. 7.

17. "League Too Big for Newspapers, Can't Grasp Idea—Rube," *Chicago Whip,* October 28, 1922, p. 7.

18. "Negro National League Meets December 7 at Appomattox Club," *Chicago Whip,* November 18, 1922, p. 7.

19. "East's Baseball Teams Organize," *Chicago Whip,* December 9, 1922, p. 7; "Easterners Organize a New League," *Chicago Whip,* December 23, 1922, p. 7; "The New Eastern League," *Kansas City Call,* December 20, 1922, p. 6.

20. Foster, "'Rube' Foster Launches out against Easterners," *New York Amsterdam News,* January 17, 1923, p. 4l; Edward Bolden, "Association of Eastern Clubs Replies to Andrew Foster," *New York Amsterdam News,* January 17, 1923, p. 41.

21. W. S. Ferrance, "Says Foster Made $11,000 Commission," *Kansas City Call,* February 9, 1923, p. 7.

22. "Rube Foster Goes Eastward; Giants to Train in Texas," *Chicago Defender,* February 3, 1923, p. 10.

23. "Pitchers Brown and Rile Jump to the Outlaws," *Chicago Defender,* February 10, 1923, p. 10; "League Moguls Here This Week; Baseball War Looms," *Chicago Defender,* March 17, 1923, p. 10.

24. "American Giants Pry Lid off on Sunday, April 8," *Chicago Defender,* March 31, 1923, p. 10; "Foster to Give Fans Chance to Look over Team," *Chicago Defender,* April 4, 1923, p. 10.

25. "Foster Begins to Wreck Once Great Machine," *Chicago Defender*, August 11, 1923, p. 9.

26. "Foster's Ire Aroused over Ball Players' Charges," *Chicago Defender*, November 24, 1923, p. 9; "Negro National League Meeting," *Kansas City Call*, December 14, 1923, p. 7.

27. "Negro National League Season Opens April 28," *Chicago Defender*, April 5, 1924, p. 10; "Rube Foster Plans Surprise for League Fans," *Chicago Defender*, April 12, 1924, p. 10.

28. "Rube Foster's 'Sportsmanship,'" *Kansas City Call*, July 11, 1924, p. 6.

29. "Judge Landis Offers to Arbitrate Baseball Dispute," *Chicago Defender*, September 6, 1924, p. 10; Malarcher to Peterson, January 16, 1969, p. 3, David Malarcher File, Ashland Collection, National Baseball Hall of Fame Library; "Hilldale and Chicago Get the World's Series Apple; We Get the Core—If There Is One!" *Kansas City Call*, September 12, 1924, p. 6.

30. Foster, "Rube Foster Reviews the World Series and Tells a Little Baseball History," *Chicago Defender*, November 15, 1924, p. 10; "World's Champions," *Kansas City Call*, October 24, 1924, p. 6.

31. "Release of Umpires Was Necessary," *Chicago Defender*, August 22, 1925, p. 8; "Negro National League in Harmonious Meeting; Plan Two Fifty-Game Schedules," *Chicago Defender*, February 7, 1925, p. 10.

32. "Foster Releases Seven," *Chicago Defender*, March 7, 1925, p. 12.

33. "Gas Nearly Kills Andrew Rube Foster," *Chicago Defender*, June 6, 1925, p. 9.

34. "The Standing," *Chicago Defender*, June 6, 1925, p. 9.

35. David Malarcher Notes from tape, "And then in 1920," p. 1.

36. "Rube Foster Wants Clubs of Winners," *Chicago Defender*, January 2, 1925, p. 8; "American Giants to Start Practice April 1st; Bobby Williams to Indianapolis," *Chicago Defender*, March 27, 1926, p. 10; Fay, "Fay Says," *Chicago Defender*, May 1, 1926, p. 10.

37. Fay, "Fay Says," *Chicago Defender*, June 19, 1926, p. 10.

38. Peterson, *Only the Ball Was White*, p. 114; "Gilmore Seeks to Be Head of National League; Takes Rap at Weekly Newspaper," *Chicago Defender*, September 11, 1926, p. 10; Frank A. Young, "Directors of National League Hold Future of Our Baseball in Their Hands," *Chicago Defender*, September 11, 1926, p. 11; "Tape of Earl Foster," p. 1, Andrew (Rube) Foster Special Collection, National Baseball Hall of Fame Library; Malarcher Notes from tape, "And then in 1920," p. 1.

39. Holway, *Blackball Stars*, p. 33; Gardner and Shortelle, *The Forgotten*, p. 30; Ribowsky, *A Complete History of the Negro Leagues*, pp. 130–131; Ira F. Lewis, "The Passing Review," *Pittsburgh Courier*, January 1, 1927, part 2, p. 6.

40. Peterson, *Only the Ball Was White,* p. 114; Malarcher to Peterson, March 20, 1969, p. 2.

41. "Defeat Atlantic City Club in Deciding Game, 1 to 0, in Last Half of 9th Inning," *Chicago Defender,* October 23, 1926, p. 11; Malarcher to Peterson, December 16, 1968, p. 2.

42. Malarcher to Peterson, January 16, 1969, pp. 1–2; Malarcher to Peterson, November 20, 1968, pp. 8–9; Malarcher to Peterson, December 16, 1968, p. 2.

43. "'Rube Foster Day,' 'C. I. Taylor Day' to Be Observed," *Pittsburgh Courier,* February 12, 1927, sec. 2, p. 4; "Chicago Loses Deciding Game of Series, 9 to 2," *Chicago Defender,* October 13, 1928, p. 8; "New Faces to Be Seen in American Giants Line-Up as Result of Drastic Shake-Up," *Chicago Defender,* August 23, 1930, p. 8.

44. "No East vs. West Baseball Series," *Chicago Defender,* August 31, 1929, p. 8; "Taylor Tells What's Wrong in Baseball," *Chicago Defender,* February 1, 1930, p. 8; "Baseball Is in Need of Good Housecleaning," *Chicago Defender,* March 1, 1930, p. 9.

Notes to Chapter 13

1. W. Rollo Wilson, "Sport Shots," *Pittsburgh Courier,* February 19, 1927, part 2, p. 5.

2. W. Rollo Wilson, "Sport Shots," *Pittsburgh Courier,* April 2, 1927, part 2, p. 6.

3. Ibid; W. Rollo Wilson, "Sport Shots," *Pittsburgh Courier,* April 9, 1927, part 2, p. 6.

4. W. Rollo Wilson, "Sport Shots," April 2, 1927, p. 6.

5. Ibid.

6. Wilson, "Sport Shots," April 9, 1927, part 2, p. 6.

7. William Dismukes, "Ye Olde Stove League," *Pittsburgh Courier,* January 5, 1929, part 3, p. 4.

8. William Dismukes, "Immortals of Negro Baseball and Their Achievements," *Pittsburgh Courier,* December 29, 1928, part 3, p. 5.

9. "Greatest," *Chicago Defender,* May 3, 1930, p. 9.

10. Frank A. Young, "Rube Foster—The Master Mind of Baseball," *Abbott's Monthly* (November 1, 1930): 42–43.

11. Ibid., pp. 42, 49.

12. Ibid., p. 93.

13. "Rube Foster Dead," *Chicago Defender,* December 13, 1930, pp. 1, 4; "Thousands Attend Last Rites for Rube Foster," *Chicago Defender,* December 20, 1930, pp. 1, 8.

14. "Thousands Attend Last Rites for Rube Foster," pp. 1, 8.

15. Ibid; "Rube Foster Dead," p. 1.

16. "Cosmopolitan Throng Pays Final Tribute to Organizer of Negro Baseball League," *New York Amsterdam News,* December 17, 1930, p. 11; "'Rube' Foster, Former Baseball Czar, Is Dead," *Pittsburgh Courier,* December 13, 1930, pp. 1, 5.

17. Al Monroe, "What Is the Matter with Baseball?" pp. 26–29, 60–61.

18. "Rube Foster," notes, p. 2, Rube Foster Officials File, National Baseball Hall of Fame Library; Wendell Smith, "No Need for Color Ban," *Pittsburgh Courier,* September 2, 1939, p. 16.

19. Edwin Bancroft Henderson, *The Negro in Sports* (Washington, D.C.: Associated Publishers, 1939), p. 174.

20. "Courier 'Experts' Name All-Time, All-American Baseball Team," *Pittsburgh Courier,* April 12, 1952, p. 14; "Top Baseball Names Pick Greatest Team," *Pittsburgh Courier,* April 19, 1952, p. 14.

21. A. S. "Doc" Young, *Great Negro Baseball Stars and How They Made the Major Leagues* (New York: A. S. Barnes and Company, 1953), pp. 188–192.

22. A. S. "Doc" Young, "Rube Foster," *Hue* (August 1957): 55–56.

23. Ibid., pp. 56–60.

Notes to Chapter 14

1. "Pioneering Rube Foster 'Saved' Major Leagues," *New Courier,* May 18, 1968.

2. "Dave Malarcher Notes from tape," p. 1; Malarcher to Peterson, January 16, 1969, p. 1; Malarcher to Peterson, November 20, 1968, p. 6.

3. Peterson, *Only the Ball Was White,* pp. 103–115.

4. "Historically Speaking . . . 'Rube' Foster," *Black Sports* (February 1972).

5. A. S. "Doc" Young, "Good Morning, Sports!" *Chicago Daily Defender,* February 14, 1973, Foster Officials' File.

6. Ibid.

7. John Hall, "Hall of Shame," *Los Angeles Times,* February 28, 1974.

8. Ibid.

9. Robert Peterson, "Rube Foster, Best of the Black Managers," *Sport* (May 1975): 38, 40.

10. *Congressional Record—Extensions of Records,* July 9, 1975, E 3645.

11. Robert Peterson to the Sports Editor, *New York Times,* n.d., Rube Foster Officials File, National Baseball Hall of Fame Library.

12. William J. Guilfoib (National Baseball Hall of Fame), "For Immediate Release: Mize, Foster Newest Hall of Famers," March 12, 1981.

13. George Vecsey, "Welcome to the Hall," *New York Times,* August 3, 1981, Bill Madden, "Hall of Famers Win the Cheers of Bitter Crowd," Rube Foster File, Foster Ashland Collection, National Baseball Hall of Fame Library.

14. John B. Holway, "Rube Foster: Father of Black Game," *Sporting News,* August 8, 1981, p. 19.

15. Ibid.

16. Geoffrey C. Ward, *Baseball: An Illustrated History* (New York: Alfred A. Knopf, 1994), p. 157.

BIBLIOGRAPHY

Primary Documents

Abbott's Monthly
Amsterdam News
Baseball Magazine
Chicago Defender
Chicago Tribune
Chicago Whip
Crisis
Indianapolis Freeman
Indianapolis Ledger
Kansas City Call
Messenger
Negro League Files: The Ashland Collection, National Baseball Hall of Fame
   Library
New York Age
Officials' Files, National Baseball Hall of Fame Library
Oregonian
Outlook
Philadelphia Item
Philadelphia Tribune
Pittsburgh Courier
St. Paul Pioneer Press
Seattle Post-Intelligencer
Sporting Life
Sporting News

Secondary Sources

Alexander, Charles. *John McGraw*. Lincoln: University of Nebraska Press, 1988.
———. *Our Game: An American Baseball History*. New York: Henry Holt and
   Company, 1991.
———. *Ty Cobb*. New York: Oxford University Press, 1984.

Alexander, Charles. *The Baseball Encyclopedia: The Complete and Definitive Record of Major League Baseball.* 10th ed. New York: Macmillan, 1996.

Bjarkman, Peter C. *Baseball with a Latin Beat: A History of the Latin American Game.* Jefferson, N.C.: McFarland & Company, 1994.

Bruce, Janet. *The Kansas City Monarchs.* Lawrence: University Press of Kansas, 1985.

Chadwick, Bruce. *When the Game Was Black and White: The Illustrated History of Baseball's Negro Leagues.* New York: Abbeville Press, 1985.

Clark, Dennis. "Urban Blacks and Irishmen: Brothers in Prejudice." In *Black Politics in Philadelphia.* Edited by Miriam Ershkowitz and Joseph Zikmund II. New York: Basic Books, 1973.

Craft, David. *The Negro Leagues: 40 Years of Black Professional Baseball in Words and Pictures.* New York: Crescent Books, 1993.

Dixon, Phil, with Patrick J. Hannigan. *The Negro Baseball League: A Photographic History.* Mattituck, N.Y.: Amereon House, 1992.

Drake, St. Clair, and Horace R. Cayton. *Black Metropolis: A Study of Negro Life in a Northern City.* Vol. 1. New York: Harper & Row, 1962.

Du Bois, W. E. B. "The Black Vote of Philadelphia." In *Black Politics in Philadelphia.*

———. *The Philadelphia Negro: A Social Study.* Philadelphia: University of Pennsylvania Press, 1996.

Echevarría, Roberto Gonzáles. *The Pride of Havana: A History of Cuban Baseball.* New York: Oxford University Press, 1999.

Emlen, John T. "The Movement for the Betterment of the Negro in Philadelphia." In *Black Politics in Philadelphia.*

Farr, Finis. *Chicago: A Personal History of America's Most American City.* New Rochelle, N.Y.: Arlington House, 1973.

Gershman, Michael. *Diamonds: The Evolution of the Ballpark.* Boston: Houghton Mifflin Company, 1993.

Gosnell, Harold F. *Negro Politicians: The Rise of Negro Politics in Chicago.* Chicago: University of Chicago Press, 1967.

Grossman, James R. "African-American Migration to Chicago." In *Ethnic Chicago: A Multicultural Portrait.* Edited by Melvin G. Holli and Peter d'A. Jones. Grand Rapids, Mich.: William R. Eerdmans Publishing Company, 1995.

———. *Land of Hope: Chicago, Black Southerners, and the Great Migration.* Chicago: University of Chicago Press, 1989.

Hall, Alvin L., ed. *Cooperstown Symposium on Baseball and the American Culture.* Westport, Conn.: Meckler Books, 1989.

Hardwick, Leon. *Blacks in Baseball.* Los Angeles: Pilot Historical Association, 1980.

Henri, Florette. *Black Migration: Movement North, 1900–1920*. Garden City, N.Y.: Anchor Press, 1975.

Holway, John B. *Blackball Stars: Negro League Pioneers*. New York: Carroll & Graf Publishers, 1992.

———. *Black Diamonds: Life in the Negro Leagues from the Men Who Lived It*. Westport, Conn.: Meckler Books, 1989.

James, Bill. *The Bill James Guide to Baseball Managers from 1870 to Today*. New York: Scribner, 1997.

Kenney, William Howland. *Chicago Jazz: A Cultural History, 1904–1930*. New York: Oxford University Press, 1993.

Klinkner, Philip A., with Rogers M. Smith. *The Unsteady March: The Rise and Decline of Racial Equality in America*. Chicago: University of Chicago Press, 1999.

Levine, Michael L. *African Americans and Civil Rights: From 1619 to the Present*. Phoenix: Oryx Press, 1996.

Miller, William D. *Pretty Bubbles in the Air: America in 1919*. Urbana: University of Illinois Press, 1991.

The Negro in Chicago: A Study of Race Relations and a Race Riot in 1919. New York: Arno Press and the New York Times, 1968.

Ottley, Roi. *The Lonely Warrior: The Life and Times of Robert S. Abbott*. Chicago: Henry Regnery & Company, 1955.

Peterson, Robert. *Only the Ball Was White: A History of Legendary Black Players and All-Black Professional Teams*. New York: Oxford University Press, 1992.

Philpott, Thomas L. *Slum and the Ghetto: Neighborhood Deterioration and Middle-Class Reform, Chicago 1880–1930*. New York: Oxford University Press, 1978.

Pietrusza, David. *Judge and Jury: The Life and Times of Judge Kenesaw Mountain Landis*. South Bend: Diamond Communications, 1998.

Ribowsky, Mark. *A Complete History of the Negro Leagues, 1884 to 1955*. New York: Carol Publishing Group, 1997.

Rice, Lawrence D. *The Negro in Texas, 1874–1900*. Baton Rouge: Louisiana State University Press, 1971.

Riley, James A. *The Biographical Encyclopedia of the Negro Baseball Leagues*. New York: Carroll & Graf Publishers, 1994.

Ritter, Lawrence. *Lost Ballparks: A Celebration of Baseball's Legendary Fields*. New York: Penguin Studio Books, 1992.

Robinson, Ray. *Matty: An American Hero*. New York: Oxford University Press, 1993.

Rosogin, Donn. *Invisible Men: Life in Baseball's Negro Leagues*. New York: Kodansha International, 1995.

Rust, Art, Jr. *Get That Nigger off the Field.* New York: Delacorte Press, 1976.

Scott, Emmett J. *Negro Migration during the War.* New York: Arno Press and the New York Times, 1969.

Seymour, Harold. *Baseball: The Early Years.* New York: Oxford University Press, 1989.

———. *Baseball: The Golden Age.* New York: Oxford University Press, 1989.

———. *Baseball: The People's Game.* New York: Oxford University Press, 1991.

Solomon, Burt. *The Baseball Timeline: The Day-by-Day History of Baseball, from Valley Forge to the Present Day.* New York: Avon Books, 1997.

Spear, Allan H. *Black Chicago: The Making of a Negro Ghetto, 1890–1920.* Chicago: University of Chicago Press, 1969.

Thorn, John, et al. *Total Baseball: The Official Encyclopedia of Major League Baseball.* 6th ed. New York: Total Sports, 1999.

Trouppe, Quincy. *Twenty Years Too Soon.* Los Angeles: S&S Enterprises, 1977.

Tuttle, William M., Jr. *Race Riot: Chicago in the Red Summer of 1919.* Urbana: University of Illinois Press, 1996.

Ward, Geoffrey C. *Baseball: An Illustrated History.* New York: Alfred A. Knopf, 1994.

Ward, Geoffrey C., and Ken Burns. *Jazz: A History of America's Music.* New York: Alfred A. Knopf, 2000.

White, G. Edward. *Creating the National Pastime: Baseball Transforms Itself, 1903–1933.* Princeton: Princeton University Press, 1996.

White, Sol. *Sol White's History of Colored Base Ball, with Other Documents on the Early Black Game, 1886–1936.* Lincoln: University of Nebraska Press, 1995.

Whitehead, Charles E. *A Man and His Diamonds.* New York: Vantage Press, 1980.

INDEX

ABOUT THE AUTHOR

Robert Charles Cottrell is Professor of History and American Studies at California State University, Chico. He is the author of *Roger Nash Baldwin and the American Civil Liberties Union, Izzy: A Biography of I. F. Stone, The Social Gospel of E. Nicholas Comfort,* and *1920: The Black Sox, Blackball, and the Babe.*

B   Cottrell, Robert C.
FOSTER   Best Pitcher in
           Baseball, The : The Life
           of Rube Foster, Negro ...

46854

$24.95   46854

DATE			